The First Book of

Quicken® in Business

Includes Version 4.0

The First Book of

Quicken® in Business

Includes Version 4.0

Gordon McComb

A Division of Macmillan Computer Publishing
11711 North College, Carmel, Indiana 46032 USA

©1990 by SAMS

FIRST EDITION
FIRST PRINTING—1990

International Standard Book Number: 0-672-27331-4
Library of Congress Catalog Number: 90-63193

Acquisitions Editor: *Marie Butler-Knight*
Manuscript Editor: *Sara Black*
Cover Art: *Held & Diedrich Design*
Production: *Jeff Baker, Brad Chinn, Sally Copenhaver,*
Tami Hughes, Bill Hurley, Sarah Leatherman,
Matthew Morrill, Dennis Sheehan
Indexer: *Sherry Massey*
Technical Reviewer: *C. Herbert Feltner*

Printed in the United States of America

Contents

V

vi

4 *Writing Checks,* 67

5 *Maintaining the Check Register,* 85

viii

ix

10 *Creating and Printing Reports, 207*

xii

11 *Setting Up a Business Accounting System,* 249

12 *Business Reporting with Quicken,* 273

xiii

xiv

Introduction

Money. Bread. Cash. Dough. Booty. Moolah. Dollars. Whatever you want to call it, the world revolves around money. If you're like most people, you want to spend your productive hours *making* money, not figuring out where your money goes or how it's spent. With the advent of the personal computer, software publishers have developed programs to make money management easier. Though it was a good thought, the approach taken by these programs left a lot to be desired. They were difficult to use, offered little or no flexibility, and required in-depth knowledge of financial matters and accounting practices.

Quicken, from Intuit, offers something different. This one program for the IBM PC lets you track your checking account, savings, cash, credit cards, investments, rental property, business accounting, payroll, and much, much more. Yet it does this job with surprising simplicity. Quicken is designed to make child's play out of money matters—giving you the ability to track, print, and review all of your financial business.

This is a book on learning Quicken on the IBM PC. With the information contained in this book, you'll be able to use Quicken to create checkbook and savings account registers, print checks, manage cash and credit card accounts, track business accounts receivable and accounts payable, print financial reports, and lots more. *The First Book of Quicken in Business* is a beginner's guide to get you started using Quicken for all your financial affairs.

Though Quicken is not an overly complex program, it does have many features and capabilities that can confuse first-time users. This book pares it all down to manageable size. You'll learn everything you need to know to use Quicken to track all types of finances, including checking and savings accounts, cash, investments, income rental property and even business payroll.

How to Use This Book

xvi

The chapters in *First Book of Quicken in Business* are organized in the same manner that you are likely to use the Quicken program.

Chapter 1, "An Introduction to Quicken," is an overview of Quicken. It provides a quick summary of the program, how it works, and what it does.

In Chapter 2, "Getting Started with Quicken," you'll learn how to install the program on floppy or hard disks, how to set up the program to match your computer and printer, how to activate Quicken's commands and menus, and how to access on-line help.

Chapter 3 is "Setting Up Accounts." Here, you'll discover Quicken's six account types and what they're used for. You'll also learn how to start new accounts, maintain accounts, and back up account data.

Chapter 4, "Writing Checks," explains the heart and soul of Quicken: how to prepare checks and record them as transactions in a check register.

"Maintaining the Check Register," Chapter 5, explains how to access the check register, edit transactions, find transactions using specific search criteria, and more.

Chapter 6 is "Keeping Track of Transactions." This chapter details some of the finer points of Quicken, writing memos in checks, splitting transactions, using categories and classes, and reconciling the checking account to the bank statement.

Chapter 7, "Transaction Shortcuts," highlights two of Quicken's time-savers: memorized transactions and transaction groups.

In Chapter 8, "Printing Checks," you'll learn how to print checks you've written with Quicken. You'll learn how to print all the checks that are waiting to be printed and how to select only those checks for printing that you want. You'll also learn how to make sure your printer is properly aligned for check printing and how to diagnose potential problems.

Chapter 9 is "Working with Other Quicken Accounts." Here, you'll discover the ins and outs of using Quicken's cash, credit card, other asset, other liability, and investment account types and how they are used.

Chapter 10, "Creating and Printing Reports," tells you everything you need to know to produce printed reports with Quicken.

xvii

Chapter 11 is "Setting Up a Business Accounting System," where you will learn how to develop cash accounting strategies, use Quicken's post-dated check feature to create a versatile accounts payable system, and create A/R and A/P accounts.

In Chapter 12, "Business Reporting," you'll learn how to create reports from the A/R and A/P accounts developed in the previous chapter, preparing reports of the general journal, producing trial balances and cash analysis reports, and more.

"Quicken Applications," in Chapter 13, describes some of the other ways you can use Quicken in real-world situations, including monthly budgeting, tracking home improvements (your own home or rental property), and developing a business payroll plan.

Appendix A lists the preset home and business income/ expense categories provided with Quicken. Appendix B lists the on-line help topics found in Quicken, while Appendix C reviews the command-line options that can be used to start Quicken.

Although you don't have to read this book from cover to cover and in order, at the very least you should start by reading Chapters 1 and 2. These provide an overview of Quicken and how to access its features and capabilities.

Conventions Used in This Book

You need little advance information before you can dive head first into this book. We've used the following conventions to make your trip with Quicken more enjoyable and effective.

This is a beginner's quick start guide to Quicken, but it assumes you are familiar with the IBM PC and its disk operating system. If you are unfamiliar with DOS or how to use your computer, read the instruction manual that came with the computer or consult one of the many fine books on using the PC and DOS. A good place to start is *Understanding MS-DOS*, published by SAMS.

The First Book of Quicken in Business is written for Quicken version 4.0. Users of version 3.0 can still apply many of the methods and techniques found in this book, but some commands may be different. Among the main changes in 4.0 are:

xviii

▶ A new investment account type for tracking stocks.

▶ Increased support for Checkfree, an option for electronic bill payments.

▶ Redefined categories for home and business. Specifically, a number of standard categories for business have been deleted. This is not a problem if you have Quicken version 3.0 and use one or more of the deleted categories, as the program will re-enter them for you automatically.

▶ Memorized reports.

▶ Redefined functions for the Home and End keys.

Many chapters include step-by-step "Quick Steps" that help you promptly master a particular command or function of Quicken. The Quick Steps outline only the most commonly used Quicken procedures. Refer to the inside front cover of this book for an alphabetical list of Quick Steps.

Trademark Acknowledgments

All terms mentioned in this book that are known to be trademarks or service marks are listed below. In addition, terms suspected of being trademarks or service marks have been appropriately capitalized. SAMS cannot attest to the accuracy of this information. Use of a term in this book should not be regarded as affecting the validity of any trademark or service mark.

IBM, IBM PC, and IBM PC AT are registered trademarks of International Business Machines Corporation. IBM PC XT and PS/2 are trademarks of International Business Machines Corporation. Lotus 1-2-3 is a registered trademark of Lotus Development Corp. Microsoft Works is a trademark of Microsoft Corp. Quicken is a registered trademark of Intuit.

xix

Chapter 1

An Introduction to Quicken

In This Chapter

1

▶ *Using Quicken in home or business*
▶ *What Quicken will do for you*
▶ *A typical application of Quicken*
▶ *Computer hardware you'll need*
▶ *Terms you'll want to know*

Quicken. Even the name promises fast results. Speed and ease-of-use are the secrets behind Quicken, the number one best-selling home/business finance program for the IBM PC and compatibles. In one package, you get all the tools you need to keep track of money matters at home or in a small business. Quicken lets you juggle just about any number of checking and savings accounts, credit cards, and even cash and miscellaneous income and expenses.

While Quicken was designed so that you could install it in your computer and be crunching numbers in less than 15 minutes, its finer points are slightly more obscure. In this book, you'll learn everything you need to know about using Quicken in your day-to-day affairs, along with some tricks of the trade that will make you a Quicken pro.

This chapter introduces you to Quicken: what it does, how it does it, and what you can expect from it. You'll see how Quicken lets you set up flexible accounts for your income and expenses, how you can automate check-writing, and ways in which Quicken makes bank statement reconciliation child's play.

What Is Quicken?

Quicken is a home and business finance program that helps you keep track of expenses and income. No matter where you use Quicken, it has features of particular interest to both the home and the business user. Throughout this book we will emphasize business applications, but you can use many of the same techniques in the home.

2

In the Home

On the home front, you can use Quicken to maintain your checking and savings accounts, track the checks you write (or withdrawals you make from savings), and balance that against your deposits.

Just as in real life, Quicken uses checks for paying out money and a check register to keep track of everything. The check-writing screen, shown in Figure 1.1, is one of Quicken's strong points. To pay a bill, you just fill in the check. Quicken automatically catalogs it in the register, which is illustrated in Figure 1.2.

Quicken can print your checks for you—using almost any dot matrix, ink jet, daisywheel, or laser printer on the market. You can order specially printed checks that are suitable for use with Quicken. Several styles are available, including wallet-size, standard (three checks per 8-1/2 by 11-inch sheet), and payroll/voucher.

Of course, you don't need to use Quicken to print the checks, but you'll find it makes bill-paying much easier.

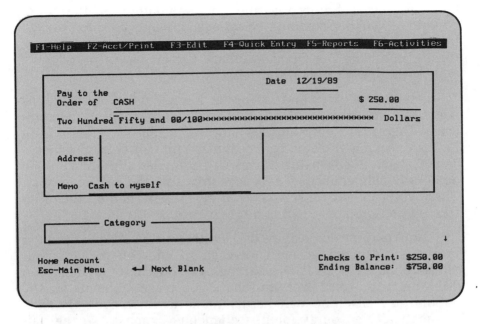

Figure 1.1. A sample of the check-writing screen.

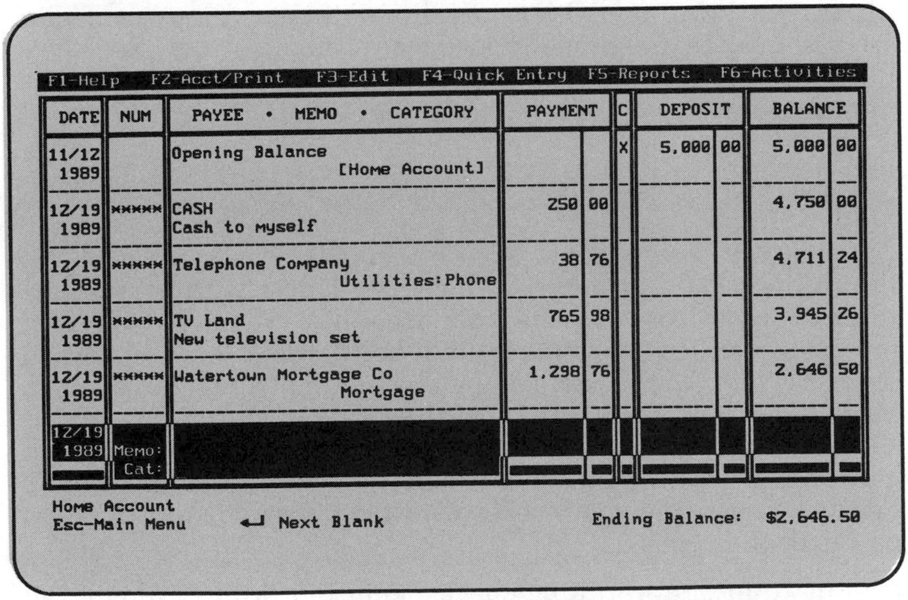

3

Figure 1.2. A sample of the check register screen.

Quicken checks follow the rules and regulations of the North American banking community, so even though you don't order the checks from your bank, your bank will still honor them. (Intuit, publisher's of Quicken, offers a money-back guarantee if your bank doesn't honor your checks.)

Besides checking and savings accounts, just about everyone has the extra burden of keeping track of one or more credit cards. Credit card accounts are handled in much the same fashion as checking and savings accounts. You can enter purchases as you make them—using the credit card sales slip—or you can defer all maintenance of the account until the bill comes in. Then, you can tack on service charges, interest, and all the other fees that accompany owning a credit card.

You may prefer to pay cash whenever you can. Quicken provides a separate account for cash so you can prevent your "loose change" from falling through the cracks. Of course, you don't need to record every purchase you make (10 cents for the bubble gum machine will hardly make a difference). Quicken automatically accounts for miscellaneous expenses so the balance is always correct.

Quicken offers two additional account types: Other Assets (things you own) and Other Liabilities (things you owe). These are best used by the property manager or home owner, for example, or to maintain a running list of money spent on home improvements.

In Business

In business, Quicken serves as a general ledger with payroll features. You still use the checking account to monitor expenses, but you can easily differentiate between general operating expenses and payroll. By using a post-dating technique, you can keep a watch on cash flow by writing checks ahead of time and seeing what expenses you'll have throughout the month (you can even project several months in advance). When your bills are due—assuming you receive your money as you expect—you can mail the checks.

In addition to printing checks, Quicken prints a number of reports. These reports can be used by both the home and business user, but they really make a difference in a business environment. For example, you can quickly prepare a payroll expense report, an accounts receivable or accounts payable report, a cash flow report, or a breakdown of spending by job, client, department, property, or project. A sample business report (a profit and loss statement) is shown in Figure 1.3.

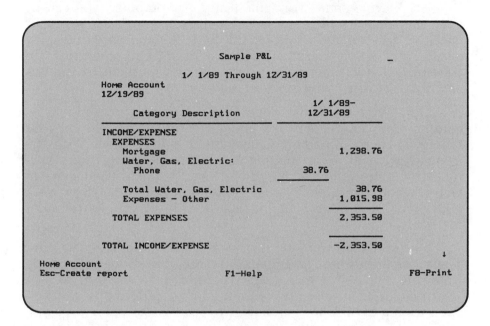

```
                          Sample P&L                    _

                    1/ 1/89 Through 12/31/89
          Home Account
          12/19/89
                                              1/ 1/89-
                 Category Description         12/31/89
          ──────────────────────────────    ──────────
          INCOME/EXPENSE
            EXPENSES
              Mortgage                             1,298.76
              Water, Gas, Electric:
                Phone                    38.76
                                        ────────
              Total Water, Gas, Electric            38.76
              Expenses - Other                   1,015.98

            TOTAL EXPENSES                        2,353.50
                                                 ────────

            TOTAL INCOME/EXPENSE                 -2,353.50
                                                              ↓
          Home Account
          Esc-Create report            F1-Help              F8-Print
```

Figure 1.3. This profit and loss report is just a few keystrokes away.

For Investments

Quicken can also be used to track stocks and bonds using a special investment account. In this account you can track an entire protfolio of stocks and bonds, monitoring buy and sell shares, dividends, splits, and other transactions. Quicken lets you monitor your actual investment purchases or make "paper" investment purchases in trial-runs at the stock market. Quicken is smart enough to know the difference between a real stock and a play stock.

5

What Quicken Will Do for You

At its most basic level, Quicken is a glorified calculator, automatically tallying your income and expenses and providing an instant balance. Barring some freak glitch in your computer, you can be sure the balance will be correct. If you started with $100 in your checking account and wrote a check for $30, Quicken will display a balance of $70. It doesn't mistake $30 for $50 and report that you have only $50 left, nor does it press the wrong calculator buttons and arrive at some wild amount.

Quicken also allows you to know where your money is coming from and where it's going. Getting a handle on your money is more important today than it's ever been. With the average price of a car topping $20,000 and house prices skyrocketing more than $50,000 in one year, it makes good sense to watch where every penny goes. That's not easy when you work with pencil and paper, but Quicken does it for you almost automatically.

Quicken lets you set up income and expense categories. These *categories* help you identify where your money is coming from and where it's going. For example, let's say you receive your regular salary each week from your employer plus an extra $200 from a trust fund. You have two sources for income, so you create two income expenses: payroll and trust fund. With each deposit you make into your checking or savings account, you use the categories to identify where the money came from.

The same applies to expenses, although you're likely to have far more expense categories than income categories. For instance, you may have categories for rent, food, car payment, clothing, and entertainment. With each check you write, you record the category in the memo area of the check—rent, car payment, whatever.

At the end of the week, month, or year—or any other time frame for that matter—you can use Quicken to list expenses and income by category. The report, like the one in Figure 1.4, will include all the deposits you've made and all the checks you've written. Each category will be totaled for you, so you can quickly see how your money was spent.

```
                              Sample Category
                          1/ 1/89 Through 12/31/89
  Home Account                                                    Page 1
  12/19/89

     Date   Num         Payee            Memo        Category    Clr  Amount

                  INCOME/EXPENSE
                    EXPENSES
                      Mortgage

   12/19  *****  Watertown Mortgage                  Mortgage        -1,298.76

                    Total Mortgage                                   -1,298.76

                  Water, Gas, Electric:

                      Phone

   12/19  *****  Telephone Company              Utilities:Phone        -38.76

                    Total Phone                                        -38.76

                    Total Water, Gas, Electric                         -38.76

                  Expenses - Other

   12/19  *****  CASH              Cash to myself                     -250.00
   12/19  *****  TV Land           New television                     -765.98

                    Total Expenses - Other                          -1,015.98

                  TOTAL EXPENSES                                    -2,353.50


                  TOTAL INCOME/EXPENSE                              -2,353.50


                  BALANCE FORWARD
                    Home Account

   11/12         Opening Balance               [Home Account]    X  5,000.00

                    Total Home Account                              5,000.00

                  TOTAL BALANCE FORWARD                             5,000.00


                  OVERALL TOTAL                                     2,646.50
```

Figure 1.4. Sample category report.

Quicken lets you set up categories as you go. Even if you initially established just ten categories, you can expand it to dozens or even hundreds, if necessary.

In addition, you can create categories under other categories—*subcategories*—to keep track of similar but separate items. This is most helpful in a small business where you may want to separate the expense of, say, printing by the type of printing done. Here's an example:

7

Main Category	Subcategories
Printing	Postcards
	Envelopes
	Letterhead
	Business cards

Akin to categories are *classes.* These help you assign kinds of expenses to people, places, or times. You most often will use classes as individual entries under categories. For instance, under the category of printing, you could assign the expenses to individual jobs ("people"). In that way, when you get ready to bill for the job, you can easily extract all the expenses for the particular job.

Main Category	Subclasses
Printing	Anderson Meat Packing
	Bill's Garage Door Opener Co.
	Uncle Walter's Newsstand

No matter how you decide to set up Quicken for your home or business, the end result of tracking your income and expenses is to make your money last longer. You may not be aware of how much money is spent each month on eating out, for example. Upon seeing the facts, you may have second thoughts the next time you don't see anything appetizing in the kitchen and suggest a quick bite to eat at the corner restaurant.

Or, you may find that you're not spending as much money on clothing or vacations as you could. With the figures in front of you, you can prepare a quick budget for redistributing your expenses among some of the items you didn't think you could afford.

Quicken can practically automate tax calculations, which is a feature that is as important as regular check-ups on your financial health. If you've indicated those items that are tax deductible and those that are not, Quicken will prepare a report that itemizes your income and expenses and lists how you can apply them to your tax forms. Quicken provides data-compatibility with the JK Lasser's Your Income Tax and TurboTax packages. Use of these ancillary programs is not covered in this book.

The Process of Using Quicken

The way you use Quicken depends on the kinds of accounts you're tracking with it. The most straightforward application of Quicken is to maintain a single checking account. To open the account:

1. Provide the opening balance.
2. Identify the income and expense categories (you can add or remove categories at any time).

You can now write one or more checks. Quicken automatically numbers and dates the checks, but you can change these if you like. To write a check, you enter the payee, the amount, and optionally an address and memo. If you're using Quicken to print checks, you can either print the check now or wait until you've written more and print them all at once.

9

The check register lets you make changes to checks you've written but not yet printed, void checks, write in deposits, include automated teller machine (ATM) withdrawals, add service charges, and perform all other regular check register duties. Quicken initially organizes the transactions (e.g., checks you've written and deposits you've made) in the order you entered them. When you print checks, the checks are re-ordered by number. Other transactions are re-ordered by date, so you can find them easily.

Use the list of transactions compiled by Quicken to make sure that your balance corresponds to the balance the bank says you have when you receive your bank statement. This entails subtracting deposits that have not yet shown up in the statement, adding checks that have not yet cleared, and making adjustments for any service fees. If the reports match, the balances agree. If Quicken and the bank disagree, the program tells you the amount of the error. You can then look for items you missed.

You can print reports that show how your money is coming and going at any time, but preferably after you're sure the Quicken check register accurately reflects the condition of your checking account. Quicken provides the following personal, business, and investment reports:

Personal	Cash flow
	Monthly budget
	Itemized categories
	Tax summary
	Net worth
Business	Profit and loss statement
	Cash flow
	Accounts payable, by vendor
	Accounts receivable, by customer
	Job/project
	Payroll
	Balance sheet
Investment	Portfolio value
	Investment performance
	Capital gains (Schedule D)
	Investment income
	Investment transactions

10

These reports are generated by Quicken using predesignated defaults. If you don't like the way Quicken prepares a report, you can design your own custom reports of transactions, summaries, budgets, and account balances. For example, as shown in Figure 1.5 for the create summary report, you can restrict transactions between certain dates, control row and column headings, and indicate which accounts to include in the report.

The Quicken Way

Quicken is completely menu driven. Your available choices are shown on the screen. Quicken has two types of menus:

▶ Pop-up box.
▶ Pull-down.

The pop-up box menu, such as the one shown in Figure 1.6, presents a list of commands. Beside each option is a number or letter. You select the command by pressing the appropriate key on the keyboard. You can also select the command by moving the selector (a highlight or arrow) over the item and pressing the Enter key. Quicken uses pop-up box menus when it's not displaying anything else on the screen.

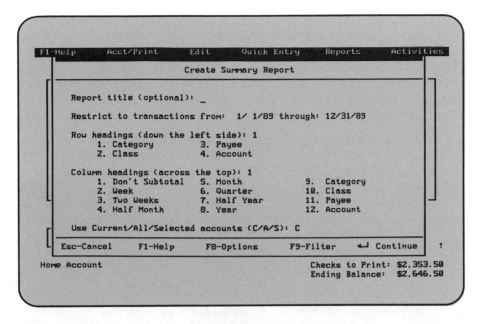

Figure 1.5. The Create Summary Report window.

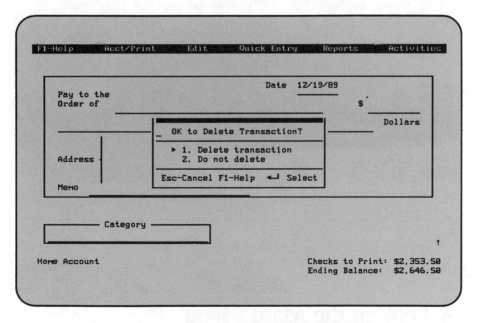

Figure 1.6. Sample pop-up box menu in Quicken.

11

Pull-down menus, like the one in Figure 1.7, are used to select an option or command while writing checks or working an account register. You "pull" the menu into view only when you need it. Pull-down menus are activated by pressing one of the function keys on the keyboard. For example, to choose the Reports menu, press the F5 key when in the Write Checks or check register screen.

Quicken uses numerous quick-keys to activate common commands directly from the keyboard. The quick-key for a given command is always shown by the command in the menu. As illustrated in Figure 1.8, you press Ctrl-P (the control and P keys together) to print checks. A complete list of available quick-keys appears on the inside back cover of this book. The Quicken manual also provides the quick-keys, in a different arrangement, on its back cover.

12

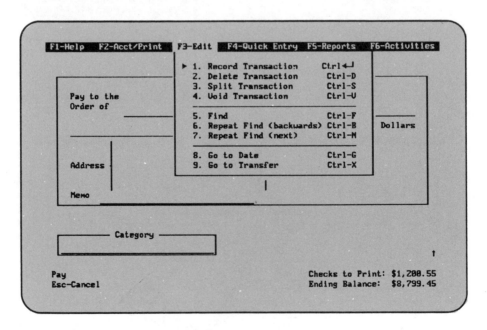

Figure 1.7. Sample Quicken pull-down menu.

A Look at the Main Menu

When you start Quicken, it displays the main pop-up box menu shown in Figure 1.9. This is the main menu and serves as a bridge to all of Quicken's features. Note that you can also access many of the program's features directly by using quick-keys. The menu serves as a convenient basis until you get used to Quicken.

The main menu contains six commands, all of which are self-explanatory. We'll take a moment now to introduce these commands and to note where to find more information about them in the remainder of this book.

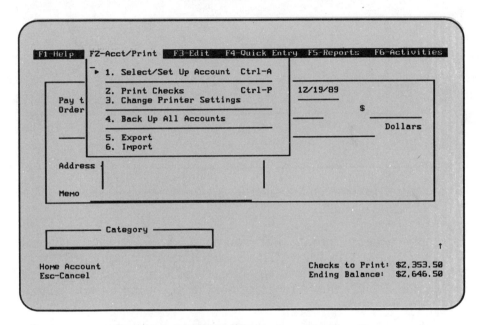

Figure 1.8. The Acct/Print menu.

1. Write/Print Checks—This command lets you write checks and optionally print them. When you write a check, it's automatically added to the register. See Chapters 4 and 8 on writing and printing checks, respectively.

2. Register—The register is where you maintain all checking account transactions. If you are using Quicken to maintain other account types, you record the transactions in their respective registers. For more information on registers see Chapter 5.

3. Reports—Reports provide a convenient summary of your account transactions. See Chapter 10 on how to prepare printed reports.

4. Select Account—You can maintain any number of accounts with Quicken. (You are limited to 255 accounts

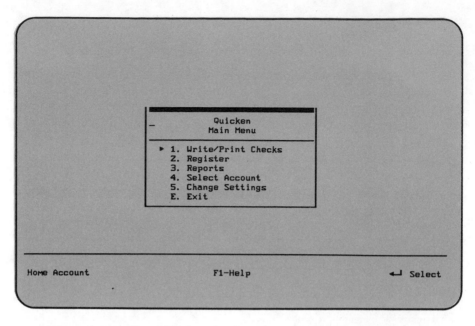

Figure 1.9. The Quicken main menu, the bridge between Quicken's functions.

per account group, but you can have as many account groups as you want.) The Select Account command allows you to select a previously created account or to start a new one. See Chapter 3 for information on setting up and changing accounts.

5. Change Settings—Quicken permits a moderate amount of customization, so that you can tailor the program to your computer, tastes, and requirements. Refer to Chapter 2 on how to set up Quicken.

E. Exit—This command lets you leave Quicken.

Hardware You Need

The PC version of Quicken works on any IBM PC or compatible. You actually need very little additional hardware to make Quicken work for you. Here's what you'll need:

IBM PC, XT, AT, PS/2, or a close compatible.

At least 320 kilobytes of RAM.

Monochrome or color monitor.

DOS 2.0 or later (3.0 or later is recommended).

Quicken will work from either floppy disks or a hard disk. Your work will go faster if you use a hard disk. The Quicken program and data files consume less than 1 megabyte of hard disk space. If you don't have a hard disk, you can still achieve good results using floppy disks. You'll need a minimum of two 5-1/4-inch drives or one 3-1/2-inch drive.

Quicken *does not* use a mouse or other alternate input device, nor does it need a graphics monitor and display adapter. The Write Checks and check register screens are produced using standard display characters. Of course, if you happen to have a mouse connected to your computer, you can leave it there; Quicken won't mind. You can also use a graphics display with Quicken. When you run Quicken, the display will switch to text mode automatically.

15

Quicken can be used as effectively with a color monitor as with a monochrome monitor. Note, however, that using a color display is a little easier on the eyes. Quicken allows you to select a color scheme, including light blue with dark blue, red with gray, shades of gray, and white with blue. If you have a color display, you can experiment with each color palette to find the one you like best.

If you're planning to use Quicken to print checks or reports, you'll need some type of printer. An impact printer, such as a dot matrix or daisywheel, is recommended for printing checks, although you can also use ink jet and laser printers. Because laser printers print an entire page at a time, you need to order special "laser checks."

You *cannot* use a thermal printer to print checks because the check stock is not made with thermal paper. You can, however, print with a thermal transfer printer. These produce an image by melting a waxy ink from a ribbon onto the paper. Keep in mind that both ink jet and thermal transfer printers work best with a smooth, polished paper. Nonimpact printers, which include laser, ink jet, and thermal transfer, cannot be used in multipart (NCR) type checks.

Some Useful Terms

Throughout this book we'll be using some basic financial terms. You probably know the meanings of some, if not all, of these terms, but if you don't, here's a quick review of the more common ones. Note that Quicken generally eschews the more exotic financial terms. We'll keep within that tradition, but we'll use some additional terms common in banking and financial affairs.

account   Any one of several independent records of money or financial transactions. In Quicken, accounts are subdivided into type: Bank (checking and savings), Credit, Cash, Other Asset, Other Liability, and Investment.

asset   Something you own. This includes cash, real estate, office furniture, and the clothes on your back. See also *liability*.

automated teller machine   Also called an ATM. A machine that performs the duties of a bank teller, including accepting cash and checks for deposits and paying cash for withdrawals. It is often friendlier than its human counterpart.

balance   The difference between the money that was originally in an account (called the starting balance) and the payments you made against that money. If you start out with $1,000 in the bank, and write $900 in checks, the balance is $100.

cash flow   The amount of money you receive versus the amount of money you spend. If you receive more money in a given period of time than you spend, then you have a positive cash flow. If you spend more money than you receive, your cash flow is negative.

category   A means of classifying income and expenses. As applied to income, a category indicates the source of the income; as applied to expenses, a category indicates what your money is being spent on.

class   Another means of specifying how money is spent. Classes are generally limited to classifying by people, places, or times.

clear   A check that is acknowledged by the bank and shows up as being paid on your statement. Cleared items also pertain to credit card purchases (when they show up on your bill).

credit   Apart from the usual meaning, the term also means a transaction where you add money to your account. It's synonymous with *deposit*.

debit   A transaction where you subtract money from your account. An example is a check or an ATM withdrawal.

deposit   A transaction where you add money to your account.

ending balance   The money you end up with after you've tallied up all credits and debits.

liability   Something you owe. This includes the things you haven't yet paid for in full, including real estate, office furniture, and the clothes on your back. See also *asset*.

overdraw   To withdraw more funds from your account than you have. If you write a check and don't have funds to cover it, the check "bounces" back from your bank as an overdraft.

payee   Who you're writing the check to. It can be a person or a company.

17

payment   A transaction subtracted from your account. A typical payment is a check you write.

post-date   To provide some future date on a transaction. With Quicken, post-dating is most often used to maintain a positive cash flow. For example, you write all the checks for a given month but date the checks for the days they are due. This helps Quicken to know that you're not overdrawn, even if you don't currently have enough money in the bank to pay all the checks. As money that you're expecting comes in, you can mail the checks.

reconcile   To compare the ending balance the bank says you have against the one you say you have. If the ending balances are the same, the account is reconciled. Differences often occur because of check charges, service fees, and other debits that you may not have included in your ending balance.

register   A place to record the transactions in an account. In a checking account, the register contains the checks you write, your deposits, and additional debits and credits including ATM withdrawals, service fees, and check charges.

split   Dividing a single transaction (such as a check) among several categories or classes.

statement   A balance sheet provided by your bank or other financial institution that itemizes your deposits and with drawals. The statement also shows a beginning and ending balance. A bill from a credit card company serves as a statement.

transaction Any payment from, or a deposit to, an account. A transaction is anything that affects the ending balance of your account, whether it's a $1,200 monthly mortgage payment or a five-cent check charge.

transfer To withdraw money from one of your accounts and deposit it into another. You can readily transfer money from your savings to your checking account, for example. (The complete transfer is performed in one step, assuming Quicken is handling both accounts.)

withdrawal Removal of money from. It usually refers to a savings account.

18 What You Have Learned

This chapter introduced Quicken and its various capabilities. Here's what you have learned:

▶ Quicken keeps track of six types of accounts: banking (checking and savings), cash, credit cards, miscellaneous assets, miscellaneous liabilities, and investments.

▶ Quicken can print your checks using almost any printer.

▶ By using a post-dating technique, you can keep a watch on cash flow by writing checks ahead of time and seeing what expenses you'll have throughout the month. When your bills are due and you have the cash to cover them, you can mail the checks.

▶ An important use of Quicken is to keep track of where money is coming from and where it's going.

▶ Categories and classes let you catalog your money so you can more easily track its origin and destination.

▶ After setting up your checking account with Quicken, paying bills is a four-step process: write the check, print the check (optional), record any other transactions in the register, and reconcile the register when your statement comes in.

▶ Quicken provides the following personal reports: cash flow, monthly budget, itemized categories, tax summary, and account balances.

▶ Quicken provides profit and loss statements and balance sheets as well as the following business reports: cash flow, accounts payable, accounts receivable, job/project, and payroll.

▶ At a minimum, Quicken needs an IBM PC, XT, AT, PS/2, or compatible with DOS 2.0 or later, 320 kilobytes of RAM, a monochrome or color monitor, and two 5-1/4-inch floppy disk drives (or one 3-1/2-inch floppy disk drive).

19

20

Getting Started with Quicken

In This Chapter   21

- ▶ *Installing Quicken*
- ▶ *Customizing the program*
- ▶ *Starting Quicken*
- ▶ *Accessing on-line help*
- ▶ *Moving around within Quicken*

Quicken is almost ready to use right out of the box. But if your computer is equipped with a hard disk drive, you'll want to install the Quicken files on the hard drive before using the program. Quicken also works with dual-floppy disk drive systems. If you're using floppy disk drives, you should make working copies of the Quicken distribution disks before proceeding.

This chapter tells you how to install Quicken on floppy or hard disks, how to set up and customize Quicken for your computer and printer, and how to use Quicken's basic operating conventions. You'll also get to know a little more about Quicken by creating a "trial" checking account and printing several sample checks.

Installation

Quicken comes on two distribution diskettes. Among the files included on the distribution diskettes is an installation program. This program, called INSTALL, automates the installation process for hard and floppy disk computer systems. INSTALL serves three functions:

▶ Copies the Quicken files to the appropriate drive and/or directory.

▶ Updates the CONFIG.SYS file (if any) on your hard disk to ensure that it contains the minimum settings for the FILES = and BUFFERS = commands.

▶ Optionally installs the Billminder program on your hard disk and adds a command line to your AUTOEXEC.BAT file to run BILLMINDER automatically each time your computer is started.

22

To use INSTALL, insert the Quicken Install/Startup disk into drive A and type

```
INSTALL
```

at the A> prompt. If you are installing Quicken on floppy disks, format one 3-1/2- or two 5-1/4-inch diskettes ahead of time. If you're using a hard disk, you don't need to create a Quicken sub-directory ahead of time. INSTALL will do that for you.

After starting INSTALL, it tells you what it will do before it happens, as shown in Figure 2.1. At any time you can cancel the installation by pressing the Escape key. To go on, press the Enter key.

Floppy Disk Installation

You can install the Quicken files onto a previously formatted disk in drive A or B. At the menu prompt shown in Figure 2.2, choose option 1 for drive A or option 2 for drive B. Press the Enter key when you're done. INSTALL will prompt you when to insert the disks into the appropriate drives during the installation process.

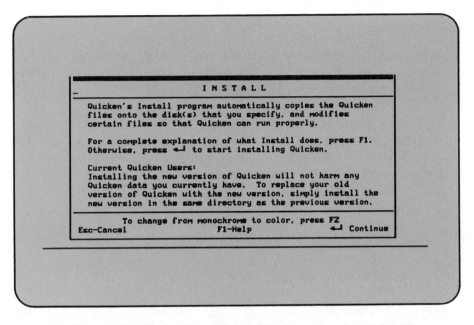

Figure 2.1. You see this opening screen when you first start Quicken.

23

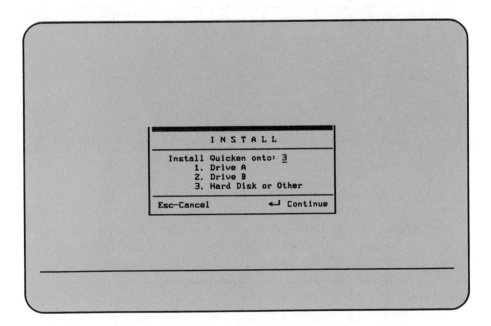

Figure 2.2. The floppy disk/hard disk installation menu.

Hard Disk Installation

Two extra steps are required when installing the Quicken files onto a hard disk: indicate the drive and subdirectory path for the files and indicate whether you want to install the Billminder program (see below) on your hard drive.

After indicating that you want to install Quicken onto a hard disk, specify the drive and directory for the files, as shown in Figure 2.3. INSTALL initially offers drive C and a subdirectory of \QUICKEN4. If you're using a different hard drive or subdirectory, edit the path as desired.

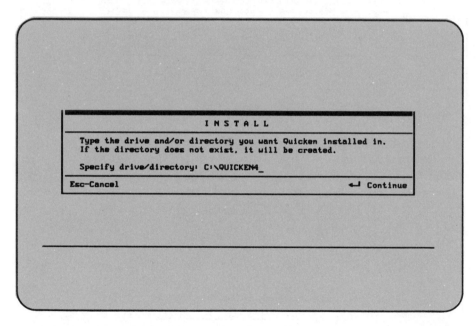

Figure 2.3. Specifying drive and directory for files.

▶ **Note:** The subdirectory *does not* need to exist before installation. INSTALL will create the subdirectory for you if one doesn't already exist on your hard disk.

Installing Billminder

For hard disk drive users, one of the options during the installation process is whether to include the Billminder program. BILLMINDER is a small program that runs each time your computer is started. The program checks the current date (as set by the DOS clock) and locates recurring bills (like car and mortgage payments) in any of your Quicken registers. If a bill is due, you're prompted to run Quicken so that you can pay it.

You have the option, as shown in Figure 2.4, of either installing BILLMINDER on your hard disk or leaving it off. If you enter No, the Install program does nothing. If you enter Yes, INSTALL places the Billminder program (BILLMIND.EXE) in the root directory of your hard disk and adds a command line to your AUTOEXEC.BAT file. This command line, shown in the example in Figure 2.5, executes BILLMINDER each time you run your computer. (To view this file, type AUTOEXEC.BAT at the DOS prompt.)

25

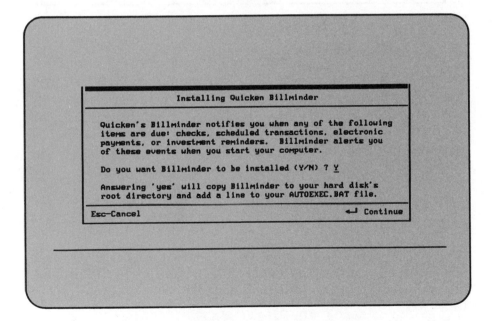

Figure 2.4. The Billminder program install option screen.

```
C:\>type autoexec.bat
ECHO OFF
path C:\UTIL;C:\;C:\PCTOOLS;C:\DOS;
Mirror C:/TC
PC-CACHE /IA /IB /SIZEXP=512K
cd \batch
prompt $p$g
\us4\uf
billmind


C:\>_
```

Figure 2.5. The BILLMIND command line in the
AUTOEXEC.BAT file.

Depending on how you've structured your AUTOEXEC.BAT
file, you may wish to omit the BILLMIND command line or to
move it to another spot in the file. For example, if the last line of
your AUTOEXEC.BAT file initiates a menu or starts a DOS shell
program, you'll want to place the BILLMIND command line earlier in the AUTOEXEC.BAT file.

Manual Installation

If your computer is equipped with a hard disk drive, you can
also manually install the Quicken files and by-pass the automated Install program. Manual installation takes a little less
time.

The following steps create a subdirectory to hold the
Quicken files and copy the files from the distribution disks to
the hard disk. Before starting, place the Quicken Help disk into
drive A or B. Keep the Program disk handy; you'll be copying
files from it, too.

Q Installing Quicken Manually

1. Type CD \ and press Enter. | Moves to the root directory on your hard drive.

2. Type MKDIR QUICKEN4 and press Enter. | Creates a subdirectory called QUICKEN4 to hold the Quicken files. (You can use a subdirectory of your own choosing if you wish.)

3. Type CD \QUICKEN4 and press Enter. | Moves to the QUICKEN4 subdirectory, making it current.

4. Type COPY A:*.* and press Enter. (Substitute B for A if you're copying files from drive B.) | Copies all files from the disk in drive A.

☐

After copying is complete, remove the Help disk from the drive, insert the Program disk, and repeat step 4. If you want to use the Billminder program, add the following command line to your AUTOEXEC.BAT file:

`C:\QUICKEN4\BILLMIND`

This automatically runs BILLMINDER at startup.

> ▶ **Note:** If you've placed the Quicken files in a subdirectory other than QUICKEN4, edit the AUTOEXEC.BAT command line as required.

About the Q.BAT File

If you're installing Quicken onto a hard disk drive, the Install program automatically adds a batch file to the root directory of the drive. The Q.BAT batch file starts Quicken quickly. The Q.BAT file works best when the AUTOEXEC.BAT file contains a PATH statement that includes the root directory. With the root included in the PATH statement, you can start Quicken from any subdirectory of your hard disk.

If the AUTOEXEC.BAT file on your hard disk lacks a PATH statement, you can add it easily enough. Using any word processor that can save files in standard DOS (plain text or ASCII format), open the AUTOEXEC.BAT file and, near the end of the file, add

`PATH=C:\`

This assumes that drive C is the hard drive you want to use. If it's not, substitute the appropriate drive letter.

If the AUTOEXEC.BAT file already contains a PATH statement, you can include the root directory as an alternate path. For example,

Before   `PATH=C:\DOS`
After   `PATH=C:\DOS;C:\`

As shown in the example, you can extend the PATH parameters by adding a semicolon, then entering the full DOS path—in this case simply `C:\`.

Customizing Quicken

Once installation is complete, you can immediately use Quicken to handle your financial affairs. But first, you'll probably want to alter some of its preset options to conform to your particular computer and printer. You change Quicken's setting directly inside the program. Although you can change the settings at any time, take a moment right now to familiarize yourself with the available options and how to modify Quicken to suit your needs. Among the settings you can alter are screen color, monitor speed, printer, and password. To make any changes to Quicken, you must first start the program, then choose the Change Settings command.

Q Changing Quicken Settings

1. Press Q then Enter.   Starts Quicken.
2. Press 5.   Chooses Change Settings command. The menu in Figure 2.6 appears. □

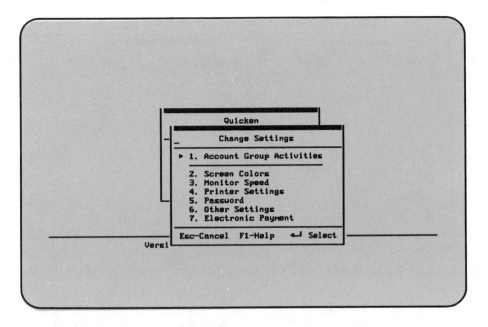

Figure 2.6. The Change Settings menu.

To select one of the subcommands in the Change Settings menu, type the corresponding number or press the Up or Down arrow keys to highlight the option you want, then press the Enter key.

Setting the Screen Color

Quicken offers a choice of five "palettes" for displaying its screens. Your choices are monochrome, navy/azure, white/navy, red/gray, and shades of gray. You can use any palette with any type of monitor—color or black & white. Even so, you should avoid using the color palettes if your computer is equipped with a monochrome monitor or you are using a color monitor in monochrome mode. Table 2.1 shows recommended settings for different monitor types.

Table 2.1. Recommended Screen Color Settings.

Settings	Color	Color/Monochrome*	Screen Snapshot**
Monochrome	R	R	R
Navy/Azure	R	NR	NR
White/Navy	R	NR	NR
Red/Gray	R	NR	NR
Shades of Gray	R	NR	NR

Notes:

R = Recommended

NR = Not recommended

*Color/monochrome applies to both color monitors operated in monochrome mode (using the MODE=MONO DOS command) or standard monochrome monitors.

**Screen snapshot includes Hijaak, Hotshot, and many other screen memory programs that take a "snapshot" of the display and store it on disk or print it on a printer. Unless the image is saved in color, highlighted text within Quicken will not appear.

30

Quicken uses a patterned background (see Figure 2.7) when you select any but the Monochrome setting. If you don't want the background, choose Monochrome. Note that the screen shots throughout this book were made with the Monochrome setting—the pattern does not appear.

To change the screen color (from the Change Settings menu):

1. Press 2. This selects the Screen Colors option.
2. In the Screen Colors menu, press the number that corresponds to the screen color you want. For example, to choose Red/Gray, press 4.

Setting the Monitor Speed

If you're using a Color Graphics Adapter (CGA) monitor, you can select Fast or Slow monitor speed.

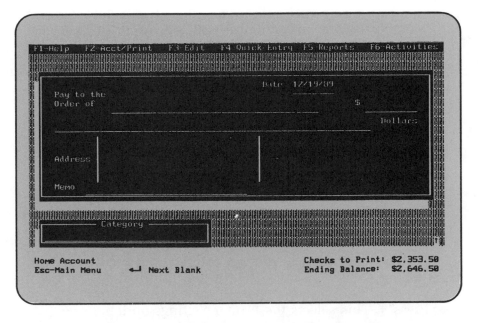

*Figure 2.7. A sample of the patterned background
provided by Quicken.*

The Slow setting causes the display to write text somewhat slower than normal, but "snow" (caused by the flicker of the cursor as it scans across the screen) *does not* appear during text scrolling and changes.

The Fast setting causes the display to write text at the usual speed, but snow appears when scrolling or changing text.

The Fast and Slow settings make no difference if you're using a display adapter other than the CGA.

To change the monitor speed (from the Change Settings menu):

1. Press 3. This selects the Monitor Speed option.
2. You have two choices, Fast or Slow. Choose the speed you want from the Screen Update Speed window.

Setting Printer Functions

Quicken is designed to print checks and reports. You don't have to print anything with Quicken, if you don't want to, but you'll

get the most from the program if you take advantage of its printing features. Before you can use Quicken to print checks or
reports, however, you must indicate the type of printer you have
and how it's connected to your computer.

You must furnish four main tidbits of information to
Quicken about your printer:

▶ *Type of printer,* usually by make and model.
▶ *Printing style,* such as normal or compressed.
▶ *Interface port* used to connect the computer to the printer.
▶ *Settings for general printing,* including lines per page, mar-
   gins, and standard print pitch (normally 10 characters per
   inch).

Follow these steps to select a printer from the Change Settings menu:

32

1. Press 3. This selects the Printer Settings option.
2. Choose a printer setting type, as shown in Figure 2.8.
   Quicken separates its printing functions into three discrete
   areas: check printing, report printing, and alternate printing.
   The remaining steps are the same no matter which printer
   setting type you select. However, if you plan on using
   Quicken to print both checks and reports, you need to
   change the settings for both Check Printer and Report
   Printer.
3. From the list shown in Figure 2.9 (not all of the available
   printers are displayed at once), select the printer you wish
   to use. To select a printer, highlight it (with the cursor keys)
   and press the Enter key. See Table 2.2 for a directory of
   printers Quicken supports.

The printer list provides three "blanks" where you can use
Quicken with your printer, even if your printer is not listed.

Use the *IBM Compatible* printer selection for any dot matrix
or daisywheel printer that uses the standard IBM character set
and IBM printer control codes (IBM ProPrinter compatible).

Use the *Unlisted* printer selection for any dot matrix, daisywheel, thermal transfer, or ink jet printer that is not listed and
that is not compatible with the IBM ProPrinter.

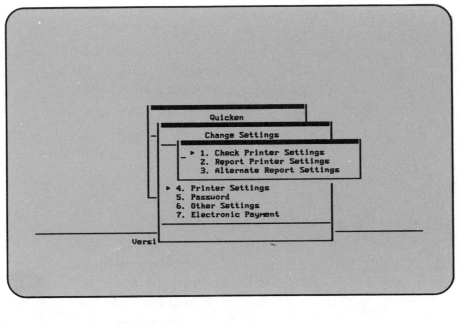

33

Figure 2.8. Setting the printer type.

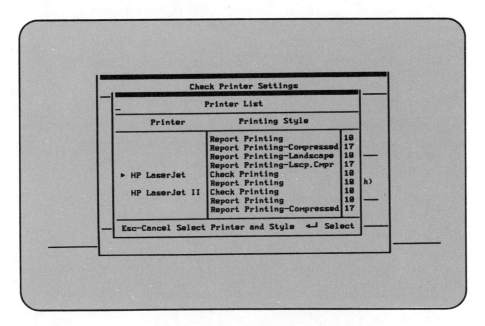

Figure 2.9. One screen of Quicken's printer list.

Table 2.2. *Printers Supported by Quicken.*

Brand	Model	Print Style	Pitch
Canon	LPB-II	Check printing	10
	LPB-III	Report printing	10
		Report/compressed	17
		Report/landscape; compressed	17
Epson	All	Checks & Reports; normal	10
		Compressed	17
Hewlett-Packard	Deskjet	Check printing	10
		Report printing	10
		Report/compressed	17
	Deskjet Plus	Check printing	10
		Report printing	10
		Report/compressed	17
		Report/landscape	10
		Report/landscape; compressed	17
	LaserJet	Check printing	10
		Report printing	10
	LaserJet II	Check printing	10
		Report printing	10
		Report/compressed	17
		Report/landscape	10
		Report/landscape; compressed	17
	LaserJet IIP	Check printing	10
		Report printing	10
		Report/compressed	17
		Report/landscape	10
		Report/landscape; compressed	17
	LaserJet III	Check printing	10
		Report printing	10

34

Continued

Brand	Model	Print Style	Pitch
		Report/compressed	17
		Report/landscape	10
		Report/landscape; compressed	17
IBM Compatible		Checks/reports; normal	10
		12-pitch printing	12
		Compressed printing	17
IBM	ProPrinter	Checks/reports; normal	10
		Compressed printing	17
		Near-letter quality	10
	4216	Check printing	10
		Report printing	10
	4019	Check printing	10
		Report printing	10
		Report/compressed	17
		Report/landscape	10
		Report/landscape; compressed	17
Kyocera	F-1000A	Check printing	10
		Report printing	10
		Report/compressed	17
		Report/landscape	10
		Report/landscape; compressed	17
NEC	3530	Checks & reports; normal	10
		Compressed printing	17
	8023A	Checks & reports; normal	10

Continued

35

Table 2.2 *continued*

Brand	Model	Print Style	Pitch
		Compressed printing	10
Okidata	83,92,182, 192, 292	Checks & reports; normal	10
		Compressed printing	17
	320	Checks & reports; normal	10
		Compressed printing	17
Star	All	Checks & reports; normal	10
		Near letter quality	10
Unlisted		Checks & reports; normal	10
		Wide carriage	10
Unlisted Laser		Normal	10
		Compressed	17

Notes:

Quicken uses "pitch" to indicate the number of characters printed in 1 inch. A pitch of 10 means 10 characters per inch.

"Normal" printing is standard portrait orientation without print compression.

"Wide carriage" printing is landscape orientation.

"Compressed" printing is 17 pitch.

36

Use the *Unlisted Laser* printer selection for any laser printer other than the LaserJet I or II. It's acceptable to use the LaserJet printer settings if your laser printer is HP LaserJet compatible, but be sure your printer is *truly* LaserJet compatible.

Once you've selected a printer (for checks or reports), you need to tell Quicken how it's set up and how your computer attaches to it. Press the F8 key at the Change Settings window to get in the Check Printer Settings window. It appears after you select a printer (see Figure 2.10), you set:

Name of the printer (optional).

Port connecting the computer to the printer.

Indent margin, if any.

Page size—Length is expressed as number of lines from top to bottom, and width is expressed as number of characters from left to right.

Print pitch, or the number of characters printed per inch (normally 10 or 12, but you may want to select a condensed or compressed pitch—15 or 17 pitch).

Whether you'd like the printing to *pause* between each page (if you're hand-feeding the paper into the printer, for instance).

Page orientation of the printer (e.g., a laser printer ejects no less than an entire page).

Whether the printer supports *IBM graphics characters.*

37

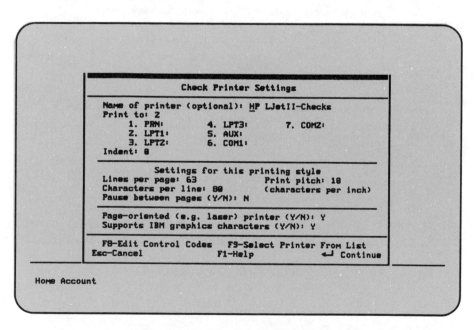

Figure 2.10. The Check Printer Settings screen.

To fill in the settings, place your entry at the appropriate *data field* (entry blank), and press the Enter key when you're done. If the setting is already the way you want it, just press Enter to confirm the default.

You can optionally edit the control codes Quicken sends to the printer prior to, during, and after check and report printing. Quicken already provides the necessary control codes to use with the printers listed in Table 2.2. If you need to change the codes—or need to enter codes for a printer not on the list—you should refer to your printer's manual on the codes that are necessary for each of the functions Quicken supports.

As shown in Figure 2.11, you can enter control codes that are sent before printing starts, after printing finishes (to reset the printer, for instance), and at the start of each page. If your printer is capable of *landscape* (sideways) printing, you can insert the control codes for that function in the appropriate blank.

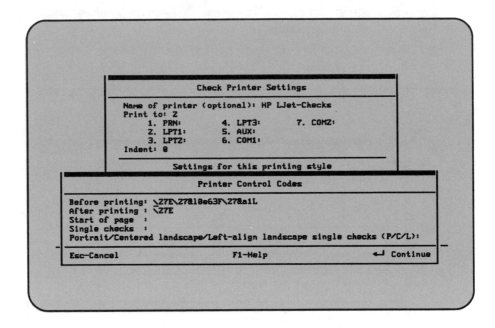

Figure 2.11. The Printer Control Codes screen.

Setting Passwords

Quicken lets you set passwords for accessing the program and for changing transactions. The use of a password is strictly optional. For most home and many business users, a password is unnecessary. You will want to use a password if you want to prevent unauthorized persons from accessing or changing the information in your Quicken accounts. Quicken offers two levels of password protection: main and transaction.

The *main password* allows access to all your accounts in the current Quicken account group. (An account group is a collection of all your accounts. You'll create additional account groups if you are tracking the finances of several different people, households, or businesses.)

The *transaction password* allows access to transaction records and enables you to make changes to those records even if the account period for those transactions has been "closed." With password protection on, no one else can make changes to transactions that are dated prior to the closing period.

Both passwords are set using the Password menu. Follow these steps to set the main password from the Change Settings menu:

1. Press 5. This selects the password option.
2. Press 1, for Main Password.
3. Enter a password. You can type any word or phrase, up to 16 characters. Check it carefully. Press the Enter key to record the password. Quicken asks that you enter the password a second time for verification.

39

Follow the same general steps to set a transaction password at the Change Settings menu:

1. Press 5, for Password menu.
2. Press 2, for Transaction Password.
3. Enter a password (up to 16 characters).
4. Enter a closing date for transactions. Transactions prior to this date will be locked out from future changes, unless you provide the transaction password. Press the Enter key when done.

> ▶ **Tip:** Don't choose a password carelessly. If you forget your main password, you will not be able to access *any* of your accounts, and your Quicken files will be useless. Choose a password that others won't be able to guess easily (your first or last name is out, for instance) but that you won't forget. If necessary, write it down in an inconspicuous place—on the back of a picture you carry in your wallet or purse or as a "fake" name in your Rolodex file.

You can change or remove your main and transaction passwords at any time. You need the original password to do it, however. If you want to change your password, repeat steps 1 and 2 above (for either main or transaction password), and enter the current password into the Old Password slot. Enter a new password into the New Password slot. If you'd like to delete the password, leave New Password blank.

Additional Settings

As shown in Figure 2.12, Quicken allows you to select a number of other settings. To get to the Other Settings menu, enter 6 at the Change Settings menu. You can leave the settings as they are or change them. Their use is fairly self-explanatory, but here's a summary:

40

Beep when recording and memorizing—Sounds a beep when Quicken is recording and memorizing transactions. Set to Yes or No.

Request confirmation—Displays a yes/no query when Quicken is about to record or delete data. Set to Yes or No.

Require Category on transactions—Forces Quicken to ask for a category name for each transaction. Set to Yes or No.

Extra message line on check—Allows you to write and print an extra message line on the check; Quicken does not record the line in the register. Set to Yes or No.

Days in advance to remind of postdated checks and scheduled groups—Sets the number of days in advance Quicken will alert you to print checks you've entered into the check register. If you use your computer every day, you don't need to be reminded more than 1 or 2 days in advance. Set a number from 0 to 30.

Change date of checks to today's date when printed—Prints all checks with the current date, as set by DOS. It is used mostly when printing post-dated checks. Set to Yes or No.

MM/DD/YY or DD/MM/YY date format—Sets month/day/year format for checks and registers. Set to M (month first) or D (day first).

Billminder active—Tells Quicken that Billminder is active (for hard disk users only). Set to Yes or No.

Print categories on voucher checks—Prints category names (that you've typed in the Split Transaction window) on voucher checks. Quicken always prints text entered into the Description column of the Split Transactions window. Set to Yes or No.

43 line register/reports—Displays register and reports in 43 lines. For use only with EGA and VGA monitors that are supplied with appropriate 43-line display drivers. Set to Yes or No.

Show Memo/Category/Both—Determines the information displayed on the second line of the Payee-Memo-Category in the register (when the transaction is not selected). Set to M (for memo), C (for category), and B (for both memo and category).

In reports, use category Description/Name/Both—Determines how classes and categories are labeled in printed reports. Set to D (for description), N (for name), or B (for description and name).

Warn if check number is reused—Sounds a beep if you attempt to enter a check number that already exists. Answer Yes or No.

41

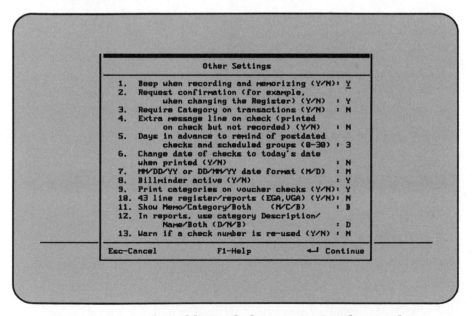

```
                    Other Settings

  1.  Beep when recording and memorizing (Y/N):  Y
  2.  Request confirmation (for example,
          when changing the Register) (Y/N)   :  Y
  3.  Require Category on transactions (Y/N)  :  N
  4.  Extra message line on check (printed
          on check but not recorded) (Y/N)    :  N
  5.  Days in advance to remind of postdated
          checks and scheduled groups (0-30)  :  3
  6.  Change date of checks to today's date
          when printed (Y/N)                  :  N
  7.  MM/DD/YY or DD/MM/YY date format (M/D)   :  M
  8.  Billminder active (Y/N)                 :  Y
  9.  Print categories on voucher checks (Y/N):  Y
 10.  43 line register/reports (EGA,VGA) (Y/N):  N
 11.  Show Memo/Category/Both    (M/C/B)      :  B
 12.  In reports, use category Description/
          Name/Both (D/N/B)                   :  D
 13.  Warn if a check number is re-used (Y/N) :  N

 Esc-Cancel          F1-Help            ←┘ Continue
```

Figure 2.12. Make additional changes in Quicken at this screen.

Table 2.3 lists the miscellaneous option settings offered by Quicken. Shown are the default (factory) settings, as well as suggested settings for expert Quicken users. Of course, you should configure Quicken in the way you like best; use the suggestions in the table as a guide only.

Table 2.3. Default and Suggested Expert Miscellaneous Settings.

	Setting	
Option	Original	Expert
Beep when recording...	Y	N
Request confirmation	Y	N
Require Category on transactions	N	N
Extra message line on check	N	N
Days in advance to remind...	3	0
Change date of checks...	N	Y
MM/DD/YY or DD/MM/YY date format	M	M*
Billminder active	Y	N
Print categories on voucher checks	Y	Y
43 line register/reports	N	N**
Show Memo/Category/Both	B	B
Use category Description/Name/Both	D	B
Warn if check number is reused	N	N*

Notes:

*Depends on personal tastes and conventions used in your country.

**Depends on your personal tastes and the capabilities of your display adapter.

Electronic Payments

The Change Settings menu provides a seventh option for setting up Quicken for electronic bill paying using the Checkfree system. Checkfree can be used by individuals and businesses, although most businesses will prefer to have more control over their accounts payable than Checkfree provides, so it is only briefly mentioned here. Checkfree requires a telephone modem (1200 or 2400 bps recommended) and a phone line. You do not need a tele-communications program; the facility for contacting Checkfree via the modem is built into Quicken.

Selecting the Electronic Payment command from the Change Settings menu displays an additional set of two options: Modem Settings and Account Settings. You must sign up with the Checkfree system before attempting to use this feature of Quicken. They will provide a phone number for your use as well as additional information on how to make contact.

The Modem Settings command lets you set up the serial port used by the modem, the modem speed (either 300, 1200, 2400, or 9600 bps), tone or pulse dialing, and the phone number for the Checkfree center nearest you. The Account Settings command lets you select accounts and payments to make through the Checkfree system.

43

Starting Quicken

The way you start Quicken depends on how you've installed the program: on a hard disk or on floppy disks.

 Starting Quicken, Hard Disk Installation

1. Turn on your computer (if it's not already on).
2. Press Q then Enter.   Quicken starts.   ☐

> ▶ **Note:** The Q.BAT file must be in the current directory, or the PATH statement (in the AUTOEXEC.BAT file, as detailed earlier in this chapter) must include the root or other directory that contains the Q.BAT path file.

Starting Quicken, Floppy Disk Drive

1. Start computer with system
   disk (if it's not already on).
2. Replace system disk with
   Quicken Program disk.
3. Type A: and press Enter.   Logs onto drive A.
4. Press Q then Enter.   Quicken starts.   ☐

 Note: If your computer is equipped with two floppy
disk drives, you should place the data disk in drive A.

44

 Note: You can start Quicken using special command-
line options, as detailed in Appendix C.

First Time Startup

If this is the first time you're using Quicken, the program asks if
you have a color monitor. Press 1 (if color) or 2 (if monochrome).

▶ **Tip:** Quicken's settings are stored in a file called
Q.CFG. If this file is ever lost, damaged, or erased,
Quicken will revert to its original settings, and you'll have
to select printer and screen options again. In addition, some
programs on your computer may reset the DOS display
mode to MONO, even if your machine is equipped with a
color monitor. Should this happen, Quicken may load and
display either a blank screen or a screen with only partial
characters. You need to either reset your computer or
change Quicken's display options. After Quicken loads
(even if you can't see the main menu), type 5 2 1. This sets
the monitor type to monochrome.

Date Set

Some computers—particularly the IBM PC and clones—lack a built-in clock/calendar. If the computer has a clock/calendar function, it is provided by an accessory card, which is optional. Without a clock/calendar card, DOS has no means to remember the date each time the computer is turned on or off. Unless you manually set the date when the computer is first turned on, DOS will think the date is January 1, 1980—the first day of DOS's time-keeping clock.

Quicken tracks financial data by date, and the setting of the current date is important. Quicken is designed to detect if the DOS clock is set to January 1, 1980; if it is, you're asked to provide the current date, as shown in Figure 2.13. The program initially provides the date of the last transaction. You can either type the date explicitly or use the + and − keys to set the date one day at a time.

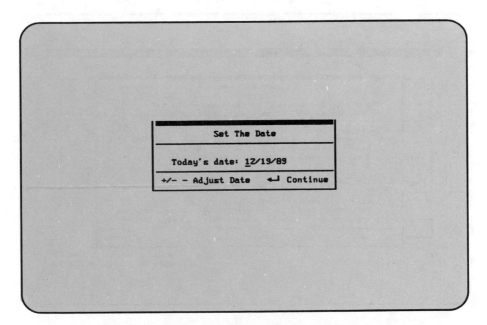

Figure 2.13. Quicken requests that you enter the current date if the clock in your computer is set to 1/1/80.

If your computer is equipped with a built-in clock/calendar, the battery used to retain the date and system information will eventually fail. When it does fail, the computer will lose the current date information. Each time you start your computer, the clock/calendar will reset to January 1, 1980. Again, Quicken will recognize that the date is not valid and ask you to update it.

Accessing On-Line Help

Quicken provides an on-line, context-sensitive help feature for times when you need a little nudge to get you going in the right direction. At just about every screen and menu in Quicken, you can access help by pressing the F1 key. A help window, like the one in Figure 2.14, splashes on the screen. If the help message is too long to fit in one window, you can scroll to see the remainder of its contents with the Page Down key. Conversely, press the Page Up key to scroll back through the help window.

46

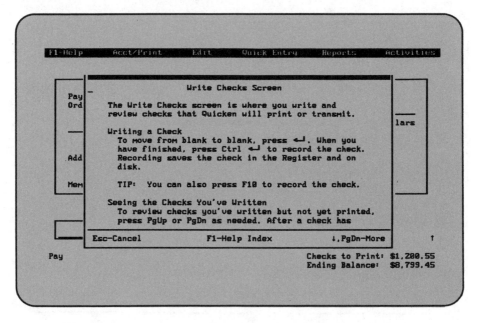

Figure 2.14. Sample of Quicken's on-line help.

When you're done reading help, press the Escape key to return to Quicken. Refer to Appendix B for a quick reference of topics covered by Quicken's on-line help feature.

> ▶ **Note:** Because Quicken's help feature is context-sensitive, it always displays a help message about the current screen, window, or menu. If you'd like to see an index of available help topics, press the F1 key again. Scroll through the help index, as illustrated in Figure 2.15, and press the Enter key when you find the topic you want. Quicken will then display the help window for that topic.

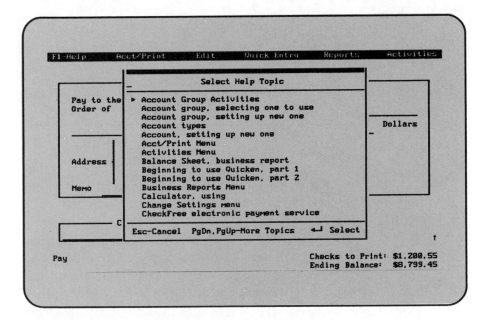

Figure 2.15. The help index.

Anatomy of a Screen

Most Quicken screens are similar to the one shown in Figure 2.16. The screen contains several components that are used frequently throughout the Quicken program. Get to know them.

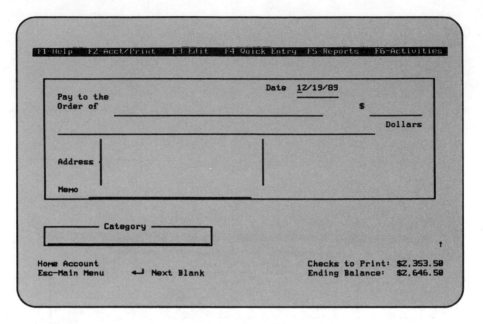

Figure 2.16. A sample Quicken screen.

Menu bar—The menu bar, which is displayed at the top of the screen, shows the menus currently available. To select a menu, press its corresponding function key.

Menu—A pull-down menu provides additional commands you can select at the current screen. The commands listed in all of Quicken's menus can also be accessed directly from the keyboard or from a submenu under the main menu.

Main screen window—The main window displays the dominant information of the screen. In this example, the main window displays a check, for you to enter a payee, dollar amount, address, and category.

Status—Most screens provide a status report at or near the bottom of the screen. Most often, it reports a balance or an amount.

Data fields—A data field is any portion of the screen where Quicken expects you to provide an entry. In the example, the date, payee, dollar amount, address, memo, and category blanks are data fields.

Moving Around Quicken

One of the strongest features of Quicken has nothing to do with money: it's the way you move around the program. Quicken employs an intuitive and consistent interface to help you maneuver from one screen and command to the next. Quicken uses the same keys for the same functions, no matter where you are in the program. Table 2.4 lists most of the functions within Quicken and the keys you'll press to activate those functions.

Table 2.4. Common Quicken Functions and Associated Keys.

Function	Keys
Help	F1
Help topics	F1, F1 (press the F1 key twice)
Access Account/Print menu	F2 (from selected screens only)
Access Edit menu	F3 (from selected screens only)
Access Quick Entry menu	F4 (from selected screens only)
Access Reports menu	F5 (from selected screens only)
Access Activities menu	F6 (from selected screens only)
To select a command in an item	Highlight the command or press the corresponding number
To move to the next data field	Tab or Enter
To move to the preceding data field	Shift-Tab
To select a command, complete an entry, or advance to next data field or screen	Enter
Delete character at cursor	Delete
Delete character to left of cursor	Backspace
Move to next word	Ctrl and right arrow keys
Move to previous word	Ctrl and left arrow keys
Move to start of entry blank	Home
Move to end of entry blank	End
Move to first entry blank	Home, Home

Continued

49

Table 2.4   *continued*

Function	Keys
Move to last entry blank	End, End
Delete all data from a field	Ctrl and Backspace
Cancel current screen and go back to previous screen or menu level	Esc
Confirm all data field entries on the screen	Ctrl and Enter

For a summary of Quicken keys and their uses, see the inside back cover of this book.

50   Leaving Quicken

When you're done with Quicken, press the Escape key to return to the main menu (if necessary), then press E to quit. Quicken automatically saves all of your data as you use the program and upon exiting, so you don't have to worry about doing it manually.

You can also make safety backups of your Quicken account files prior to leaving the program. To make a backup and remain in Quicken, press Ctrl-B at the main menu. To make a backup and leave Quicken (return to DOS), press Ctrl-E at the main menu.

For the backup, Quicken prompts you to insert a formatted data diskette. Be sure to have a formatted data diskette ready before requesting the backup. In addition to making quick backups using the Ctrl-E and Ctrl-B keys, you should make periodic backups of all Quicken program and data files, as detailed in Chapter 3, "Setting Up Accounts."

Do not leave Quicken by turning off or resetting your computer. Doing so may cause serious data loss.

What You Have Learned

This chapter examined the basics of getting started with Quicken. Here's what you have learned:

▶ The Quicken Install program copies the Quicken files to your disks, updates your CONFIG.SYS file (if necessary), and optionally installs a command line to run the Bill-minder program whenever you start your computer.

▶ When using a hard disk drive, the Q.BAT file lets you quickly start Quicken without having to be in the Quicken directory.

▶ Quicken lets you set screen color, monitor speed, printer type and settings, and password to suit your needs and hardware requirements.

▶ To start Quicken from a hard disk, press Q then Enter.

▶ To start Quicken from a floppy disk, insert the Quicken program diskette in drive A, then log onto drive A. Press Q then Enter.

▶ Press the F1 key to access Quicken's on-line, context-sensitive help. Press the F1 key again when in the help window to view the available help topics.

▶ When you're ready to leave Quicken, press the Escape key to return to the main menu (if necessary), then press E to quit.

51

52

Setting Up Accounts

In This Chapter

53

▶ *Setting up Quicken accounts*
▶ *Identifying account types*
▶ *Using account groups*
▶ *Maintaining account files*
▶ *Backing up account files*

Now that you've installed Quicken on your computer, you're ready to use it to keep track of your financial affairs. Quicken needs very little advance information about your finances, but it does need to be told the kind of accounts you want to track and the beginning balances.

This chapter shows you how to set up accounts in Quicken, how to maintain account records, and ways to keep backups to protect against data loss. You'll also learn about the types of accounts Quicken can handle and the information you should have on hand when you actually enter new account data into Quicken.

Types of Accounts

Quicken lets you track your finances regardless of their form or content. While the program is ideally suited for tracking your checking account, you can also use it to maintain savings accounts, record assets and liabilities, provide budgetary projections, handle payroll accounts, and much more. Quicken is designed to work with six specific types of financial accounts, although you are free to use any of these account types for other purposes. The six account types directly supported by Quicken are:

▶ Checking or savings account (called "Bank Account" by Quicken).

▶ Credit Card.

▶ Cash.

▶ Other Asset.

▶ Other Liability.

▶ Investment.

54

The first time you start Quicken, it asks you the type of account you'll be using, either business or personal, as shown in Figure 3.1. This helps Quicken set up standard categories for you. Choose

1 to use Quicken's standard home categories.

2 to use Quicken's standard business categories.

3 to use standard home AND business categories.

4 to omit all standard categories.

If you're just starting out with Quicken, choose option 3, both account types. Appendix A lists the categories Quicken automatically provides for home and business use. Remember that you can always delete categories you don't want and add new categories. For now, you don't need to worry about categories.

In this same screen, Quicken asks where the data files are located. If you're computer is equipped with:

Two floppy disk drives (any capacity), specify drive B (which should contain the data disk).

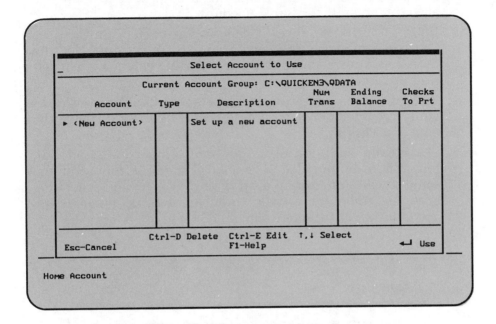

Figure 3.1. Screen shown on first time setup.

One high-capacity drive, specify drive A.
Hard disk, specify the drive letter (usually either C or D) and the full path, normally \QUICKEN4\.

Press Enter to go on to the next step. The Set Up New Account screen, shown in Figure 3.2, appears. Follow these steps to complete the entries in this screen. With the exception of selecting the account type, press the Enter key after providing the necessary information.

1. Provide a name for the account. Account names can have up to 15 characters and can use any characters except [ ] / : . Quicken uses the brackets to denote transfers between categories; the slash to enter main categories, subcategories, and class names; and the colon to separate category names from class names.

2. Indicate the account type, either Bank Account, Credit Card, Cash, Other Asset, Other Liability, or Investment. If you'll be using Quicken to maintain a checking or savings account, enter 1, for Bank Account.

3. Enter a starting balance, if known. Most often, this will be the actual money you have in your bank account. See the note that follows about entering a starting balance when setting up Quicken accounts.

4. Enter the date of the starting balance. Quicken automatically provides the current date (as set by DOS). Change the date if necessary.

5. Provide a description of the account. This step is optional, but it is recommended if you have many accounts of the same type. For example, if you have several checking accounts, enter the account number or bank name (if the accounts are at different banks).

56

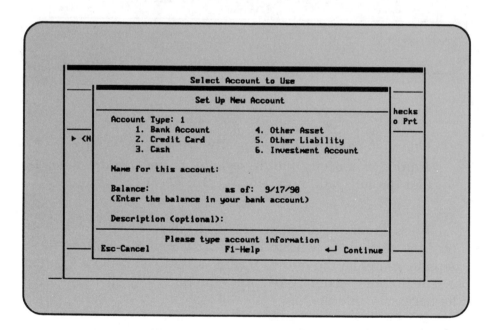

Figure 3.2. Set Up New Accounts screen.

When you're done filling in the new account information, press the Enter key one more time. Quicken then takes you to the Write Checks screen, where you can immediately use your new account. We'll save actually using the account for the next chapter.

Setting Up a Starting Balance

Although it seems a trivial matter, setting the starting balance for a new account can be a tough proposition. Normally, when dealing with checking and savings accounts, the starting balance is the amount of money you currently have in the bank. But the amount your bank says you have and the amount indicated in your checkbook or savings passbook may be wildly different.

If you are charged a monthly checking fee or are charged for each check you write during the month, your bank may have a slightly different balance than the one reflected in your check register. If your checking account is interest-bearing (and the same applies to savings accounts, which always accrue interest), your check register won't reflect the actual balance held by your bank's computer.

The best time to set up a new Quicken account is right after you've received the checking or savings account statement from the bank. Reconcile it against your own register, to make sure there are no errors, and enter the remaining balance into the starting balance data field in the Set Up New Account screen.

You will then need to enter into Quicken all those transactions that are listed in your paper register, but that have not yet shown up in the bank statements. For instance, if you've written five checks that are listed in your old register but aren't shown as being cleared at the bank, you'll need to enter them into Quicken to keep your account straight. Do the same for deposits and other transactions, including over-the-phone transfers and automated teller machine withdrawals.

Another approach is to enter the amount shown in the last entry in your checking account register. This entry doesn't include service charges or interest, and it may be in error (due to mistakes in computing your balance, for example), but it's a good rough estimate of what you have in the bank. Then, when the statement comes in, you can make adjustments within Quicken to amend for fees, interest, and corrections.

57

A final approach is to enter 0.00 in the standard balance entry field. Quicken will accept that as a temporary balance but will still let you track checks and deposits, and even write checks. At a later date, when you receive the bank statement in the mail, you can change the starting balance to reflect the amount you really have.

Selecting the Right Account Type

Quicken offers only six account types, which at first may appear to be very limited. What if you want to track your IRA account or maintain records on a money market fund? Or what if you want one general savings account, but then separate the accounts in your own records into compartments—one for travel, one for office supplies, one for inventory, and so forth?

58

Quicken doesn't really care what the account is. As long as the account deals with money—how and when it's spent and received—Quicken can handle it. While Quicken is not a full-fledged accounting package that can be used by Fortune 500 companies for their budgetary, payroll, and expense accounts, it is perfectly suited to personal and small business use.

Although you are free to try different approaches, here are some real-world financial records and the Quicken account types you may want to use when maintaining them:

Account	Quicken Account Type
Checking	Bank Account
Savings	Bank Account
Money market fund	Bank Account
Certificate of deposit	Bank Account, Other Asset
Real estate holdings	Other Asset
Spending cash	Cash
Petty cash (as used in business)	Cash, Bank Account
Personal belongings (antiques, jewlry, etc.)	Other Asset
Business property	Other Asset
Payroll	Bank Account

Account	Quicken Account Type
Income (regular income, plus income from alimony, royalties, trust funds, sponsorships, grants, etc.)	Bank Account, Other Asset
Revolving credit accounts (department store cards, Visa, MasterCard, etc.)	Credit Card
Closed-end accounts (credit cards, car loan, boat loan, personal line of credit)	Other Liability, Credit Card
House/property mortgage	Other Liability
Leases (you pay on)	Other Liability
Leases (you get paid)	Other Asset
Stock/bond portfolio	Other Asset, Investment
Personal debts (you pay on)	Other Liability
Personal debts (you get paid)	Other Asset
Stocks and bonds	/Investment

59

Here are some general guidelines to help you select the best Quicken accounts to take care of your financial matters:

An *asset* is something you own.

A *liability* is something you owe.

If the money is in a bank and you can write checks or make regular withdrawals to get it out, it's a *Bank Account*.

Other Assets are money that belongs to you or property (real or personal) you own. You can, with varying degrees of difficulty, withdraw the money or sell the property and receive the money for it.

Other Liabilities are money you've borrowed or property you are still paying for. If you sell the property, some or all of the money you get may have to be paid back to the lender.

Cash is usually considered *liquid* (easy to get at) money. This money is not in a bank account but rather can be readily found, say, in your wallet or under your mattress. Quicken is designed to treat the money in a Cash account as dispensable—you can spend some and just list it under "miscellaneous."

If the money is in a bank but you are restricted from withdrawing it, it's an *Other Asset*.

Your income (like your paycheck) can be applied to almost any account, depending on where it goes. Income can be applied to a Bank Account (the most frequently used), Credit Card, Cash, or Other Asset. If you get special income you want to track (e.g., grants, royalties for best-selling books, or scholarships), you can record it as an Other Asset.

About Account Groups

You can define any number of accounts in Quicken, limited only by disk space and your willingness to spend endless hours behind a computer. However, Quicken can handle accounts only when they are in groups. Most likely, you'll be using just one account group to hold all the accounts you create in Quicken.

60

You may, however, want to create separate account groups if you handle financial matters for others. As you learned in Chapter 2, "Getting Started with Quicken," Quicken lets you select a password to prohibit access to account information. You can give each account group its own password, for protection purposes.

Quicken *is limited* to holding no more than 255 accounts in any single account group. As even 255 accounts is far beyond the needs of the average Quicken user, this limitation is of no consequence.

Keeping Double Books

The first tenant of "computerizing the books" is to maintain the old-fashioned paper ledger while you enter the same transaction information into the computer. The same is true when starting out with Quicken. While it's not Quicken's style to record data incorrectly or to miscalculate balances, your newness to the program can cause an occasional slip-up.

For at least the first few weeks of using Quicken, record your transactions in your checkbook and savings passbook registers, as you've always done. Then, when you feel comfortable that you've gotten the hang of using Quicken, you can store the registers in a safe place (you'll want to keep them at least until the bank statement comes) and use Quicken to record all your financial transactions.

Maintaining Account Files

The accounts you create in Quicken are recorded as files on your data disk or hard disk. Quicken is designed so that you never have to copy, rename, or delete these files manually; you can do it all within the program using menu commands.

When you initially use Quicken and make your first account, it is stored in an account group named QDATA. Most likely, this is the only account group name you'll work with, but you can create a new account group, edit an account group file you no longer need, and more.

61

Making a New Account Group

You need to create a new account group before you can stash accounts in it. From the main menu:

1. Choose 5 for Change Settings.
2. Choose 1 for Account Group Activities.
3. Choose 1 for Select/Set Up Account Group.
4. Select Set Up New Group in the window that appears and press the Enter key.

The Set Up Account Group screen is displayed, as shown in Figure 3.3. Note that this screen is almost the same as the First Time Setup window that is displayed when you initially install Quicken. The only addition is that you can provide a unique DOS name for the account group. Provide a name, using up to eight characters, following standard DOS file name practices. Do not provide an extension.

Selecting an Account Group

If you have more than one account group stored on your data disk or hard disk, you can easily switch between them. Quicken allows you to use only one account group at a time. You can't access a checking account in account group A at the same time that you access a savings account in group B.

To select an account group, start at the main menu, then:

1. Choose 5 for Change Settings.
2. Choose 1 for Account Group Activities.
3. Choose 1 for Select/Set Up Account Group.

62

The window shown in Figure 3.4 appears. All of the account group files currently on your disk are shown. Use the up and down arrow keys to select the account group you want to use and press the Enter key. If there's more than one account in the group, Quicken also asks you to select the specific account you want to access.

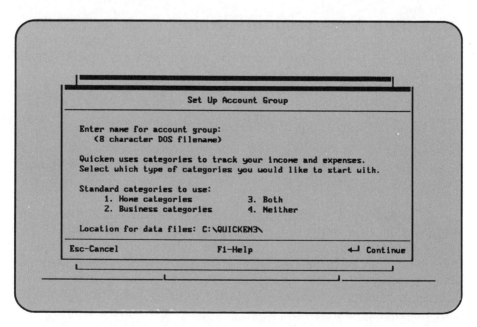

Figure 3.3. Fill in this blank to set up account group.

> **Tip:** If you don't see the account group you want in the
> list, and you have other Quicken data files stored in
> another directory or disk, press the F9 key and indicate the
> directory/disk you want to view.

Other Account Group Activities

At the Select/Set Up Account Group window, Quicken also
allows you to rename and delete account groups. To delete an
account group, highlight it at the Select/Set Up Account Group
window, then press Ctrl-D. Answer Yes to the prompt. To
rename an account group, highlight it, and press Ctrl-E. Enter a
new name (up to eight characters, following all standard DOS
file name restrictions). Press the Enter key when you're done.

63

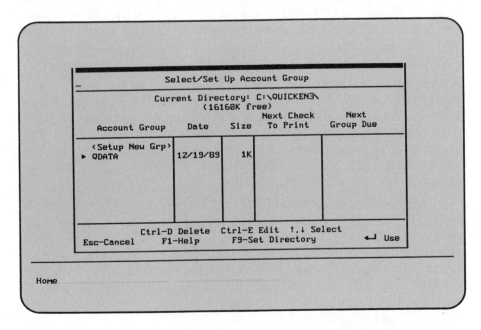

*Figure 3.4. Select the account group you want to use at
this Quicken screen.*

Backing Up Account Information

As with all the data stored on your floppy disks and hard disk, you should periodically make backup or archival copies, in case something should ever happen to the original files. This is especially critical with Quicken files because they represent your or your company's financial position.

The easiest way to make backups of your account data is to use the Ctrl-E and Ctrl-B quick backup shortcut keys. To make a backup and remain in Quicken, press Ctrl-B at the main menu. To make a backup and leave Quicken (return to DOS), press Ctrl-E at the main menu.

For the backup, Quicken prompts you to insert a formatted data diskette. Be sure to have a formatted data diskette ready before requesting the backup.

64

In addition, you can make backup copies of Quicken data manually. Use DOS to copy the data files to a floppy disk. Or, if you use floppy disk drives, simply make a copy of the entire data disk (use the DISKCOPY command). Hard disk users should use a reliable hard disk backup program, such as Fastback Plus or PC Tools Deluxe.

How often should you back up your Quicken data? An ideal backup plan for hard disk users is to archive all the files on the hard disk once a week and to archive just the files that have been created or modified once a day. All of the commercial hard disk backup programs for the PC allow selective archives in this manner. If you are a floppy disk user, you should make a copy of the Quicken data (or the complete data disk) every time you use the program and enter transactions.

While all this may seem like a lot of work, sooner or later it will pay off. By keeping vigilant watch over the data on your disks, you'll never lose more than a day or two of work. And should your entire computer go on the fritz, you can use the backup to re-install your data on a different computer. You can continue to use Quicken (as well as all your other programs) while your computer is in the shop.

What You Have Learned

This chapter examined how to set up accounts and maintain files in Quicken. Here's what you have learned:

▶ Quicken can handle any financial account, but it is specifically built to maintain checking, savings, and cash accounts, as well as general asset and liability accounts (e.g., home loan and real estate) and accounts for stocks and bonds.

▶ The starting balance indicates the amount you have in an account when you begin using Quicken. You can alter the starting balance at a later date, should it be necessary.

▶ You can define any number of accounts in Quicken, limited only by disk space.

▶ Quicken can handle accounts only when they are in groups. An account group can hold up to 255 separate accounts.

65

▶ When first starting with Quicken, maintain a separate paper ledger of your accounts. This helps prevent errors while you learn to use the program.

▶ You should periodically back up your Quicken account file. Quicken provides a quick method of making backups (press Ctrl-E or Ctrl-B at the main menu).

66

Chapter 4

Writing Checks

In This Chapter

▶ *Selecting the account to use*
▶ *Writing checks*
▶ *Check-entering shortcuts*
▶ *Reviewing, editing, and recording checks*

What better way to pay bills with your computer than filling out and printing an "electronic" check. Quicken's check-writing screen is as easy to use as your checkbook, and you don't have to worry about remembering to enter the transaction in the register. Quicken does all the bookkeeping for you.

In this chapter, you'll learn how to select the account you want to use, write checks, provide memo and category information, and more.

Check-Writing Procedure

Writing a check with Quicken is almost as easy as writing a check in your checkbook. You must follow these five steps to write a check:

1. Select the account to use. Once you have selected the account, you can write a series of checks.
2. Access the Write Checks screen.
3. Fill out the check by providing a dollar amount, payee, payee's address, and other information.
4. Review the check for errors or omissions and correct any mistakes.
5. Record the check in the Quicken register.

Selecting the Account to Use

68

Quicken can maintain an unlimited number of different accounts; your checking account may be just one of many. You may also have more than one checking account and want to use Quicken to track each one.

However you use Quicken, you need to select an account to use before you can write checks. Once you have selected this account, Quicken remembers it for subsequent checks you write. (If you've just created one account, Quicken automatically assumes it's the one you want to use; if you have only one account, you can skip this section and proceed directly to the section entitled "Writing the Check.") Quicken even recalls the account each time you start the program. Once you've selected an account, Quicken assumes you want to keep using it, until you tell it otherwise.

If you have not yet set up any accounts with Quicken, you need to refer to Chapter 3, "Setting Up Accounts." There you'll learn how Quicken handles accounts, how you can create accounts for almost any financial need, and how to maintain accounts in discrete account groups. The following quick step assumes you are at Quicken's main menu.

Q Selecting an Account

1. Press 4.

Chooses Select Account command and displays the Select Accounts screen, as shown in Figure 4.1.

2. Press up or down arrow
   keys to select an account to
   use.

3. Press Enter.   Selects the highlighted
                              account and makes it
                              current. Quicken
                              remembers your choice
                              until you explicitly change
                              it again. Quicken
                              immediately takes you to
                              the check register screen.

4. Press Esc.   Exits the check register
                              screen and returns to the
                              main menu.

69

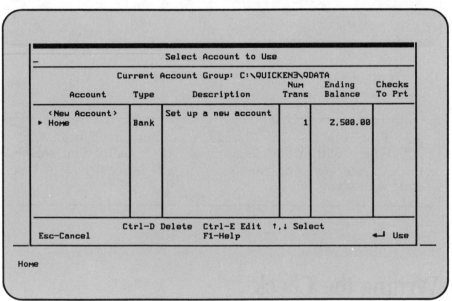

*Figure 4.1. The Select Accounts to Use screen. Use this
screen whenever you want to create or change accounts.*

While in the Select Accounts screen, you can also either
delete accounts or edit them. To delete an account you no longer
need, highlight it and press Ctrl-D. Answer Yes to the prompt
that appears. To edit an account, highlight it and press Ctrl-E.
The editing screen, as shown in Figure 4.2, appears. Here, you
may change the name and description of the account.

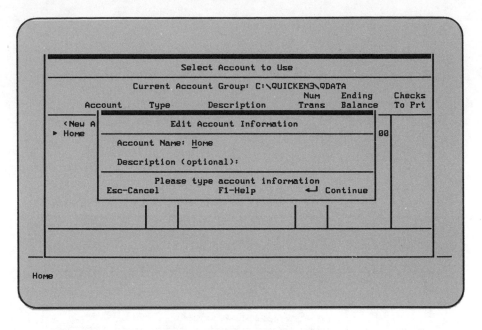

Figure 4.2. The select accounts window.

> ▶ **Tip:** To access the Change Accounts screen from any-where within Quicken, press Ctrl-A. After you select the account you want to use, you will be returned to the spot where you left off.

Writing the Check

With the proper account selected, you are now ready to write checks. At Quicken's main menu, press 1 to select the Write/Print Checks command. Quicken presents the checking-writing screen shown in Figure 4.3. You may now fill in the check as desired.

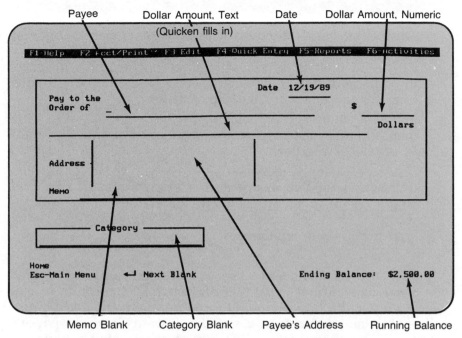

Figure 4.3. The Write Checks screen, with important points identified.

> ▶ **Tip:** You can immediately transfer to the Write Checks screen from almost anywhere in Quicken by pressing Ctrl-W.

The Write Checks screen contains seven entry blanks. Here's what you enter into each of the blanks.

Date—The current date or, optionally, some date in the future. Quicken automatically enters the current date here, but you can post-date the check so you can write the check ahead of time, but not actually include it in your current transactions.

Payee—Who you're writing the check to.

Dollar amount, numeric—The amount of the check, in numeric format (e.g., 123.45). You don't need to enter the dollar sign.

Dollar amount, text—The amount of the check, in text format (e.g., One hundred twenty-three & 45/100). You *don't* need to enter this yourself; Quicken does it for you.

Payee's address—Address of the payee, if necessary. You can enter the name and address line by line or use Quicken's memorize transactions feature, which will insert the full address automatically. You can enter up to five lines for the payee's name and address.

Memo—A message or notation for you or the payee. The memo is recorded as part of the transaction and shows up in the check register.

Category—The category and/or class you're assigning this transaction to. You also use the Category blank to apply a single check to many categories or classes or to indicate whether the check represents a transfer of funds from one of your accounts to another.

72

Although the Write Checks screen contains seven entry blanks, you need to complete only two of them. At a minimum, you need to enter the dollar amount (as a number) and the payee's name. Quicken automatically sets the current date; the payee's address, memo, and category information is completely optional.

Follow these steps to write a check. In all cases, press the Enter or Tab key when you are finished filling out a data field.

Q Writing a Check

1. Type date. If you don't use the current date, enter a new date. Or, press the + or − keys to go forward or back one day at a time. To accept the date that Quicken provides, press Enter.	Enters the desired date.
2. Type payee's name.	Enters the payee's name—either one or more individuals or a company.
3. Type the dollar amount in numerals.	Enters dollar amount, in numeric format.
4. Type address of payee. This step is optional.	Provides address of payee.
5. Type memo. This step is optional.	Adds memo when check is printed.

6. Type the category. This step is optional (but highly recommended).

Assigns the check to one or more categories or classes.

7. Press Ctrl-Enter. You can also choose the Record Transaction command under the Edit menu (press the F3 key then 1).

Records the check.

▶ **Tip:** If you're entering a whole dollar amount in the Dollar Amount data field—such as 100.00 or 1000.00, you can omit the decimal point and the two zeros to the right. Likewise, you don't need to enter commas when writing checks larger than "three figures." For example, to enter 1,005.00, just type 1005. Quicken will add the commas, decimal point, and trailing zeros automatically. The largest dollar amount Quicken can handle is 9,999,999.99.

73

A sample of a filled-out check is shown in Figure 4.4. Table 4.1 provides the maximum length (in characters) for each data field in the Write Checks screen.

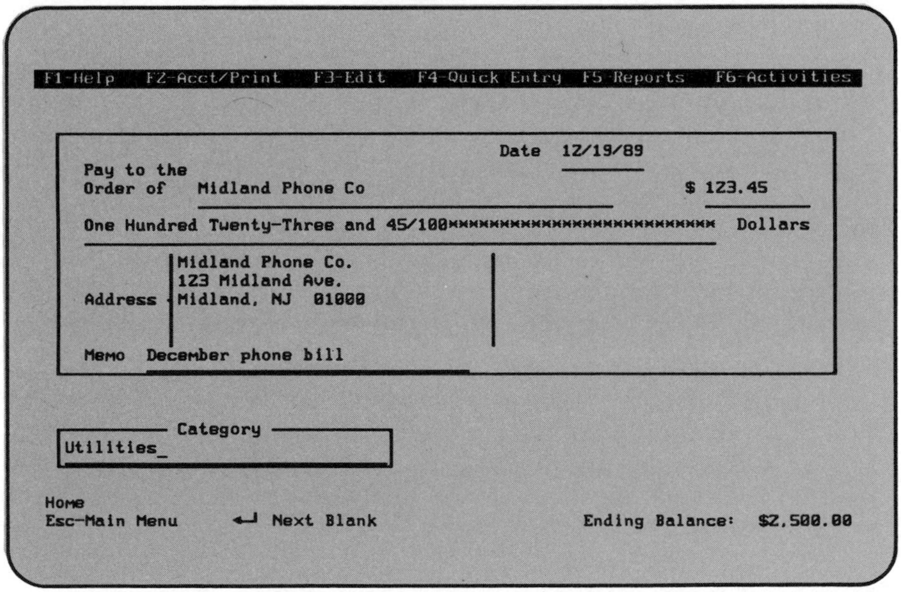

Figure 4.4. A sample of a filled-out check.

Table 4.1. Maximum Length of Data Fields in Write Checks Screen.

Field	Maximum Length (in characters)
Date	8
Payee	40
Dollars	10 (up to 9,999,999.99)
Address	Five lines of 30 characters each (total: 150)
Memo	31
Category	31

Setting the Date

Quicken automatically inserts the date into each check it writes. Initially, the date shown is the current date, as set by DOS. If your computer lacks a battery backup clock/calendar, or you don't manually set the time and date every time you start your computer, Quicken will display 1/1/80 on each check it prepares. Obviously, you can't write a check that's more than 10 years old, so you'll have to change it.

You may also wish to back-date or post-date a check you write with Quicken. *Back-dating* is selecting a date before today. You may wish to back-date a check for bill-paying purposes or when you're entering a check into Quicken that you wrote out of your pocket checkbook a few days before. *Post-dating* is selecting a date after today. Post-dating is helpful in Quicken when you want to write checks for all your bills at once, even though you don't have money to cover them all.

As shown in Figure 4.5, Quicken will display your current balance, which reflects checks you've written and printed that are not post-dated. These are the checks that you must have sufficient funds for. Quicken also displays the amount of checks yet to print. These are checks that have been post-dated. If you use post-dating, you can also use Quicken to keep tabs on accounts payable and cash flow.

Another use of post-dating has been to write someone a check, with the clear understanding that it should not (and theoretically could not) be cashed before a certain date. While you can always use Quicken's post-dating feature for this, most banks no longer recognize post-dating as a means to restrict honoring a check.

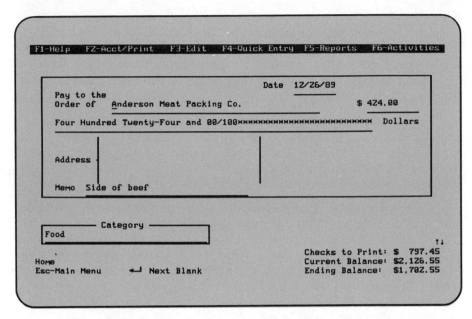

Figure 4.5. Quicken displays the current balance with each check you write.

You can set the check date in either of two ways: by typing the date explicitly in the Date field (you can selectively change the month, day, or year) or by incrementing/decrementing the date by pressing the + and − keys. You can press the + and − keys that are located along the top row of the keyboard or the keys in the numeric keypad.

About Checking Numbering

Checks aren't given numbers until they are printed. That way, you don't "waste a check" because you made a mistake. Most banks require that check numbers be preprinted on each check. Others allow you to provide your own check numbering, as long as you are careful not to duplicate the numbers. Check numbering isn't a consideration until you actually print the checks, so we'll defer discussion of the topic until Chapter 8, "Printing Checks."

Entering Payee's Name and Address

Checks for payroll and accounts payable are often mailed in convenient window envelopes. On the check is the name and address of the payee. This information shows through to the outside of the envelope. That way, you don't have to prepare a separate label or envelope to mail the check or, worse, write the name and address by hand.

All of the preprinted checks you can purchase from Intuit for Quicken have a space for the name and address (window envelopes are available separately), including the personal wallet-size checks, although you probably won't bother with the payee's address for routine home bill paying.

To enter data in the Address data field, move there using the Enter, Tab, or cursor keys and start typing. You are limited to no more than five lines, which should be sufficient for most instances. You can include a personal name or company, a department, suite number or apartment, street address, city, state, ZIP, and country. You may need to combine information on some lines if the address takes up more than five lines. For example, you can combine

555 Mill Road
Suite 1098

on just one line:

555 Mill Road, Suite 1098

> ► **Tip:** If the name in the first line of the Address data field is the same as the name in the Payee data field, you can use a handy Quicken shortcut to copy the payee's name into the address. In the first line of the Address field, type a double-quote character ("). Quicken automatically copies the entry in the Payee field and pastes it into the Address field. Press the Enter key to move down one line and enter the rest of the address.

If you send checks to the same payee on a regular basis and you need to provide the full mailing address, use the memorize transaction feature of Quicken to fill in the required data automatically. See Chapter 7, "Transaction Shortcuts," for more details on memorized transactions.

Including a Memo

Almost all checks—personal and business—provide a blank line for a memo. You can use the memo to provide an account number when paying a bill or to remind you what the check is for (e.g., "radiator, car repair" for a check written to Bill's Garage). Quicken lets you include a memo of up to 31 characters. The memo is printed along the bottom of the check and is also recorded in the check register, so you can refer to it later.

Quicken allows you to search for a specific character, word, or phrase while in the check register (more about this in Chapter 5, "Maintaining the Check Register"), so the information you write in the memo blank can be located quickly, even if the register contains thousands of old check transactions.

Note that you should not use check memos to categorize or classify checks. Save that task for Quicken's category/class feature.

77

About Categories

As you write checks with Quicken, you'll want to include a notation of where the money is going. This helps you view the "big picture" on how you spend your money. It also helps at tax time to separate those items that are tax deductible from those that aren't.

Quicken lets you assign any check you write to one or more categories. As listed in Appendix A, Quicken comes with several dozen categories for business and home use. You can assign any check to one of Quicken's ready-made categories, or you can create a new category of your choosing.

Q Entering a Category

1. Move to the Category blank.

Readies Quicken for a category entry.

2. Enter a category.
OR
If the category does not already exist, choose an option from the window that appears (see Figure 4.6).

Enters a category.

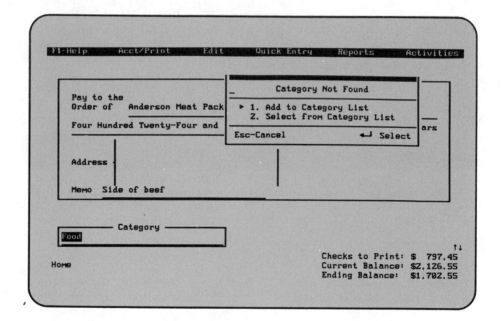

Figure 4.6. Quicken displays this window when the category you have provided can't be found.

If you choose the Add Category to List command, the category name you entered into the data field will be included in Quicken's category list. The next time you enter the category name, Quicken will recognize it, and the Category Not Found window will not appear.

If you choose the Select from Category List command, Quicken will display the Category and Transfer List window, as shown in Figure 4.7. The program automatically selects the category name that's closest to the one you entered. Use the cursor keys to select another category. Press Enter when you find the category you want. It will be inserted automatically in the Category blank in the current check.

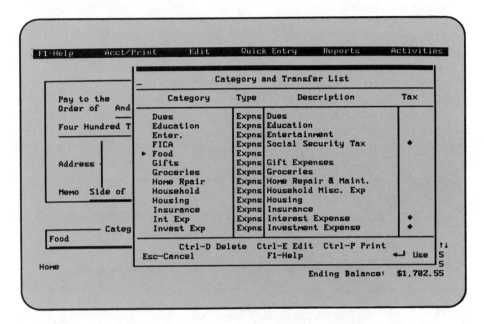

Figure 4.7. The Category and Transfer List window.

> ▶ **Tip:** You can use the Select from Category List command to help you locate and enter categories. When filling out the check, type the first two or three letters of the category you want to use. Press Enter then press 2 to choose the Select from Category List command. OR, press Ctrl-C to access the Category and Transfer List window directly.

Before creating a new category, see if it exists already, under a slightly different name (whether the category was provided by Quicken originally or is one you created). The reason: You'll want to apply categories to checks as consistently as possible.

For example, let's say that one month you apply the *Rent* category to your monthly rent check. In another month, you for-

get you've used the Rent category, and you assign the check to a
new category called *Office Rent*. When you prepare reports with
Quicken, the categories will be separate, and the total for each
won't accurately represent the money you've paid on rent. When
running Quicken, you may want to keep handy a notebook of the
categories you use.

If you're creating one of your own categories, Quicken presents the window shown in Figure 4.8. The Set Up Category
window lets you enter a name (up to 15 characters) and an
optional description (up to 25 characters) for the category. You
also indicate whether the category represents an expense item,
an income item, or a subcategory. Should the category be important when you fill out your tax return (money you can save or
money you must pay), indicate Y by the Tax-related data field.

80

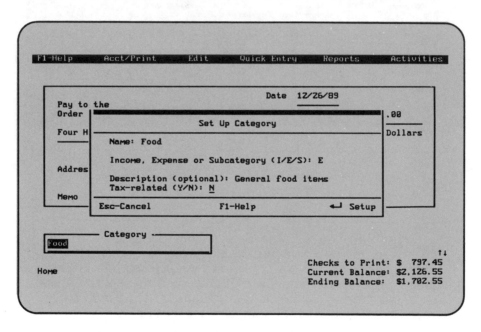

Figure 4.8. The Set Up Category window.

The topic of categories is an involved one and is central to
getting the most out of Quicken. Chapter 6, "Keeping Track of
Transactions," leads you through the maze of categories and also
explains the use of subcategories and classes, as well how to
split a check into several categories and to use categories to
transfer funds from one of your accounts to another.

Reviewing the Check

Once you've filled out the check, take a few moments to check the data and be sure you've entered everything correctly. Review the following items:

Is the date set correctly? Most often it will be today's date.

Is the payee name's entered properly? Check the spelling.

Have you entered the dollar amount correctly? There's nothing like adding a zero to the dollar entry and writing a check for $5,000 instead of $500. Suffice to say, it leads to some surprises come check statement day.

If you've provided a name and address or a memo, double-check that the entry is satisfactory. Verify the address so the check finds its way to the payee.

Be sure that the check is applied to the appropriate category or class. (This is an optional step.)

81

To edit the check, use the cursor keys to move from one entry blank to another. Quicken provides a number of shortcut keys you can use to maneuver quickly around the check-writing screen, as detailed in Table 4.2.

Table 4.2. Moving Within the Write Checks Window.

Press	To
Ctrl-Right	Move one word or blank to the right
Ctrl-Left	Move one word or blank to the left
Enter	Move to the next blank
Tab	Move to the next blank
Shift-Tab	Move to the preceding blank
Ctrl-Backspace	Erase all text in the current blank
Home	Move to start of entry blank
End	Move to end of entry blank
Home, Home	Move to Date entry blank (top of check)
End, End	Move to Category entry blank (bottom of check)

Recording the Check

With the check written and verified, you can now record it. There are three methods:

▶ Press the Enter key after providing a category name. (You can leave the Category data field blank, if you wish.) Quicken will automatically ask if you are ready to record the check. Unless you've turned off Quicken's confirm feature (with the Other Settings window under the Change Settings command), the program will ask if it's OK to record. Press 1 (or Enter) to record; press 2 (or Esc) to go back to filling out the check.

▶ Press Ctrl-Enter. This is the fast-record method and can be used when the cursor is in any data field in the Write Checks screen. You are not asked to confirm check-recording.

▶ Choose the Record Transaction command in the Edit menu. Press the F3 key then 1. This is the same as pressing the Ctrl-Enter keys. You are not asked to confirm check-recording.

82

Reviewing All Checks in Current Session

Most likely, you'll use Quicken to write several checks in one sitting. Table 4.3 provides a list of the quick-keys you can use if you'd like to review the other checks you've written. You can review all the checks you've written in the current session, as well as all other checks that are stored in the check register.

When you make changes to a check, be sure to re-save the alterations. Press Ctrl-Enter (or use one of the other check-recording methods detailed in the previous section) before viewing another check.

Table 4.3. Review Checks Quick-Keys.

Press	To
Page Up	See the previous check
Page Down	See the next check
Ctrl-Home	See the first check
Ctrl-End	See the last check (always blank)

Deleting and Voiding a Check

Suppose you wrote a check in Quicken, then realized you already paid the bill. If you were using your regular checkbook, that would mean a wasted check and a mess in the check register. With Quicken, you can delete any check up until the time it is printed. (After it is printed you should void it.)

To delete a check:

1. Display the check you want to delete in the Write Checks screen. (You can also delete checks from the check register.)
2. Press Ctrl-D or choose the Delete Transaction command from the Edit menu.
3. Quicken checks to make sure you really want to delete the check. Answer yes (press 1) at the prompt.

The check is no longer part of your checking account and is deleted from the check register. The ending balance shown in the lower right-hand corner of the Write Checks screen is updated.

If you've printed the check or you've had one of your checks returned to you uncashed, you should mark it void in the register. The transaction will remain, but the ending balance will be updated to reflect the return of the money to your account. Also void a check if you've stopped payment on it or if it's been lost in the mail and never recovered. You can void a check only within the check register.

To void a check:

1. Press Ctrl-R to switch to the check register. (We'll talk about the check register more in the next chapter.)

83

2. Press the up or down arrow keys to highlight the check you want to void.
3. Choose the Void Transaction command from the Edit menu.
4. Press Ctrl-W to return to the Write Checks screen.

Quicken marks the check as void by placing a VOID in the payee's name.

What You Have Learned

This chapter explored check-writing procedures in Quicken. Here's what you have learned:

84

▶ The check-writing procedure has five steps: selecting the account to use, accessing the Write Checks screen, filling out the check, reviewing the check, and recording the check.

▶ Once you select an account, remember the account name for subsequent sessions.

▶ At a minimum, for each check you write you must provide the payee's name and the amount of the check.

▶ Optionally, you can set a different date for the check than the one provided by Quicken. You can also enter the payee's address, a memo, and the category/class information.

▶ To set another date quickly, move the cursor to the date blank and press the + or − key to go forward or back one day at a time.

▶ The memo blank lets you write a short notation about the check to yourself or to the payee.

▶ The category blank lets you assign checks to specific account categories, to help you review your expenditures and draw up budgets.

▶ After writing a check, you should always review it to make sure the information is correct.

▶ To record the check (enter it into the check register so it can be printed), press Ctrl-Enter. You can also choose the Record Transaction command under the Edit menu.

Chapter 5

Maintaining the Check Register

In This Chapter

▶ *Accessing the check register*
▶ *Examining the contents of the check register screen*
▶ *Adding, editing, and deleting transactions*
▶ *Using Quicken find*

The Quicken check register automatically records the checks you write and tabulates the balance for you. While you can write all your checks using the Quicken Write Checks screen, you'll enter deposits, adjustments, ATM withdrawals, and other transactions directly in the register. To make it as easy as possible to use, the Quicken register functions like the paper checkbook register you're used to.

In this chapter, you'll learn how to use the register to enter all transaction types. The methods outlined here for managing the check register apply also to other Quicken account types, including Credit Card, Cash, Other Assets, Other Liabilities, and Investments.

Accessing the Check Register

The check register is never far away. You can access it directly
with a keyboard shortcut or from the main menu.

> *Keyboard shortcut*—Press Ctrl-R from almost any screen.
>
> *Main menu*—Press 2, for Register.

The check register appears, as shown in Figure 5.1. The
actual contents of the register will differ, depending on the
transactions it contains.

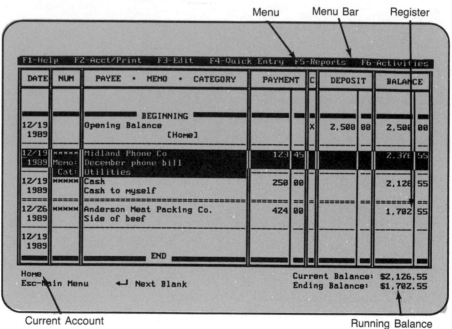

*Figure 5.1. A sample check register, with important
points identified.*

The check register screen is divided into three major parts:

▶ *Menu bar*, where you can access the Quicken pull-down
menus. (These menus are the same as those available during
check-writing.)

▶ *Transaction columns*, listing important information about the check or other transaction type.

▶ *Status*, located at the bottom of the screen, showing the account currently in use, the current balance, and the ending balance. The current balance shows the amount you have in the bank before deducting any post-dated checks. The ending balance includes *all* transactions listed in the register, including post-dated checks.

Use the cursor keys to move around the check register screen. Table 5.1 lists those keys you can use to maneuver within the register and what they do. As you press the cursor keys, you move two types of cursors:

▶ The *highlight bar* indicates the transaction you're working on.

▶ The *blinking cursor* indicates where the next character you type will be entered.

87

Table 5.1. Check Register Keys.

Key	What It Does
Up arrow	Previous transaction
Down arrow	Next transaction
Right arrow	Right one character or column
Left arrow	Left one character or column
Ctrl-Right arrow	Right one word
Ctrl-Left arrow	Left one word
Enter	Accept entry; go to next transaction
Tab	Go to next column
Shift-Tab	Go back one column
Ctrl-Home	Move to top of register
Ctrl-End	Move to end of register
Page Up	Move up one screen
Page Down	Move down one screen
Ctrl-Page Up	Go to start of previous month
Ctrl-Page Down	Go to start of next month

The *dotted horizontal lines* in the check register indicate separate transactions. While checks will be the most common transaction, you'll also include deposits, transfers, adjustments, ATM withdrawals, and so forth. A *double-dotted line* indicates that transactions listed below it are post-dated. You can have both post-dated debits (checks, fees, etc.) and credits. Each will be shown under the double-dotted line, as shown in Figure 5.2.

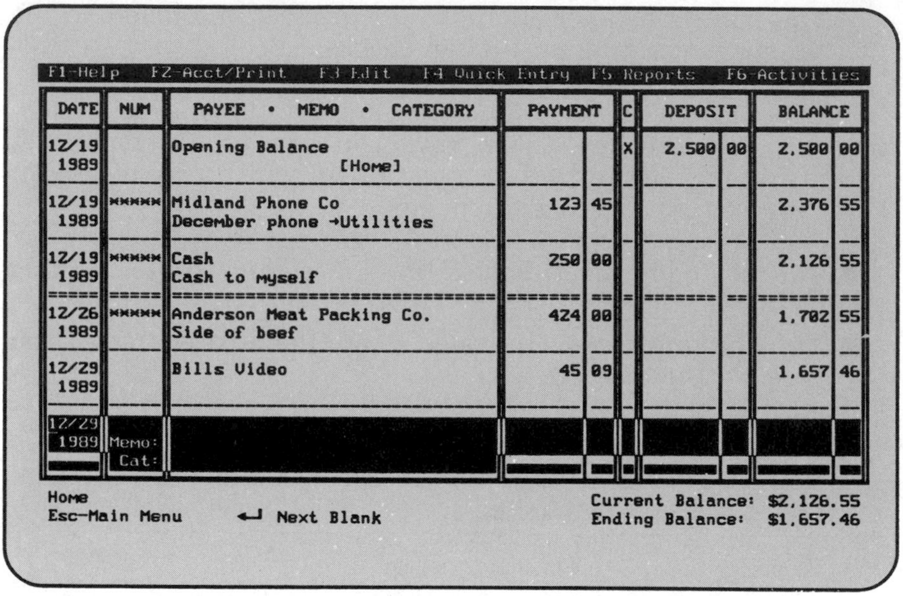

Figure 5.2. Register transactions are divided by double- and single-dotted lines; the double-dotted lines mean post-dated checks appear below.

Items in the Register

The check register records nine important tidbits about your checks or other transactions. These are date, number, payee, memo, category, payment, clear, deposit, and balance. This information is provided in the columns of the check register. The memo and category information is optional and is shown in the second line of the Payee column.

Date

The date is the date of the transaction. When writing checks, the date is normally the date you wrote the check. You can always change the date—to an earlier or later day. All other transactions in a checking account also occur on a specific date, so these each will include an entry in the date column as well.

For example, on a particular day you make a cash withdrawal from an automated teller machine. You enter the date of that withdrawal in the register. Similarly, adjustments to your checking account, including check fees and interest are usually dated as taking place on the last day of the account period. You enter that date as appropriate.

As in the Write Checks screen, you can change the date by writing a new one from the keyboard or by pressing the + or − key. Each press of the + or − adds or subtracts a day, respectively.

89

Number

Checks aren't given numbers until they are printed. In the check register, checks that have been printed are shown with a number in the NUM column. Checks that haven't been printed are shown with a ***** in the NUM column. When you print a check, Quicken asks for the check number. That number is inserted automatically in the NUM column for that check.

When you write a check by hand (it's hard to carry your computer and printer with you to the supermarket), you can manually enter its number by typing it from the keyboard. If the transaction is not a check (e.g., an ATM withdrawal, service fee, or counter check), press the Enter key to move the cursor to the next column.

> ▶ **Tip:** Use the + and − key shortcuts to select a check number quickly. With the cursor in the NUM column, press the + key; Quicken automatically looks up the number of the last check, adds 1 to it, and inserts that number in the current NUM column. Keep pressing the + key to advance the number. Press the − key to decrement the number.

Payee

The payee is the first line in the PAYEE/MEMO/CATEGORY column. It lists who you wrote the check to. Or, if the transaction is a deposit, ATM withdrawal, service charge, or the like, the Payee column will include a description of that transaction. Figure 5.3 shows some examples. For clarity, the illustration does not include entries for the memo or category.

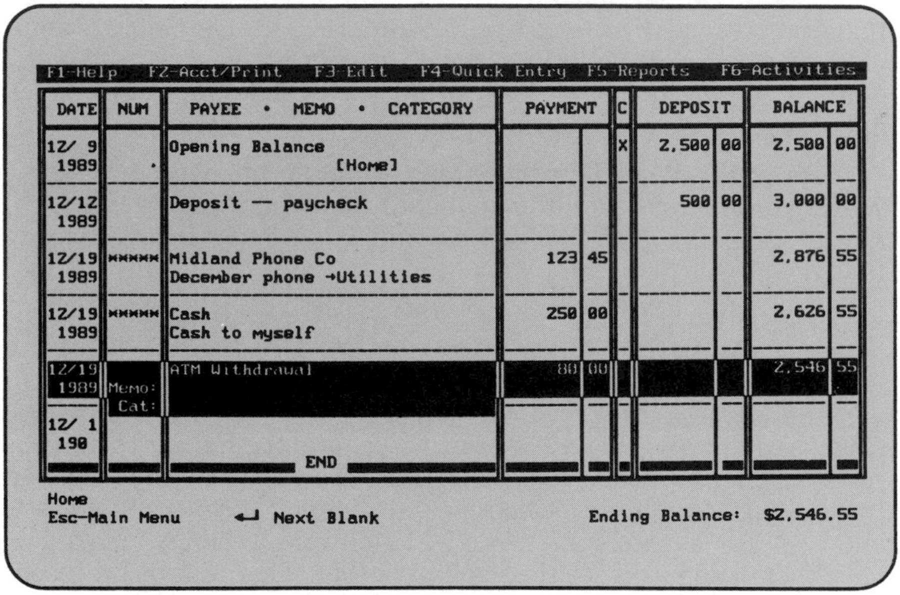

Figure 5.3. Some examples of payee entries.

> ► **Note:** You can alter the contents of the PAYEE/MEMO/CATEGORY column with the Other Settings window, located under the Change Settings menu. Specifically, you can show the memo, the category, or both on the second line. We will assume that you're using Quicken with the standard default of displaying both memo and category.

Memo

The memo message is optional. When you write a memo in a check, it appears on the second line of the PAYEE/MEMO/CATE-GORY column. Memos aren't just limited to checks. You can also include a memo for a deposit, ATM withdrawal, or correction. Write a memo to help you remember the nature of the transaction or to have Quicken automatically select transactions to print in its reports.

Category

The category message is optional. If you've indicated a category for a transaction, that category is shown in the PAYEE/MEMO/CATEGORY column. If you've used subcategories and classes, these too are displayed, up to the first 14 characters of the category/class name. If the transaction has been split among several categories, you must select the transaction in the register and press Ctrl-S to see all the components of the split.

91

Payment

If the transaction is a debit (e.g., a check, a service fee, or an ATM withdrawal), then the amount is shown in the PAYMENT column. A heavy line separates the dollar and cents. If you're entering the payment directly into the register, you can type it with or without dollar signs and commas. Quicken formats the entry with commas but leaves out the dollar sign.

Clear

Unless you haven't written any checks or made a deposit in a while, your check register will always be ahead of the bank's statement of your account. You may have checks, deposits, and other transactions that the bank doesn't know about yet. And, as checking account statements come only once a month, they are rarely up-to-date with the actual status of your account.

The C (for CLEAR) column indicates those transactions that the bank has acknowledged in its monthly statement. Some transactions are posted by the bank almost immediately after you make them: ATM withdrawals, check charges, fees, and most deposits. Every month, when you receive your statement and compare it against the entries in the Quicken register, you mark the transactions that appear as cleared in your register. This helps you determine which credits and debits the bank is aware of and assists you in reconciling your register.

Quicken offers a nearly automated system for reconciling accounts, where you can clear checks, deposits, and other transactions quickly. But you can also clear individual transactions by moving the cursor to the CLEAR column and pressing C to enter an asterisk.

Deposit

92

Money you put in the bank is listed in the DEPOSIT column. Other forms of transactions are also entered in the DEPOSIT column, including interest, wire transfers, and corrections where your register shows a lower balance than the bank statement says you have in your account.

Balance

Quicken automatically enters the running balance for you. You don't need to do it. Whenever you add, remove, or alter transactions, Quicken automatically updates the balance for you.

Adding a Transaction

You can add any type of transaction in the register at any time.

Q Adding a Transaction to the Register

1. Display the register (if it isn't already displayed).

2. Press End, End.	The transaction highlight bar moves to the very end of the register.
3. Enter the new transaction. Press the Enter or Tab keys to move to the next column. You can also use the left and right arrow keys to move back and forth between the columns.	Enters the new transaction information, as desired.
4. Review entry. Be sure the transaction information is correct.	
5. Press Ctrl-Enter.	Records the transaction. ☐

You can enter transactions into the register in any order. Quicken will rearrange the transactions in date order automatically. If you've written several checks on the same day, then those check transactions will be organized by number within that date. Checks that have not yet been printed, and therefore lack a check number, are kept with the other transactions you made on a particular day.

93

Editing a Transaction

Nobody's perfect. And when it comes to financial matters, you don't want mistakes to be left uncorrected. Quicken allows you to update and correct information easily at any time. (Note that you can lock out your accounts to prevent certain transactions from being changed by anybody except you; see Chapter 2, "Getting Started with Quicken," for details on the password option.)

 **Editing a Transaction in the Register**

1. Display the register (if it isn't already displayed).

2. Use the cursor keys to move the transaction highlight bar to the transaction you want to edit.

Moves to the transaction.

3. Edit the transaction information, as desired. Press the Enter or Tab keys to move to the next column. You can also use the left and right arrow keys to move back and forth between the columns.

Edits the transaction.

4. Review entry. Be sure the transaction information is correct.

94

5. Press Ctrl-Enter.

Records the transaction. ☐

> ▶ **Tip:** Normally, you'll use the Delete and Backspace keys to remove from a transaction characters you don't want. You can also replace characters as you type new data by pressing the Insert key once. With insert off, the characters you type replace existing text in the register. Press the Insert key again, and insert mode is turned back on.

If you alter the date of the transaction, Quicken will relocate it to maintain chronological order within the register.

> ▶ **Note:** The only information in the register you can't change is the balance in the BALANCE column. Quicken does that for you automatically.

Deleting a Transaction

You may have occasion to delete a transaction. For example, you may have entered an ATM withdrawal twice or written a check to someone who returned it to you. To delete a transaction, follow the same basic steps outlined above for editing a transaction. With the transaction you want to delete highlighted, press Ctrl-D (or choose the Delete Transaction command in the Edit menu). Answer Yes to the "OK to Delete Transaction" prompt. If you decide you don't want to delete the transaction, simply press the Esc key to cancel out of the delete process.

Similarly, you can void a transaction (usually a check) by highlighting the transaction then pressing Ctrl-V (or choosing the Void Transaction command in the Edit menu). Quicken doesn't double-check that you really want to void the check, so use this command carefully.

Using Find

95

The Quicken check register contains many shortcuts you can use to your advantage. Many of these shortcuts, including categories, classes, and split transactions, are detailed in Chapter 6, "Keeping Track of Transactions." Another helpful shortcut feature of the check register is find. With it, you can locate a specific transaction quickly, without having to scroll through the register manually and look for it.

To use the find feature, choose the Find command from the Edit menu or press Ctrl-F to access the Find command immediately. A find window like the one in Figure 5.4 appears on the screen.

In the columns provided, enter a word, number, phrase, or other text that matches the part of the transaction you want to locate. For example, if you want to find a check you wrote to "John Doe," type John Doe in the PAYEE/MEMO/CATEGORY column. If you think the transaction you want to find occurs *after* the current transaction in the register, press Ctrl-N. If you think the transaction you want to find occurs *before* the current transaction in the register, press Ctrl-B.

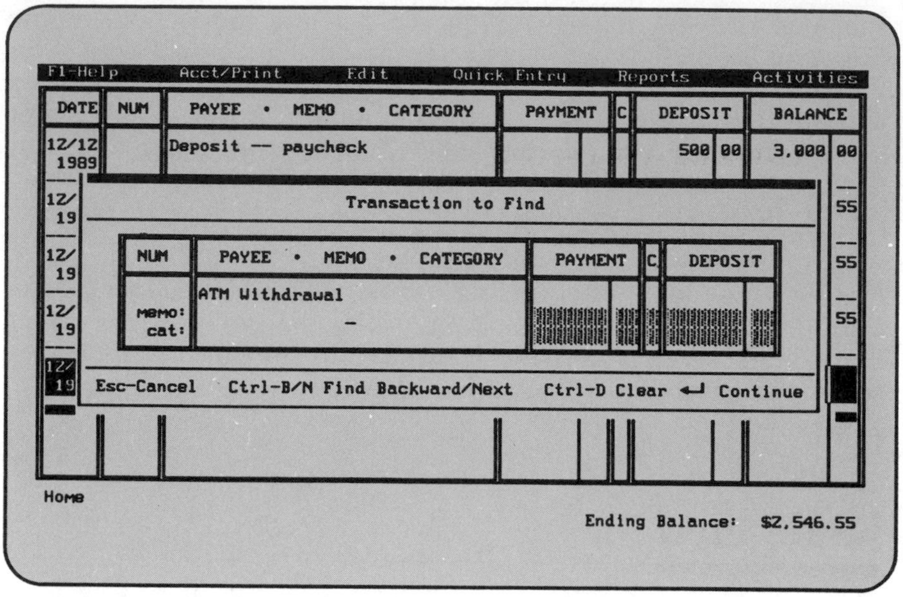

Figure 5.4. The Transaction to Find window.

> ▶ **Tip:** For the sake of simplicity and thoroughness, you may find it easier to locate transactions with the find feature by first moving to the start of the register (press Ctrl-Home) then using Ctrl-N for a forward search.

Your register may contain several transactions that match the criteria you've entered. After Quicken locates the first transaction, press Ctrl-N or Ctrl-B again to find the next one. If you want to locate a transaction using different criteria, clear the Transaction to Find window by pressing Ctrl-D.

You can look for more than one piece of information at one time. If you've written several checks to John Doe, but only want to find the ones that you entered into the Rent category, type John Doe as the payee and Rent as the category. Quicken will find only those transactions that meet all of the criteria you've entered. Using the example, only those checks with a payee of John Doe and a category of Rent are located, even if you have hundreds of checks either written to John Doe or categorized as Rent.

Wildcard Searches

Sometimes, you may not know the exact information to enter in the Transaction to Find window. Quicken allows "wildcard" searches that will help you locate transactions when you aren't sure of the exact entry. Quicken uses double periods (..) to mean "approximate." For instance, if you know that you wrote a check to a company you recall having the name "Computer" something, type `computer ..` as the payee. (You can use upper- or lowercase letters; Quicken does not differentiate.) This finds all those payees that start with Computer, and end in anything else, such as:

> Computer Depot
> Computer Specialists International
> Computers R Us

Entering the periods before the word to search

97

`.. Computer`

finds all those transactions where the payee name starts with any text and ends with Computer, as in:

> Inland Computer
> Basic Computer
> Obsolete Computer

And using double-periods on each side of the word to find locates any entry where "Computer" is merely a part:

> Touchstone Computer Center
> Your Neighborhood Computerstore
> Instant Computers, Inc.

Quicken also uses other characters as search wildcards:

Wildcard	Meaning
~	Search for everything except...
?	Replace question mark with any single character

You can combine wildcards characters to build complex search criteria. You can use these wildcards in the check register for finding transactions or when printing customized reports. For more information, see Chapter 10, "Creating and Printing Reports."

Go to Date

Similar to the find feature is Go to Date, where you can move to a specific date in the register instantaneously.

Q **Moving to a Specific Date in the Register**

1. Press Ctrl-G.
   OR
   Choose the Go to Date command from the Edit pull-down menu.

   Activates Go to Date command.
   The window box in Figure 5.5 appears.

2. Enter date.

3. Press Enter.

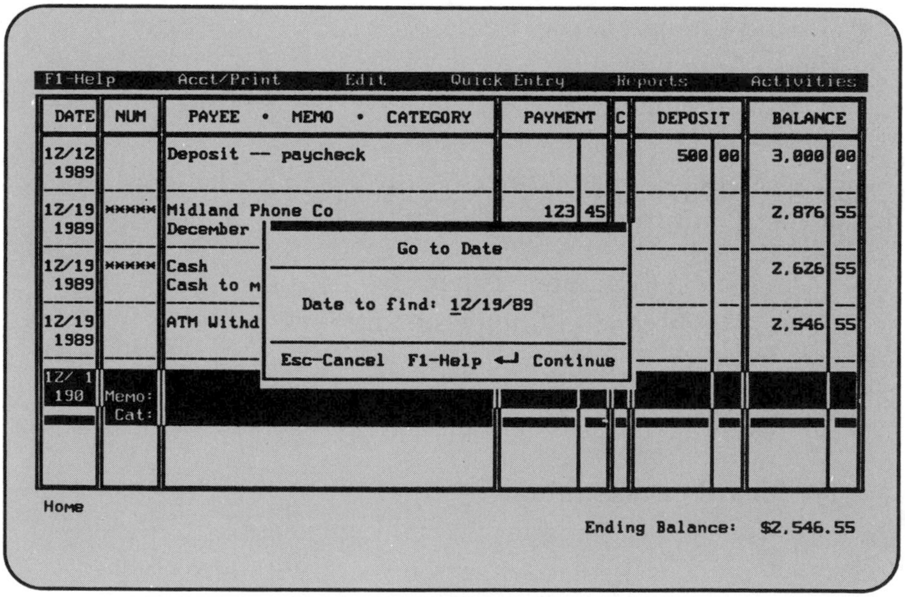

98

Figure 5.5. The Go to Date window.

Quicken takes you to the first transaction in the register with the indicated date. If no transaction was recorded on the date you specified, Quicken goes to the next nearest date.

What You Have Learned

This chapter examined the check register screen and discussed how to manipulate data within it. Here's what you have learned:

▶ You can access the Quicken check register in either of two ways: press Ctrl-R from almost any screen or press 2 from the main Quicken menu.

▶ The check register uses columns to display the following items of interest: date, check number, payee/memo/category (all in one column), payment, clear, deposit, and balance.

▶ Checks aren't numbered until they are printed. Checks that have been written but not yet printed are shown with a ***** in the NUM column.

▶ The PAYEE column lists who the check is written to. If the transaction is not a check, it indicates whether it is a deposit, ATM withdrawal, service charge, or other transaction.

▶ The C (for CLEAR) column shows those checks and other transactions that have been acknowledged in the bank's monthly statement to you.

▶ Quicken automatically enters the running balance; you don't need to calculate the balance yourself.

▶ Within the check register, you can add, edit, and delete transactions. You can also void checks.

▶ Press Ctrl-Enter to record a transaction or the changes you've made in a transaction.

▶ The find feature helps you locate a specific transaction, without having to scroll through the register manually and look for it.

99

100

Chapter 6

Keeping Track of Transactions

In This Chapter

▶ *Writing memos*
▶ *Using transaction categories and classes*
▶ *Splitting transactions*
▶ *Entering transfers*
▶ *Reconciling your account*

Quicken provides many shortcuts to keep tabs on your financial matters. By using categories and classes, you can departmentalize your income and expenses so you know—at all times—your entire financial picture. You can also write memos directly onto checks (which are recorded in the check register) and use them as notes to yourself. You will not need to scribble in the margins of your paper register. With Quicken's flexible find feature, you can search for these notes quickly and easily. This can be handy, for example, when you need to verify that you've mailed out a check.

In this chapter, you'll learn how to use categories and classes to your best advantage. You'll discover the basics of setting up categories and classes and how to apply transactions to them. We'll examine categories and classes as they relate to checkbook transactions, but the fundamentals apply to all Quicken account types.

You'll also learn the ins and outs of *transaction reconciliation*—the process of making sure you and the bank agree on the ending balance. Few people enjoy reconciling their checking accounts, but Quicken makes the process about as painless as it can possibly be.

Writing Memos in Checks

102

Check memos let you jot down a note to yourself or to the payee. They are written and printed in the lower left-hand corner of the check. One application of the memo blank is to enter an account number when paying charge accounts or the car insurance bill. The memo is for the benefit of the payee rather than you—unless you have several such accounts with the same companies and need the numbers for your own benefit as well.

Another use for the memo blank, as shown in Figure 6.1, is to write notes to yourself. For example, you might enter "Loan to Uncle Joey," to indicate a check you wrote to Uncle Joey (step brother on your mother's sister's side) as a personal loan. Not only will the memo help you to remember what the check was for, it can help at tax time or when settling your estate.

When (and if) Uncle Joey pays you back, his checks might appear as income to the Internal Revenue Service. You will need your original check—with the "Loan to Uncle Joey" memo on it—to prove that his checks to you were repayments. Should something happen to you—you die or become hospitalized and can't manage your financial affairs—your family or executor will be able to track the Uncle Joey loan and determine whether you've been paid back.

In time, your check register will become full with checks, deposits, corrections, and other transactions, and finding the one check you write to Uncle Joey may become burdensome. You can use Quicken's find feature to locate it quickly. To use find, choose the Find command from the Edit menu (or press Ctrl-F). Type Uncle Joey in the memo blank. If you think Uncle Joey's loan check is above the current transaction in the register, press Ctrl-B (for backwards search). If you think the check is below, press Ctrl-N (for next). Quicken finds the first check that lists Uncle Joey in the memo blank.

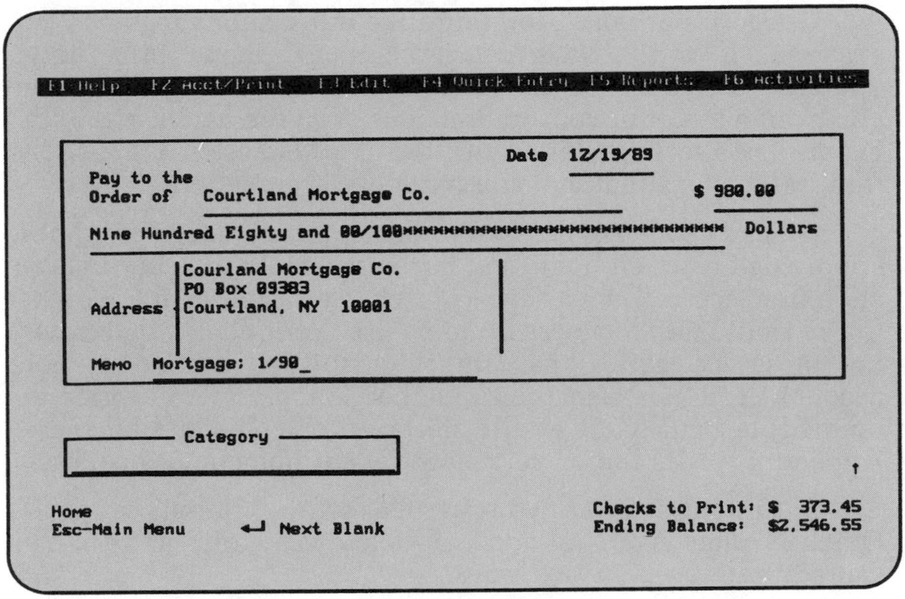

Figure 6.1. Filling in the memo blank.

Note that you can also find transactions based on other criteria: check number, date, category, and so forth. The find feature was more completely discussed in Chapter 5, "Maintaining the Check Register." Refer to that chapter for more information.

You can write a memo at the Write Checks screen or check register screen. Merely position the cursor within the memo blank and type. Press the Enter key when you are done. Because Quicken allows you to make changes to transactions even after the check has been printed, you can write memos to yourself that won't show on the check. In the case of Uncle Joey's loan, you might write "Irrecoverable loan to Uncle Joey...."

Using Transaction Categories

Categories are Quicken's "official" way of keeping track of transactions. As with memos, categories are optional: you don't have to

103

use them if you don't want to. But if you'd like to take advantage of Quicken's advanced features—particularly customized reports —you'll want to get into the habit of using categories.

Categories are used to group like transactions together. For example, if you always categorize your phone bills under "phone," all your "phone" checks will appear together when you print a report of your transactions. You can also use the find feature (as already detailed in "Writing Memos in Checks") to find transactions that match a particular transaction.

Quicken comes with several dozen preset categories. These are divided between home and business use. When you first create a new account, you have your choice of indicating whether the account is for business or home use. Your choice determines the preset categories that are automatically applied to your account. You can also select neither (all preset categories are omitted) or both (you get all categories for home and business). Appendix A lists the preset categories for home and business.

104

By no means are you limited to the preset categories Quicken offers. You can add and delete categories at will. You can add categories in two ways:

▶ Directly in the Category List window.
▶ While writing checks (in the Write Checks screen or check register).

Each account you create with Quicken has its own unique set of categories. Your checking account may have different categories than your savings account. If you also use Quicken to manage your cash, credit cards, assets, liabilities, and investments, these, too, can have their own unique set of categories.

Before you create any new categories, take a moment to jot down where your money comes from and where it goes. Leaf through the last two or three months of bank statements and note to whom you wrote checks. Make a list of recurring payments made to companies or individuals—rent, mortgage, utilities, business insurance, and so forth.

Other checks may have been written to a variety of payees, but reflect common purchases, such as gasoline, entertainment, or business supplies. If you're using Quicken to track your credit cards, go through the card statements and note your recent purchases.

Adding Categories in the Category List Window

The most direct way of adding categories is to enter them in the Category and Transfer List window. You can access the Category and Transfer List window in two ways:

▶ At the Quicken main menu, choose the Write/Print Checks or Register commands. In the Write Checks or check register screen, choose the Categorize/Transfer command from the Quick Entry menu.

▶ At the Write Checks or check register screen, press Ctrl-C.

The Category and Transfer List window appears, as shown in Figure 6.2. The actual contents of the window you see will be different, depending on the categories already assigned to your account.

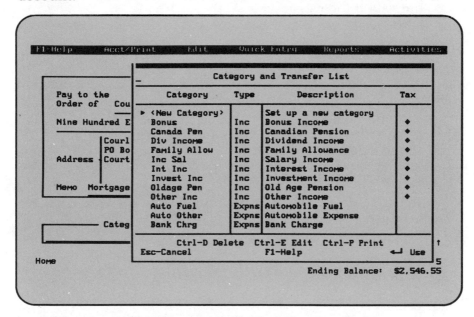

Figure 6.2. The Category and Transfer List window.

Flip through the category list with the cursor keys. Press Home or End to move to the beginning or end of the list; press Page Up or Page Down to scroll through the list one page at a time. Select a specific category to use by highlighting it with the up and down arrow keys.

Q **Adding a New Category to the Category and Transfer List Window**

1. Highlight <New Category>.

2. Press Enter.   Quicken displays the Set Up Category window, as shown in Figure 6.3.

3. Enter category name and press Enter.

4. Enter E for Expense (default), I for Income, or S for Subcategory.   Defines type of category.

5. Enter a description and press Enter. Descriptions are optional, but recommended.

106

6. Indicate if the category is tax-related.   ☐

Repeat the procedure for each new category you wish to create. If you make a mistake (misspell the category name, for example), you can either edit or delete categories, as detailed below.

Note that other accounts you have created also appear in the category list. You can see them by scrolling to the end of the list. These categories are there to allow you to transfer funds from one account to another. See the section entitled "Splitting Transactions" later in this chapter.

When you are done entering transactions, press the Escape key to return to the Write Checks or check register screen.

Adding Categories While Writing Checks

You can create categories "on the fly" while you enter checks and other transactions in the Write Checks and check register screens. Enter a new category name in the Category blank in the check register. Quicken will prompt you that it can't find the category, as shown in Figure 6.4. You have two choices:

▶ Ask Quicken to add the category name to the category list. The name, exactly as it appears in the Category blank, is appended to the Category and Transfer List window and will appear there (in proper alphabetical order) the next time you access the window.

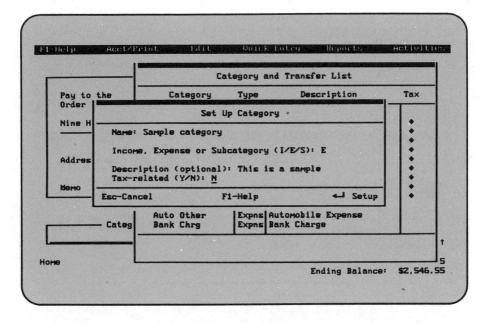

Figure 6.3. Set up categories in this window.

▶ **Tip:** Categories (as well as classes, detailed below) consume memory. Although Quicken doesn't impose a limit on the number of categories you can create, the amount of memory available in your computer will determine the maximum number of categories you can create for any one account. On a computer with 320 kilobytes of RAM (and using no terminate-and-stay resident programs), you can create approximately 150 categories and classes. A computer with 640 kilobytes of RAM can accommodate over 1,000 categories/classes. The actual number of categories you can create depends in part on the length of names you use to identify the categories. Using shorter names helps conserve some (but not much) memory. Get into the habit of choosing short names for your categories, but don't make them so short that you can't decrypt their function.

▶ Ask Quicken to display the category list so you can select another category. Use the cursor keys to select the category you want, then press the Enter key. The category you selected is inserted into the Category blank automatically.

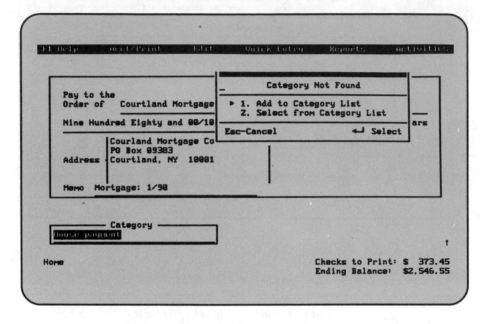

Figure 6.4. This window is displayed when Quicken can't find the category you've indicated.

You can also cancel the message and re-enter the category name. Press the Escape key to return to the Write Checks or check register screen.

The procedure for naming and describing the category is the same as it is when adding categories directly in the category list.

Proper Category Names

You can give any category just about any name you wish. Categories can include letters, numbers, spaces, and most other printable characters with four exceptions. The following keys are not allowed in category names:

[ ] / :

Quicken reserves these characters for special uses. The brackets are used to denote a transfer; the colon means you want to use a subcategory; and the slash means you want to use a class.

Editing and Deleting Categories

Let's say you no longer need a category or that you want to free up memory space and delete some of the extraneous preset categories Quicken offers. You can readily delete categories you don't want. You can also edit existing categories and change their names, descriptions, and other specifics. The following Quick Steps assume you are currently in the Write Checks or check register screen.

 Deleting a Category

109

1. Press Ctrl-C.   Accesses Category and
                                          Transfer List window.

2. Scroll to category you want
   to delete.

3. Press Ctrl-D. Quicken
   checks that you really want
   to remove the category
   permanently. Answer
   accordingly.   ☐

The category notation for transactions that was linked to this category (if any) is blanked out. For example, if you had a category called Rent and deleted it, the category blank for all rent checks would be cleared. The rest of the check remains unaffected.

 Editing a Category

1. Press Ctrl-C.   Accesses Category List
                                          window.

2. Scroll to category you want
   to edit.

3. Press Ctrl-E.

Displays the Set Up Category window, where you can edit the name and description, or change the category type (expense, category, or subcategory).

☐

The category notation for transactions that was linked to this category (if any) is updated to reflected your edits. For example, if you had a category called Rent and edited it to read "Rent—Main St.," the category blank for all rent checks would now read "Rent—Main St."

Using Categories

110

With categories in place, you can use them in your checks and other transactions. To use a transaction, type it in the Category blank of the Write Checks or check register screen. Don't worry about case—Quicken doesn't care if you use upper- or lowercase letters.

You can change category information for any transaction. Move the cursor to the category data, edit it in the normal fashion, and re-record the transaction. Quicken automatically updates all affected transactions.

You can use this approach to add categories later. Let's say that you're in a hurry and just want to write and print out a stack of checks before you go on a vacation to Hawaii. Write the checks without categories and print them. When you get back, go through the register and write in the categories, as desired. Now, when you print a transaction report, the checks are shown with the added category information.

About Subcategories

Suppose you have several sources of small business income: from your unfinished furniture store, from your import operation, and from a week-end job where you make wood name signs with your router and sell them. While you could create a different category for each source of income, a more beneficial approach is to use subcategories. Each of your sources of income comes under the main category of "Income," but each is differentiated with the use of subcategories. In the category list as well as most transaction reports, all your sources of income will be grouped together, making it easier for you to track.

▶ **Tip:** You don't need to type the entire category name when you enter it in the Category blank. Quicken can figure out what category you want when you type the first few characters of the name and press Ctrl-C. You need to enter enough characters to distinguish the category you want from others that begin with the same characters. For instance, to recall the "Freight" category, type FR and press Ctrl-C. Unless you have other categories that also start with "FR," Quicken will fill in the rest of the blank with the full name after you press Enter.

111

Quicken understands that you want to use subcategories when you add a colon (:) after the main category name. For example,

    Income:Unf. Furn.
    Income:Import
    Income:Wood Signs

These entries are shown in the category list in Figure 6.5.

You create and use subcategories the same as you do main categories. To use a particular subcategory, enter the name of the main category, a colon, then the name of the subcategory. You can theoretically add additional subcategories under other subcategories, such as:

one level of subcategories	Utilities:Phone Mortgage:Interest Computer:Supplies
two levels of subcategories	Utilities:Phone:Business Mortgage:2nd TD:Interest Computer:Supplies:Diskettes

You should limit yourself to no more than two levels of subcategories, however. Any more and you're bound to make errors.

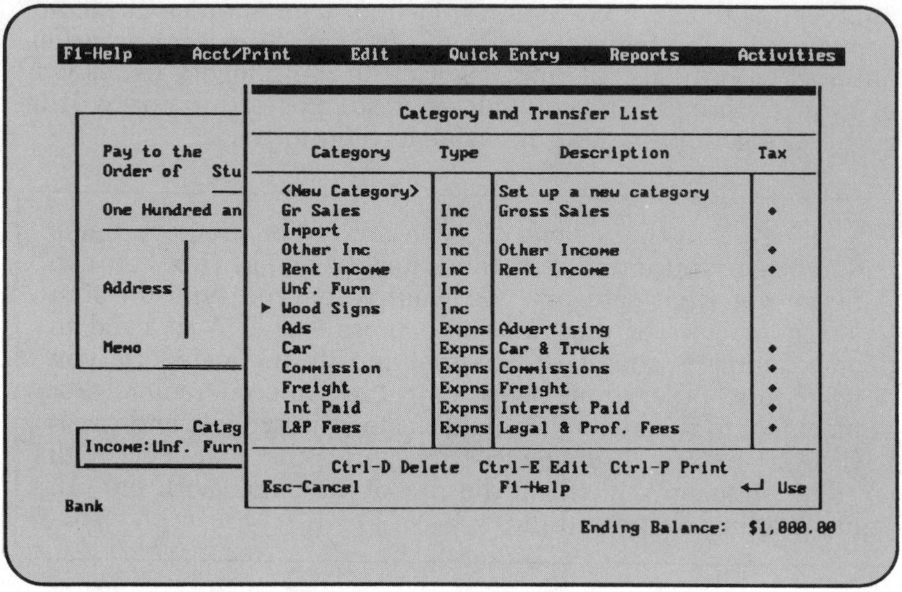

Figure 6.5. A sample of three incomes in the category
list.

> **Tip:** When creating subcategories, always put the gen-
> eral category first. Utilities:Phone makes sense, but
> Phone:Utilities does not. Although you'll be guided by com-
> mon sense to create subcategories in the proper fashion,
> some applications require forethought. For instance, do you
> enter "Alimony: First Husband" or "First Husband: Ali-
> mony"? You can always change it afterward, of course, but
> getting it right the first times makes your job that much
> easier.

The Other Category

Categories are optional in Quicken, but in fact the program
always places transactions that are recorded without a specific
category in the broad group of Other. Other doesn't appear in the
category list, but it's there nonetheless.

When you record a transaction without a category notation, it is placed in Other, but you can always move it to an established category later on. Likewise, a transaction that you previously assigned to a category can be abandoned under Other.

Printing the Category List

You'll want to keep a crib sheet of the categories you have available to you. Quicken lets you make a quick printout of the category list.

1. Press Ctrl-C to access the category list.
2. Press Ctrl-P. The Print Category List window appears.
3. Indicate the printer you are using and press Enter or Ctrl-Enter to print the list.

113

Splitting Transactions

Unless you're in the habit of writing a separate check for every small item you buy, you're bound to pay for goods with one check that should be applied to any number of different categories. If you're buying office supplies, for instance, you may need to keep separate tabs on where the supplies are going and what they are for. This is especially true if you've created categories for different departments in your company.

Quicken lets you split a transaction many ways. The split is like an itemized list of categories. A good application of a split transaction is separating the monthly combined house payment into separate categories for principal, interest, taxes, and insurance. When tax time comes, you'll know exactly how much went to the principal (which is not tax deductible), interest (which is tax deductible), taxes, and insurance. You can split a transaction up to 30 ways.

Q Splitting a Transaction

1. Move to the Category blank (Write Checks or check register screen).

2. Press Ctrl-S.

   The Split Transaction window appears, as shown in Figure 6.6.

3. Enter the splits; each on one line.

4. Press the F9 key to calculate the running total.

5. Press Ctrl-Enter when done.

   Returns you to the Write Checks or check register screen. □

114

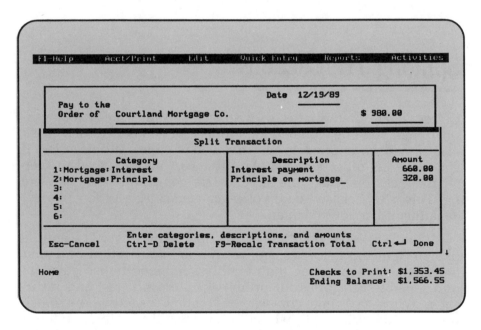

Figure 6.6. The Split Transaction window.

You need to provide three pieces of information for each tine of the split:

▶ The category name (including subcategory, if needed).

▶ A description (optional, but highly recommended).

▶ The dollar amount of the split.

In most instances, all of the splits will equal the face value of the transaction. (You can split checks, deposits, ATM withdrawals, and so forth.) You may not care to categorize all the splits, however. In that case, just enter the remainder in the next line and leave the category blank. If you've already entered the dollar amount for the transaction in the Write Checks or check register screen, Quicken keeps a running balance for you in the last line of the Split Transactions window. You can always tell when you have an outstanding balance if the amount is not $0.

In the Write Checks and check register screens, the Category blank displays the first category entered when the transaction has been split up. It shows SPLIT at the bottom of the Category blank. This does not appear when the check is printed.

115

▶ **Tip:** Quicken offers a handy shortcut when in the Split Transactions window. Enter a quotation mark (") in the Category blank, and Quicken will automatically copy the category information from the previous line. This is especially helpful for setting up split transactions because one check is often used to purchase items for one major category. Use the " method to copy the main category name quickly, then type in the subcategory.

Splits Printed on Voucher Checks

The first 15 lines of split transactions are printed on the stub of voucher checks. You can use this feature not only to keep track of your accounts payable but also to assist the payee in knowing what the check is for. You can enter account numbers, voucher numbers, invoice numbers, and so forth in the Split Transaction window, and they will appear on the voucher stub.

You'll probably want to print just the description of the split in the voucher. You can force Quicken to omit the category with the Other Settings menu, shown in Figure 6.7. Turn categories off by entering N for option 9. To access the Other Settings menu, select Change Settings at the main menu, then choose Other Settings. Refer to Chapter 2, "Getting Started with Quicken," for more information.

Making Changes to Split Transactions

At any time you can alter the information in the Split Transaction window. To edit a split, or even delete it altogether, select the transaction and press Ctrl-S to access the Split Transaction window. Move the cursor to the field you want to edit, and make your changes. When you're done, press Ctrl-Enter.

To delete one or more splits in the Split Transaction window, position the cursor on the line you want to remove and press Ctrl-D. To delete the entire split transaction, remove each line then press Ctrl-Enter. The word SPLIT disappears from the Category blank. The transaction is no longer split.

116

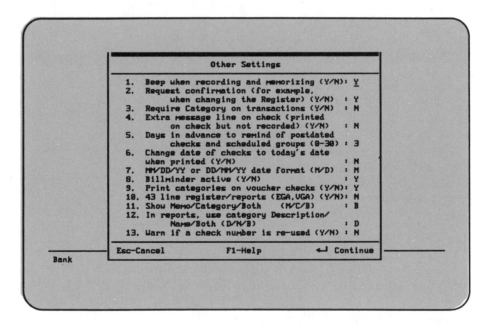

Figure 6.7. The Other Settings menu.

Entering Transfers

A *transfer* is taking money from one Quicken account and putting it into another. For example, you can write a check to your savings account or take a cash advance from your Visa (which you monitor in a credit card account) and deposit it into your checking account. You need only record the first half of the transaction; Quicken automatically records the second. That saves you time and reduces the chance of error.

To enter a transfer, merely type the name of the teamed account in the Category blank. If you're depositing money from your checking account into your savings account, for instance, enter the actual name of your savings account (Savings, My Savings Account, Money Market, or whatever) into the Category blank.

Before you can record a transfer to another account, that account must already exist. Unlike categories, which Quicken can create for you on the fly, you must specifically create new accounts ahead of time.

Accounts are always listed at the very end of the Category and Transfer List window. To see them, press Ctrl-C from the Write Checks or register screen, then press End to view the bottom of the list, as shown in Figure 6.8.

You use transfers just like categories. In the Category blank, type the name of the account you want to use. After you type the name and press the Enter key, Quicken will enclose the name in brackets, as shown in Figure 6.9. You don't have to type the brackets yourself. If you're not sure of the account name, enter a left bracket ([) in the Category blank, then press Ctrl-C. Quicken will display the account names at the bottom of the category list automatically. Scroll to the account you want to use and press Enter.

The actual transfer is not made until you record the transaction by pressing Ctrl-Enter.

117

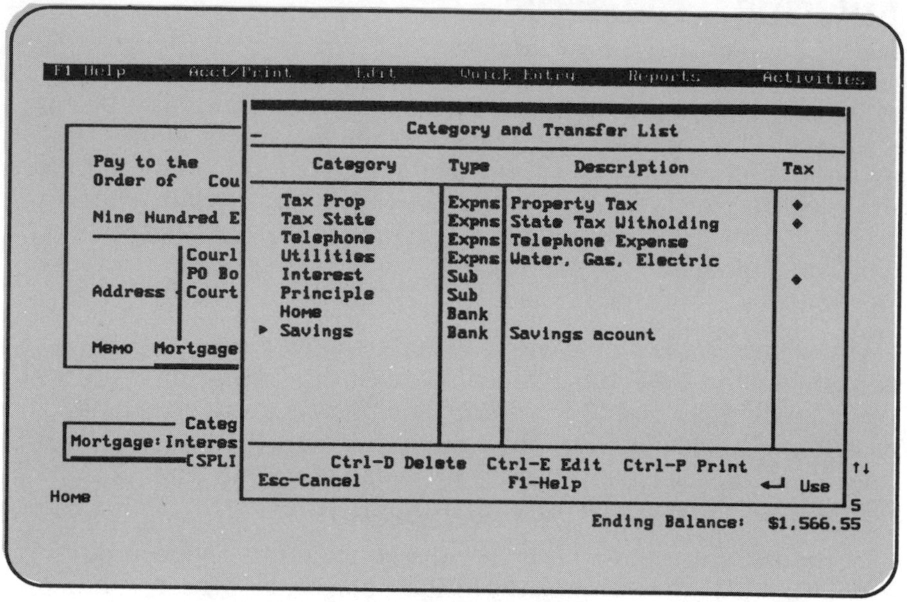

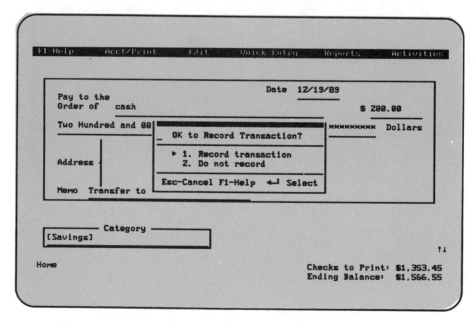

Figure 6.8. Sample accounts in the category list.

*Figure 6.9. Transfers are shown in brackets in the
Category blank.*

Splitting Transfers

Quicken allows you to split a transaction into several transfers. You might use this feature to note accounts for combined payments, for instance, or when writing a check where only part of the money is deposited into another account (when you've asked for money back when depositing a check at the bank, for instance).

To split a transaction into one or more transfers, use the Split Transaction window, as detailed earlier in this chapter. The technique is the same as splitting a transaction into several categories. You can split a single transaction into one or more categories as well as one or more transfers.

Going to a Transfer Transaction

119

Assume you're the Doubting Thomas of the family and you want to be sure that Quicken transfers your money between accounts properly. The program provides a quick and easy way of toggling between transfers.

After Quicken has recorded the transfer and while still in the Write Checks or check register screen, choose the Go to Transfer command from the Edit menu (or press Ctrl-X). Quicken immediately hauls you to the other half of the transfer transaction. While there, you can review the transaction or enter the notation as you desire. Use the Go to Transfer command again to return to your original location.

Altering Transfers

Just as Quicken automatically tracks transfers when you first create them, the link between the transactions remains in place. If you delete one of the transactions in the transfer, the opposite transaction is also deleted (e.g., you void a deposit into your savings). Changes in the amounts and account names are similarly updated automatically.

Using Classes

Classes add an extra dimension to Quicken's categories. Although you can use Quicken in any way you wish, a good application of classes is to track transactions by person, place, or time. Using the old journalistic axiom of who, what, when, where, and how, you can use categories to track the *what* and *how* and classes to track the *who*, *where*, and *when*.

Classes are created and used just like categories. Unlike categories, though, Quicken doesn't come with a preset list of classes. Classes are specific to the individual (like people's names, dates, and places), so you need to add all of them yourself.

120   *Creating Classes*

You can create a class when you're writing a check (or other transaction) or with the Class List window. To access the Class List window from either the Write Checks or check register screen, press Ctrl-L. The window in Figure 6.10 appears. Follow the same procedure outlined above under "Using Categories" to create a new class.

Using Classes

Quicken understands that you want to use a class when you enter a slash (/) in the Category blank within the Write Checks or check register screen. You can enter just a class, or a category and a class, as in

Class only	/Maple St. House
Category and class	Mortgage/Maple St. House

If you enter a class name that has not yet been defined, Quicken asks you if you want to create it or choose from among the existing class names.

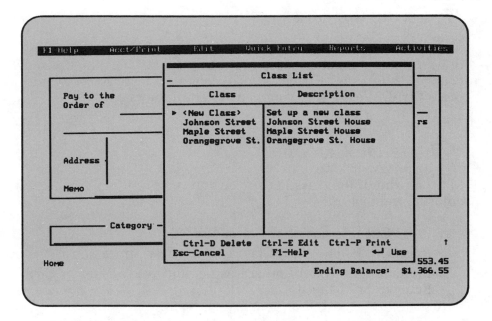

Figure 6.10. The Class List window.

Using Subclasses

As with categories, you can assign subclasses to transactions. The more subclasses you provide, the more specific the nature of the transaction. For instance,

Mortgage/Maple St. House:April '92

indicates that the transaction is listed under the broad category of mortgage and is assigned to the Maple St. House main class. The April '92 notation indicates when the mortgage payment was made.

Modifying the Class List

At any time you can modify the entries in the Class List window. To edit a class, select it and press Ctrl-E. Make the desired changes, and press Ctrl-Enter. To delete a class, select it and press Ctrl-D. Verify that you want to erase the class.

Printing the Class List

Make a print of the class list so you can refer to it when you are entering transactions.

1. Press Ctrl-L to access the class list.
2. Press Ctrl-P. The Print Class List window appears.
3. Indicate the printer you are using, and press Enter or Ctrl-Enter to print the list.

Reconciling Your Transactions

Reconciling a checkbook ranks up there with having root canal work and visiting the in-laws for the holidays. Even with Quicken, the process of making sure you and the bank agree on the ending balance is not entirely without its frustrations. But Quicken does make the task more efficient, and because it reconciles your account on a semiautomated–automated basis, you're not prone to make as many mistakes or overlook steps.

Follow this procedure when reconciling your Quicken checking accounts:

1. Choose the Reconcile command from the Activities menu.
2. Fill in the balance, service charge, and interest information, as requested by Quicken.
3. Mark those transactions in Quicken that have cleared the bank (listed in this month's statement).

4. Compare the ending balance as displayed by Quicken and the ending balance as reported by the bank. If they agree, the task is done. If they don't, you'll need to find the error(s) or adjust for the difference.

Starting Reconciliation

To start the reconciliation process, go to either the Write Checks or check register screen. Choose the Reconcile command from the Activities menu. As shown in Figure 6.11, the Reconcile Register with Bank Statement window appears. In the entry blanks provided, enter:

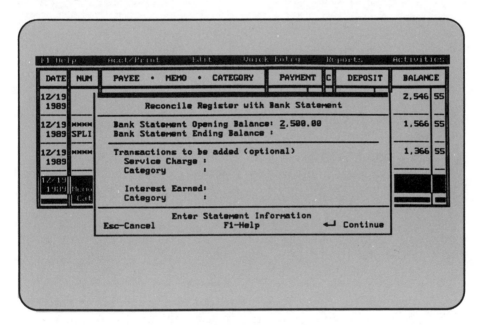

Figure 6.11. This window appears when you choose to reconcile the check register.

The opening balance, as shown on your bank statement —This amount should be displayed already and is either the opening balance you entered when you first started using Quicken or the ending balance of the preceding month. If the amount is different from what's shown in your bank statement, you may not have provided an accurate opening balance when you opened the Quicken account. You may wish to go back and check your earlier records or, if the difference is small, update the opening balance to match the bank's records.

The ending balance, as shown on your bank statement.

Service charges (combine all charges, including check charges and returned item fees).

Interest earned, if any.

Press the Enter key when done and continue to the next step. If you changed the opening balance, Quicken displays an information window to assist you in matching your old opening balance with that of the bank. You may now mark those transactions that have cleared the bank.

124 *Marking Cleared Items*

Items that have been posted in your bank statement are cleared: the bank has acknowledged them and has either added money to your account or paid money from your account. The major step of statement reconciliation is marking cleared items.

After entering opening and ending balances, Quicken automatically displays the cleared item screen, shown in Figure 6.12. This screen is a simplified version of the check register. Find those checks that are listed on the bank register as cleared and press the Spacebar. An asterisk appears in the C (for CLEAR) column. You can mark a range of checks by pressing the F8 key and entering the starting and ending check numbers.

> ▶ **Tip:** Use the Mark Range shortcut to mark as cleared all the checks you've written in a given month. Then, go back to those checks (and other transactions) that are not posted on the bank statement and press the Spacebar to erase the asterisk.

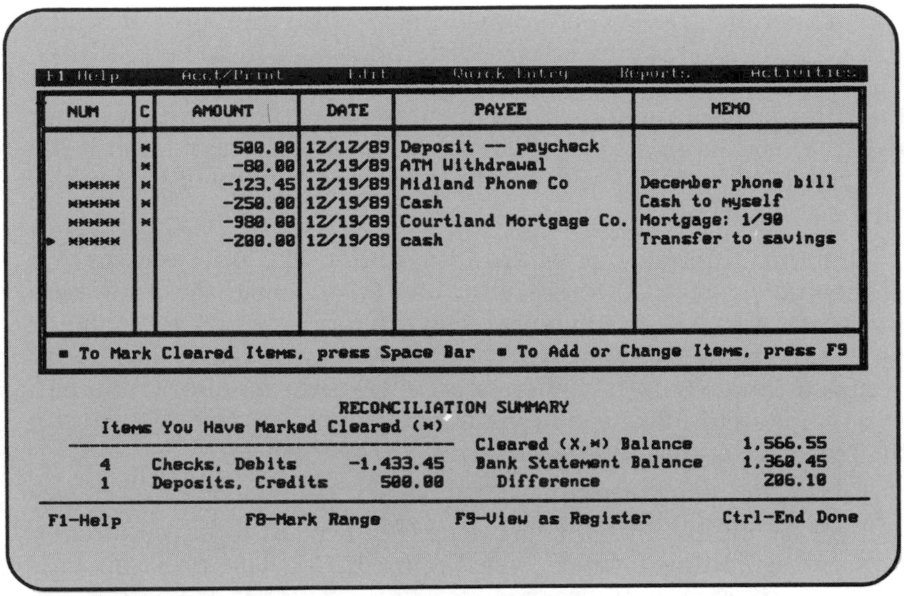

```
 F1 Help        Acct/Print      Edit       Quick Entry    Reports       Activities

 ┌──────┬───┬──────────┬─────────┬─────────────────────────┬──────────────────────────┐
 │ NUM  │ C │  AMOUNT  │  DATE   │         PAYEE           │           MEMO           │
 ├──────┼───┼──────────┼─────────┼─────────────────────────┼──────────────────────────┤
 │      │ × │   500.00 │12/12/89 │Deposit — paycheck       │                          │
 │      │ × │   -80.00 │12/19/89 │ATM Withdrawal           │                          │
 │xxxxx │ × │  -123.45 │12/19/89 │Midland Phone Co         │December phone bill        │
 │xxxxx │ × │  -250.00 │12/19/89 │Cash                     │Cash to myself            │
 │xxxxx │ × │  -980.00 │12/19/89 │Courtland Mortgage Co.   │Mortgage; 1/90            │
 │►xxxxx│   │  -200.00 │12/19/89 │cash                     │Transfer to savings       │
 │      │   │          │         │                         │                          │
 │      │   │          │         │                         │                          │
 └──────┴───┴──────────┴─────────┴─────────────────────────┴──────────────────────────┘
  ■ To Mark Cleared Items, press Space Bar  ■ To Add or Change Items, press F9

                         RECONCILIATION SUMMARY
        Items You Have Marked Cleared (×)
  ─────────────────────────────────────── Cleared (X,×) Balance    1,566.55
        4    Checks, Debits      -1,433.45  Bank Statement Balance   1,360.45
        1    Deposits, Credits      500.00  Difference                 206.10

 F1-Help            F8-Mark Range        F9-View as Register      Ctrl-End Done
```

Figure 6.12. The cleared item screen.

It often happens: when reviewing your bank statement you spot a transaction that you forgot to enter into Quicken. It may be a deposit or perhaps an ATM withdrawal. It could also be an unexpected service charge or perhaps a voided check that you forgot to update in your register. While clearing items, you can make changes to the register to update your records to match the bank's. Press the F9 key to switch to register view. In the register, you can add transactions, edit those transactions that are incorrect, and make other changes as necessary. When you're done, press the F9 key once again, and you're back in the cleared item window.

Comparing Balances

While clearing items, Quicken provides you with a running tally. It shows the amount of checks and other debits you have marked as cleared, as well as the total for deposits and other credits. Quicken calculates the bank statement balance against the items you've marked as clear and indicates the difference.

125

Theoretically, when you've marked all the posted items from the register as cleared, the difference should be zero. If it is, then your job is done. Press Ctrl-F10 to go on to the next step. If the difference is some positive or negative value, it means either that the bank is in error or that you've missed some item and it's not reflected in your Quicken register. Take a moment to double-check your records.

If the difference is small—say under $20 one way or the other—you may want to call it quits and accept that somewhere there's a mistake. You should make every attempt to look for possible errors in your bank statement or register, but there comes a time when the difference isn't worth the effort. You can ask Quicken to make the adjustment for you, or you can enter a ''correction'' transaction yourself.

To adjust the difference automatically, press Enter, and answer Yes to the prompt that asks if you want to have Quicken adjust the ending balance (see Figure 6.13). The program will add an adjustment transaction for you, indicating whether the adjustment is a credit or a debit.

126

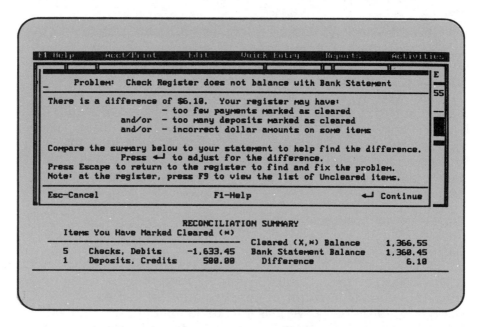

Figure 6.13. Quicken can automatically adjust for differences between your register and the bank statement.

To adjust the difference manually, switch to the register (press the F9 key) and enter a special transaction. If the difference is in the bank's favor (they say you have less money than your records show), enter the adjustment as a debit. If the difference is in your favor, enter the adjustment as a credit. Return to the cleared items list (press the F9 key) again, and mark the adjustment as cleared. Press Ctrl-F10 to finish reconciling.

Obviously, you'll want to exercise extreme care when making adjustments to your account. Just because you're using Quicken doesn't mean that errors can't occur. You may enter the wrong amount for a deposit or record an ATM withdrawal as $80 instead of $180. Or, the fault could be on the side of the banks. If the amount is considerable, you may want to examine the statement and your returned checks carefully to make sure that only your checks are listed and that the dollar amount on the checks is the amount the bank debited from your account.

Printing the Reconciliation Report

127

After reconciliation, Quicken asks if you want a detailed report. If the reconciliation went smoothly with no adjustments, you may not need the report.

But if an adjustment was necessary, print the report and keep it with your bank statement. Come next month, review the report to see if the real error has surfaced. For example, your bank may have debited your account twice for the same check, then, during their internal audits, found the error and automatically made the adjustment in the current month. The reconciliation report will help you to remember what you did to make the bank statement agree with your records.

What You Have Learned

This chapter detailed how to keep better track of your Quicken transactions. Here's what you have learned:

► You can use memos as notes to yourself or to the payee.
► Categories help you separate transactions into logical groups. You can also use categories to find a particular transaction.

▶ Quicken's preset home and business categories are optional. You can use them as you like, remove those you don't want, and add your own.

▶ The easiest way to create new categories is to enter them in the Category blank in the Write Checks or check register screen. Quicken asks if you want to add the category to your list.

▶ Transactions that fill many categories can be split. You decide how much of the transaction goes toward each category.

▶ A transfer is taking money from one Quicken account and placing it into another. Quicken automatically establishes the link between the accounts so that if you later change one side of the transfer, the other is immediately updated.

▶ Classes provide an extra dimension to Quicken's categories, letting you catalog your transactions by people, places, and times.

128

▶ Quicken greatly automates the process of reconciling your checking account statement. When necessary, Quicken can make adjustments automatically.

Chapter 7

Transaction Shortcuts

In This Chapter

▶ *Using memorized transactions*
▶ *Manipulating transaction groups*
▶ *Using Billminder*

Quicken's forte is saving you time. The program offers a number of time-saving shortcuts you can use with your checkbook account, as well as any other account maintained by Quicken. If you find yourself entering the same transactions week after week, or month after month, you'll find relief in two Quicken shortcuts: memorized transactions and transaction groups. With these two features, you can reduce repetitive bill-paying chores to an efficient science.

With transaction groups, not only can you instruct Quicken to remind you when to pay a certain bill, you can also have the program automatically prepare the check for you. And with memorized transactions, you can record the data in a check or other register entry and recall it any time in the future, just by pressing a few keys.

You can use memorized transactions and transaction groups to simplify payroll and accounts payable. Even if some of the payable information changes from month to month, you can still automatically insert the name and address of the payee, category information, and other time-consuming tasks.

In this chapter, you'll learn all about memorized transactions and transaction groups. You'll learn how to record transactions for later recall, and you'll learn how to program Quicken so that it will prepare your regular recurring payments and deposits automatically.

Memorized Transactions

130

The best way to explain the concept of memorized transactions is by example. Suppose you write salaried payroll checks twice a month. The checks are the same dollar amount month after month and are addressed to the same employees. Because each check includes gross pay, federal taxes, state taxes, and other deductions, you have set up a split transaction where the salary and deductions are divided among several different categories.

These would be time-consuming checks to fill out every two weeks. You'd be required to enter, for each employee, the following repetitive information:

Payee.
Amount.
Payee's address (you use the address in a window envelope).
Memo.
Split transaction information.

Instead of going through this hassle, Quicken can take a "snapshot" of one of the payroll checks you've filled out and record it as a memorized transaction. Next pay period, you pick the payroll transaction for each employee from a list and press the Enter key, and all of the information (except the date) is re-entered. Press Ctrl-Enter to record the new check, and you're ready to print it.

Recording a Memorized Transaction

You can fill out the entire check for a memorized transaction or just part of it. The salaried payroll scenario is a good example of a check you'd fill out completely, with dollar amount, address, memo, and category.

Q Recording a Memorized Transaction

1. Press Ctrl-M.   Highlights the data it will record and displays the memorize transaction window, as shown in Figure 7.1.

2. Press Enter.   The data in the check is memorized and added to the Memorized Transactions List (more about this later).

131

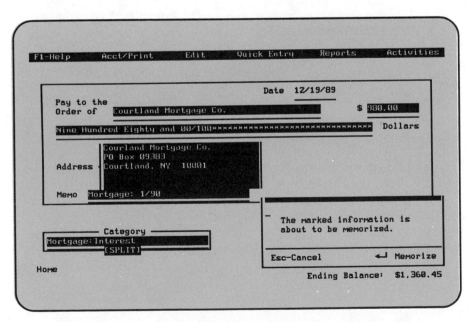

Figure 7.1. The highlighted areas of this check are about to be memorized.

Other checks don't require you to fill in all the blanks. For example, your phone bill changes every month, so you'd create a memorized transaction that contains the name of the phone company, its address (if you're not using a preprinted addressed envelope), and optionally entries in the memo and category blanks. Now, when you press Ctrl-M, as shown in Figure 7.2, Quicken highlights only those items that you filled in.

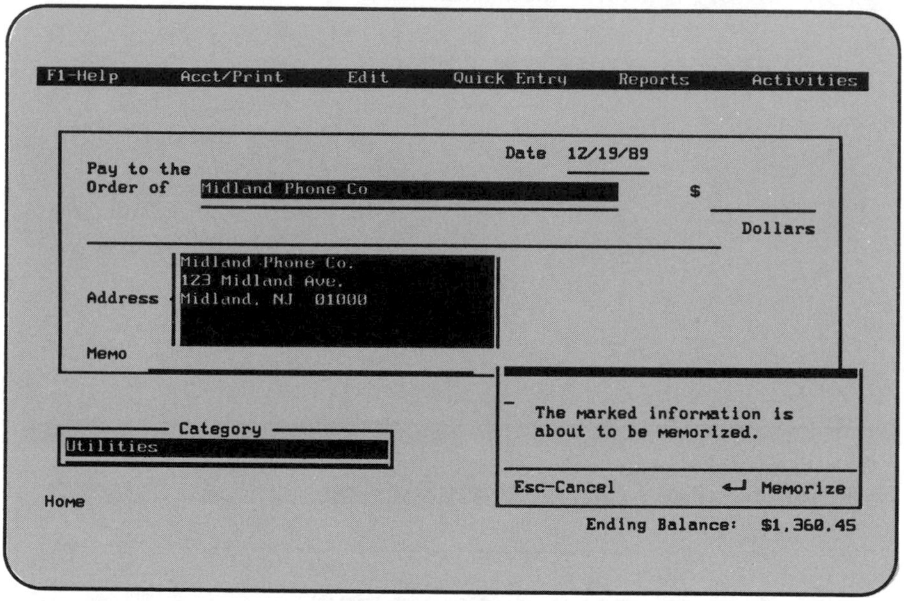

132

Figure 7.2. Only part of this check is filled in, so only part will be memorized.

Later, when you recall this memorized transaction, Quicken will fill in only those lines that you completed. To finish the check, enter a dollar amount and record it. Of course, you can modify the check in any way that you like. Just because Quicken prepared the check for you from a memorized transaction doesn't mean the entries are etched in stone.

> ▶ **Tip:** If you'd like to record several memorized transactions, but not actually prepare the checks, fill out the data as needed, memorize the transaction, then press Ctrl-D for delete. This deletes the entries in the check and lets you start all over again. If you accidentally record a check, go to the register or bring the check back into view (press Page Up until the check you want is displayed). Press Ctrl-D, and confirm that you want to delete the transaction.

Quicken stores all memorized transactions in the same pool, regardless of the account you are using. This lets you share memorized transactions between accounts—you can use the same memorized transaction for your savings and checking account, for example.

Quicken can store only a set number of memorized transactions, depending on the available memory in your computer. The more memory you have at your disposal, the more memorized transactions you can hoard. If you try to memorize a transaction, and Quicken reports an out-of-memory error, you should:

133

Remove some of the *categories* and *classes* you no longer need. (These also take up memory space.)

Remove some of the *memorized transactions* you no longer need.

Quicken stores the memorized transaction by payee's name. At the very least, you should fill in the payee's name. All other entry blanks can be empty. You should avoid entering two memorized transactions with the same or similar names for the payee. While Quicken will let you record two or more identical memorized transactions, the practice makes it harder for you to use the system.

Recalling Memorized Transactions

Recalling a memorized transaction is simple.

Q Recalling a Memorized Transaction

1. In a blank check, move to the payee blank.

2. Type the first few letters of the payee's name for the memorized transaction you want to use.

3. Press Ctrl-T.   Displays the Memorized Transaction List, as shown in Figure 7.3. The transaction you want should already be highlighted.

4. Press Enter.   Inserts the entire memorized transaction into the check. ☐

134

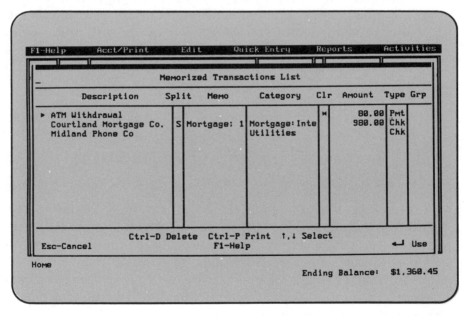

Figure 7.3. The Memorized Transaction List.

The more characters you type in the payee blank before pressing Ctrl-T, the more Quicken can differentiate between all the memorized transactions it holds. You need to type enough characters to differentiate between similar transactions, or

Quicken won't be able to decide which one you want to use. If Quicken can't decide, you'll need to select the proper transaction from the list. That entails more keystrokes and a little more work on your part.

For instance, suppose you have a memorized transaction for *Acme Rental* and another for *Acme Rents*. (As we mentioned earlier, this is not a good procedure to follow, for obvious reasons.) To differentiate between the two, you'll have to type in most of the name before Quicken can discern which one you want.

Viewing the Memorized Transactions List

You don't need to type some or all of the payee's name in the payee blank to recall a memorized transaction. From anywhere within the Write Checks screen, merely press Ctrl-T, and the Memorized Transaction List will appear. Use the cursor keys in the normal fashion to scroll through the available transactions. When you find the one you want, press Enter.

135

Editing Memorized Transactions

Things change, and you may find that a transaction you memorized months ago has to be updated. For example, your bank may have moved, or the dollar amount for the check may have changed. You can edit a memorized transaction at any time. When you recall the transaction and make the necessary changes, Quicken fills in the new information.

Q Editing a Memorized Transaction

1. In the Write Checks screen, recall the transaction using one of the methods described earlier.

2. Make the necessary changes.

3. Press Ctrl-M.

Asks if you want to Replace the transaction or Add the edited transaction to the list, as shown in Figure 7.4.

4. Answer Replace.

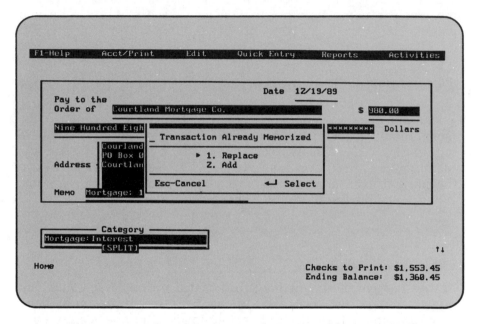

Figure 7.4. Quicken lets you Replace or Add memorized transactions.

Deleting Memorized Transactions

You can (and should) delete from the list those memorized transactions you no longer need. This clears the way for other memorized transactions and gives Quicken a little more memory with which to work. Follow these steps to delete a memorized transaction:

1. From within the Write Checks screen, press Ctrl-L to view the Memorized Transactions List.

2. Scroll to the transaction you want to erase.

3. Press Ctrl-D then Return. If you decide you don't want to delete the memorized transaction after all, press the Escape key.

You can delete any number of transactions. When you're done, press the Escape key to return to the Write Checks screen.

Printing the Memorized Transactions List

If you use Quicken to pay many checks, you'll probably forget which ones you've recorded as memorized transactions. To help you remember, print the Memorized Transactions List.

1. Press Ctrl-T while in the Write Checks screen to view the Memorized Transactions List.
2. Press Ctrl-P. The Print Memorized Transactions List window appears.
3. Indicate the printer you are using and press the Enter key or Ctrl-Enter.

137

Memorizing Other Transactions

While the memorized transaction feature is most often used to capture recurring checks, you can use it to remember any transaction you create with Quicken. While in the check register screen (or any other register screen of any Quicken account type), fill in the desired information and press Ctrl-M. Quicken will record the transaction according to the information you provided in the register.

If you indicate $500 as a deposit of your paycheck, for example, Quicken records the transaction as "Paycheck" and puts $500 in the Amount column of the Memorized Transactions List (see Figure 7.5). Quicken codes the transaction type as "Dep" rather than "Chk," so that when you recall it, the $500 will be placed in the DEPOSIT column of the register rather than the PAYMENT column.

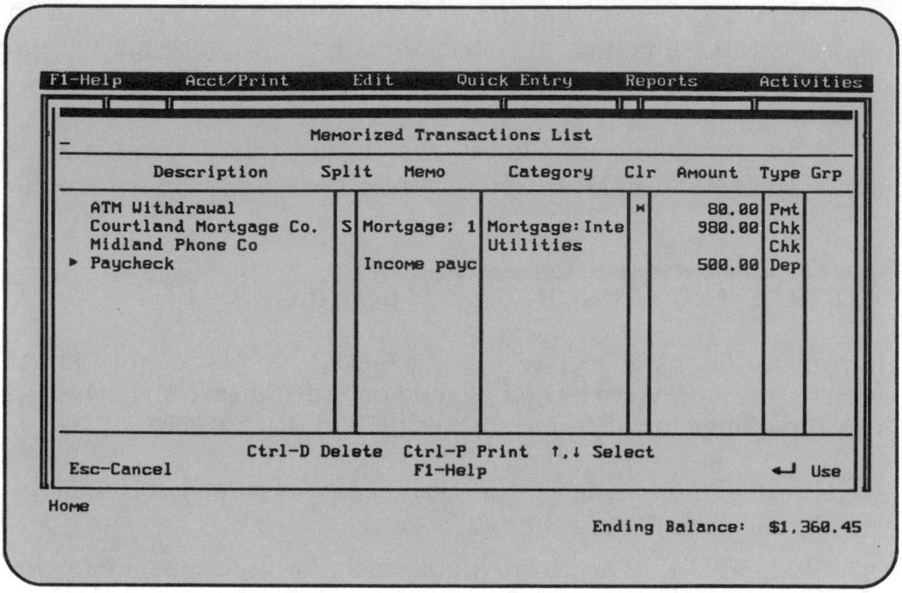

Figure 7.5. A listing of memorized transactions, including a regular deposit.

Some Handy Uses for Memorized Transactions

You probably don't need much prompting to figure out how you can best use the memorized transaction feature. But here are some ideas to start the creative juices flowing:

Record common ATM withdrawals—If you regularly withdraw, say, $60 from the ATM machine, enter an ATM payment in the register and memorize it. Then, whenever you have another ATM withdrawal for the same amount, you can recall the memorized transaction.

Record the names and addresses of regular payees—If you're in business and pay the same individuals and companies regularly, record their addresses as a memorized transaction. Each payment will likely be different, with varying memos and categories. But at least you won't have to re-enter the name and address each time. This approach also cuts down on errors.

Store common split transactions—The more ways you split a transaction, the longer it takes for you to enter all the information. If you use the split often (you buy supplies for the same departments, for example), memorize all the directions of the splits, but without dollar amounts. Recall the transaction, delete those splits you don't need, and fill in the amounts.

Use memorized transactions to maintain cash flow control —Quicken lets you post-date checks to watch over cash flow, but another method—handy for the home user who has fewer bills than most businesses—is to temporarily memorize those bills that must be paid during the month. You can do all your "paperwork" at once, then when it comes time to prepare and print the bills, you can quickly recall each memorized transaction in turn. Delete the memorized transactions, unless they are recurring.

Transaction Groups

139

An extension of memorized transactions is the transaction group. In addition to recording vital statistics about recurring transactions (e.g., checks, deposits, and ATM withdrawals), transaction groups let you consolidate those bills you pay at specific intervals or specific times of the month. When you need to pay bills, whether it's once a week, once every other week, or almost any other cycle, you can instruct Quicken to create checks for those bills. If necessary, you can fill in amounts, memos, and other variable data, then record the check for printing.

The best candidates for inclusion in a transaction group are those bills you pay every month. These include rent payments, car payments, payments for phone and other utilities, and payroll. If the bills are due at about the same time, you can include them in one transaction group. If they are due at dissimilar times, and you don't want to record the check for the transaction ahead of time, you can enter just one bill in the group.

The transaction group feature also includes an optional reminder system, using the Billminder program included with Quicken. The Billminder program (the actual DOS name is BILL-MIND.EXE) checks the scheduling of transaction groups to see if you have any bills coming due. If so, you are warned, and you can take a moment to run Quicken and print out the checks.

Even though Quicken's transaction group feature makes it easy to pay bills in chunks, you still retain control over the actual check-making process. If you decide to wait to pay a bill, that's up to you. Quicken's only interest in the matter is reminding you that the bill is due. How and when you pay it is your business.

Organizing a Transaction Group

The first step in establishing a transaction group is to gather up all the transactions you want to include. This involves memorizing each of the transactions, using the memorize transaction feature detailed in the first part of this chapter. You then select among those memorized transactions you want included in the group. Optionally, you can set a reminder frequency or date.

Q **Organizing a Transaction Group**

1. If they aren't already memorized, memorize those transactions you want included in the group.

2. From the Write Checks or check register screen, choose the Transaction Group command from the Quick Entry menu (or press Ctrl-J).

   The Select Transaction Group to Set Up/Change window appears, as shown in Figure 7.6.

3. Highlight the next available <unused> group and press Enter.

   Creates a new transaction group. The Describe Group ## (where ## is a number from 1 to 12) window appears, as detailed in Figure 7.7.

4. Provide a name for the group; the other settings are optional and discussed below.

5. Press Ctrl-Enter when done.

   Displays a list of available memorized transactions in the Assign Transactions to Group ## window (see Figure 7.8).

6. Highlight a transaction;
    press the Spacebar to select
    or deselect it.   □

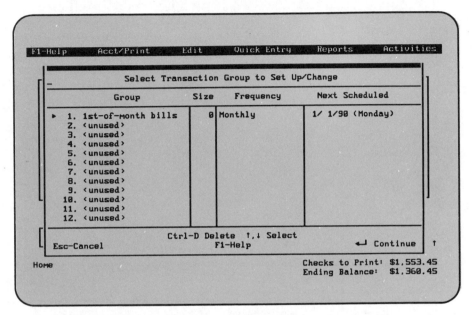

| F1-Help | Acct/Print | Edit | Quick Entry | Reports | Activities |

Select Transaction Group to Set Up/Change

	Group	Size	Frequency	Next Scheduled
▶ 1.	1st-of-month bills	0	Monthly	1/ 1/90 (Monday)
2.	<unused>			
3.	<unused>			
4.	<unused>			
5.	<unused>			
6.	<unused>			
7.	<unused>			
8.	<unused>			
9.	<unused>			
10.	<unused>			
11.	<unused>			
12.	<unused>			

Ctrl-D Delete   ↑,↓ Select
Esc-Cancel   F1-Help   ← Continue   ↑

Home

Checks to Print: $1,553.45
Ending Balance: $1,360.45

*Figure 7.6. The Select Transaction Group to Set Up/
Change window.*

Running a Transaction Group

Whenever you like, you can run the transaction group and make
checks or other transactions. Before you execute the group, open
the register for the account you want to use. As with memorized
transactions, transaction groups transcend the boundaries of
accounts; you can use the same groups in any Quicken account.

Q Running a Transaction Group

1. Select the Execute
    Transaction Group
    command from the Quick
    Entry menu (or press
    Ctrl-J).

Displays a list of available
transaction groups, as
shown in Figure 7.9.

141

2. Use the cursor keys to select the group you'd like to use.

3. Press Enter to activate the group.

Displays the Group Date window, which indicates the scheduled date for the transactions in the group (if any). This is the date Quicken will give to the transactions when they are entered into the register.

4. Press Enter to accept the date. Press Esc if you want to cancel the operation.

Announces that it is about to execute the transaction group.

5. Press Enter to execute the group.

□

142

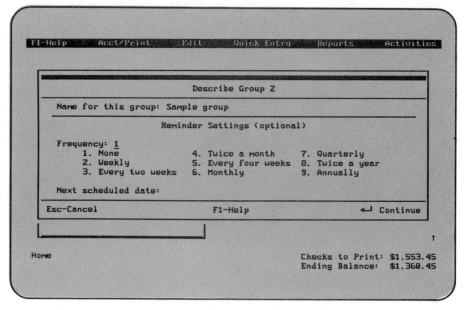

Figure 7.7. The Describe Group # window.

▶ **Tip:** If you're paying bills before or after the scheduled date, as shown in the Group Date window, you can enter a new date, if you wish, by typing it in or by pressing the + or − keys.

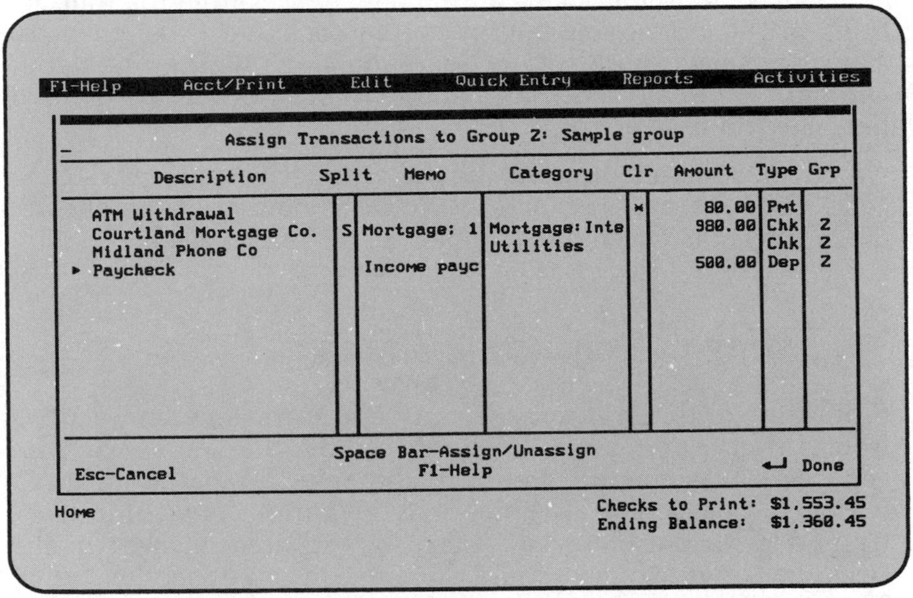

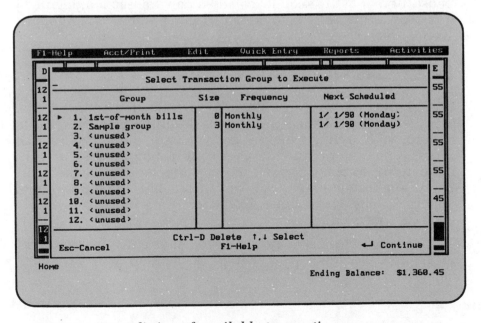

*Figure 7.8. Quicken lets you assign transactions to a
group in this window.*

Figure 7.9. A listing of available transaction groups.

Once Quicken has created the new entries from the transactions in the group, you can always go back and make changes. You can delete those transactions you don't want, edit dollar amounts, post-date checks—in short, you can do anything you'd normally do in Quicken.

If the transaction group included checks, press Ctrl-W to access the Write Checks screen. You can now print the checks. (This subject is covered in Chapter 8, "Printing Checks.")

Modifying a Transaction Group

From time to time you may wish to add or remove transactions from a transaction group. To do so, follow the same basic procedures for creating the group. At the Select Transaction Group to Set Up/Change window, highlight the group you want to modify and press the Enter key. Make any desired changes in the Describe Group window. Press Ctrl-Enter when done; the Assign Transactions window will appear.

To remove a transaction you no longer want, scroll to it with the cursor keys and press Ctrl-D. Press Enter to delete the transaction or Esc to keep it. To add a new transaction, highlight it and press the Enter key. Press Ctrl-Enter when you're done.

Setting Reminders

Quicken lets you set a specific date when the transactions in the group are due. This date is used by the Billminder program to remind you to run Quicken and prepare those checks. (Of course, you're not limited to using transaction groups and Billminder for accounts payable only, although this is the most likely application.) You can use this date to remind you of important bills, for example, like a yearly tax bill or a quarterly insurance payment.

You can also set a frequency of payment. This indicates how often the group is scheduled to be run. You have nine choices:

▶ None.
▶ Weekly.

144

▶ Every two weeks.

▶ Twice a month.

▶ Every four weeks.

▶ Monthly.

▶ Quarterly.

▶ Twice a year.

▶ Annually.

Note that Quicken makes the distinction between "every two weeks" and "twice a month," as well as "every four weeks" and "monthly." Every two weeks is every two calendar weeks —every other Monday, for example. Twice a month is two payments in any calendar month, such as the 1st and 15th. Likewise, every four weeks is four calendar weeks (such as every fourth Monday), and monthly is once a month, specifically, on a particular day of the month.

145

One of the most useful applications of transaction groups is its ability to produce payroll checks. The name and salary of every employee is memorized as a separate transaction, then all of the payroll transactions are combined into one group. If payday is once a week, set the frequency to weekly. If payday is every two weeks, or twice a month, set the frequency accordingly. When it comes time to create and print the paychecks, Quicken will do most of the hard work for you.

Normally, all transaction groups are active no matter what account you are currently using. You may want to limit a transaction group to a specific account type—payroll transactions to the payroll account, for example. In addition to setting the frequency of payment, you can indicate the name of the account to use before executing the account group. Leave the option blank if you want to apply the transaction group to any account.

About the Billminder Program

If you have a hard disk drive, you can install Billminder on the drive and run it automatically each time the computer starts. Quicken gives you the option of including Billminder on your hard disk when you install the rest of the Quicken files. Along with the actual BILLMIND.EXE program file, Quicken adds a BILL-MIND command prompt at the end of your AUTOEXEC.BAT file. The AUTOEXEC.BAT is a batch file that is executed automatically each time you start or reset your computer.

If you did not install Billminder when you installed the rest of the Quicken files, you can do so manually now. Simply copy the BILLMIND.EXE file to the root directory of your hard drive. Optionally, you can copy it into the QUICKEN4 directory. In the AUTOEXEC.BAT file, enter the line

`BILLMIND`

at the end. Or, if you use a shell program or DOS menu, add the command line above it. Type `/P` after the BILLMIND command to force the program to pause after it displays its message. Otherwise, your shell program or menu will execute before you have a chance to see the Billminder message.

146

If you have copied the BILLMIND.EXE file into the QUICKEN4 directory, you'll need to provide the full path in the AUTOEXEC.BAT file:

`/QUICKEN4/BILLMIND`

At any time, you can turn the Billminder program off and on with Billminder Active option in the Other Settings menu. Refer to Chapter 2, "Getting Started with Quicken," for more details on using the Other Settings menu.

What You Have Learned

This chapter discussed two of Quicken's most important time-shaving shortcuts: memorized transactions and transaction groups. Here's what you have learned:

▶ Quicken remembers transactions you've made in the past with its memorized transactions feature.

▶ Quicken stores all memorized transactions together, regardless of the account you are using.

▶ The memorized transaction feature is most often used to capture recurring checks, yet you can use it to remember any transaction you create with Quicken—deposits, ATM withdrawals, transfers, and so forth.

▶ A transaction group is a set of recurring transactions. The best candidates for inclusion in a transaction group are those bills you pay every month.

▶ As an option, you can use the transaction group feature with the Billminder program (which is part of Quicken) to remind you when bills need to be paid.

▶ Before you can create a transaction group, Quicken must memorize the transactions you want included.

▶ Hard disk users can install the Billminder program and use it to check for bills that are coming due.

147

148

Chapter 8

Printing Checks

In This Chapter

▶ *About Quicken checks*
▶ *Getting ready for printing*
▶ *Using a laser printer*
▶ *Printing checks*

Your efforts with Quicken culminate when you finally print the checks you've been entering, recording, splitting, categorizing, and memorizing. Check-printing is where Quicken shines, making the process as painless as possible. Quicken works with both line-at-a-time (daisywheel, dot matrix) printers and page-oriented (laser) printers. If you have more than one printer, you can select one as the reports printer and the other as the checks printer.

This chapter describes printing checks with Quicken. You'll learn how to test your printer with Quicken to make sure that the two are compatible and how to test check alignment. The Quicken package comes with several sample checks you can use for testing purposes. If you run out, you can continue your tests with plain paper. You'll need to order your own checks (Quicken comes with an order form for this purpose) when you're ready to use the program to print your real checks.

In this chapter, you'll also learn how to solve common printer alignment problems, how to use a laser printer with Quicken, how to print checks selectively, and how to reprint checks that didn't come out right.

Quicken Checks

Although Quicken can be used with a variety of preprinted computer checks, the ones Intuit offers are the best choice. Checks for dot matrix or daisywheel printers come with alignment marks on the tear-off pin-feed holes. These help you to make slight adjustments in printing to make sure that the entries align with the blanks on the check.

150

Quicken has three basic types of checks.

Regular checks—The check area is 3-1/2 inches high by 8-1/2 inches wide, as shown in Figure 8.1.

Voucher checks—The check area is the same as for regular checks, but there is an extra 3-1/2 inches high voucher stub below the check.

Wallet checks—The check area is 2-5/6 inches high by 6 inches wide with a 2-1/2 inches wide register stub at the left.

In addition, regular checks are available in a number of formats, including single-, two-, and three-part, as well as special payroll checks. Payroll checks include a pay stub voucher.

These checks are available from Intuit in two forms: *continuous,* for use in dot matrix and daisywheel printers and *full-sheet laser.* With the exception of voucher-style checks, laser checks come packed three to a sheet. Voucher checks come one to a sheet, with the check on top and the rest of the page for the voucher stub.

Quicken checks look just like the Write Checks screen. There's a place for the date, payee, dollar amount (numerals and words), and memo. Your personalized checks include:

Preprinted name and address for you and your bank.

Check number—Quicken doesn't print the check number.

Bank routing and account number digits—These digits identify you as the originator of the check and help banks locate your account.

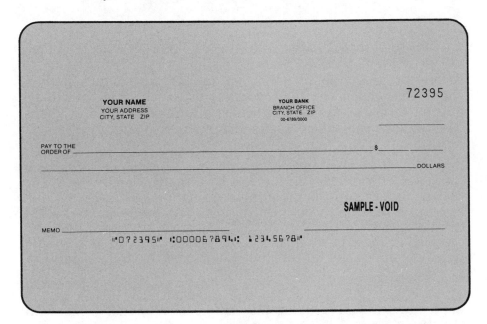

Figure 8.1. A sample check; these are provided with the Quicken package.

151

Getting Ready to Print

Quicken comes set up for use with an IBM compatible printer set at 10 characters per inch (10 pitch). If your printer matches this description, you can use the program without further setup. Most likely though, you'll want to customize Quicken for use with your specific printer. This is especially necessary if you are using a laser printer, such as the Hewlett-Packard LaserJet. Laser printers and dot matrix/daisywheel printers function in completely different ways. Using the IBM compatible printer settings with a laser model may cause jams and incomplete printing.

Refer to the section on printer selection and setup in Chapter 2, "Getting Started with Quicken," if you need to set up your printer with Quicken. You can also access the printer setup menus from within the Write Checks or check register screen, through the Acct/Print menu, but this requires that you have checks recorded and ready to print.

Loading Your Printer with Sample Checks

Before printing one of your real checks with Quicken, you should test that everything works and that the checks will be aligned properly. Quicken provides a number of helpful shortcuts to make check testing and alignment easier.

152

For daisywheel and dot matrix printers, load the checks in the printer as you would any continuous form paper. Make sure the holes on the sides of the checks line up properly with the platen sprockets inside the printer. Adjust the first check so that the top is flush with the print head. Then, loosen the sprocket clamps and slide the checks back and forth to center them on the platen. Most printers allow 1/2 inch or more of side-to-side play, to compensate for different paper sizes. Lock the clamps in place.

For laser printers, place one sheet of check stock in the paper tray. If you're using the sample checks that came with Quicken, tear off a set of three and remove the sprocket holes. These should feed properly through your printer. Note: For best results, keep at least 25 sheets of paper in the paper tray. This helps reduce paper jams, especially when using the fairly slick check stock.

If you don't have a check waiting to print in the register, write a dummy check. To print the check, follow these steps.

1. From the Write Checks screen, choose the Print Checks command from the Acct/Print menu (or press Ctrl-P).
2. Indicate the number of the printer you are using. If you don't see it listed, press Esc, then choose the Change Printer Setting command from the Acct/Print menu (the printer setup procedure is the same as outlined in Chapter 2, "Getting Started with Quicken").
3. If you're using wallet or voucher checks (as opposed to the sample regular checks that came with Quicken) or a laser printer, press the F8 key to display the Select Check Type screen. Select the check type and press Enter.

4. Press the F9 key to make a sample check.

Assuming your printer is turned on and working properly, Quicken should print one sample check, as shown in Figure 8.2.

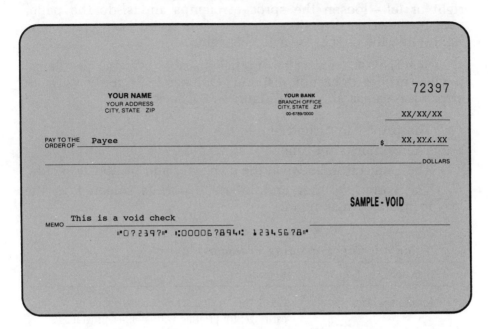

Figure 8.2. A sample printed check.

Diagnosing Alignment Problems

The first sample check you print may not be aligned properly. Don't worry; it's fairly easy to fix. If you're using a laser printer and the print is not aligned or is skewed, the most likely problem is *misfeed*—the paper went through the printer crooked. Try another sheet. Note that you can print a single check at a time if you have a manual feed tray. This feature does not work when printing sample checks. See "Using a Laser Printer," later in this chapter, for more information on tips when using a laser printer.

If you're using a dot matrix or daisywheel printer, note the position of the POINTER LINE, printed about half-way down the check (in a properly printed check, the POINTER LINE should point to number 26 in the alignment marks on the side of the check). If the POINTER LINE is too low or too high, enter the

153

number the line points to at the prompt that appears. Quicken will make the adjustments automatically so that the next check it prints will be aligned properly.

Should the check be *off-center*—the print is too far to the right or left—loosen the sprocket clamps and slide the paper over in the same direction. That is, if the print is too far to the right, slide the checks over to the right.

See Table 8.1 for a list of other possible printing problems. If your printer does not respond, Quicken will reply with an error message, as shown in Figure 8.3. Check that:

The printer is turned on.
The printer is on-line.
The connection between the computer and printer is secure.
The correct printer and interface port is selected in the Printer Settings menu.

154

Table 8.1. Check-Printing Problems.

Symptom	Remedy
Checks are blank	Check printer connection; check ribbon or cartridge; try printing with another program
Prints too far to the right	Slide checks over to the right
Prints too far to the left	Slide checks over to the left
Prints below lines	Indicate new POINTER LINE setting
Prints above lines	Indicate new POINTER LINE setting
First line prints OK but prints above other lines	Printer set to eight lines per inch (must be set to six lines per inch)
Prints over right or left sides	Print pitch setting too large, adjust
Prints OK on left side, but doesn't reach right side	Print pitch setting too large, adjust
Too much space between lines	Printer is sending extra line feed, adjust printer

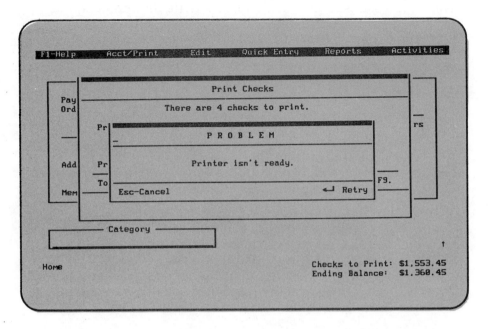

Figure 8.3. Quicken warns you when the printer is not responding.

Keep printing new samples until the checks come out right. If you're using a dot matrix or daisywheel printer, note the starting position of the checks in the printer. For example, if the top left-hand corner of the checks just reaches the left edge of the print head, make a note of that for future reference. Then, when you re-load the printer with check stock, you'll be able to return to that setting and make perfect prints.

If there doesn't seem to be a convenient alignment cue, you can make one yourself. Place a piece of masking tape or white paper tape toward the rear of the printer where the checks enter. On the tape, draw a line marking the tear-off between checks.

Handling Paper Jams

It seems that frequent jamming is the nature of some printers. Ordinarily, printer jams that occur when using regular paper are merely a frustration; the cost of the paper is minimal compared to your anger. But wasting preprinted check stock is a different matter. Not only are the checks fairly expensive (you don't pay a service charge on a check unless it goes through your bank, of course), but wasted checks throw off the counting sequence.

155

Instead of a series of checks that starts with 1000 then counts up by ones, your check register shows printed check numbers of 1000, 1003, 1008, 1014, 1015, 1019, and so forth. That makes it harder to manage your books.

If you are plagued by paper jams, take a few moments to discover the cause.

Look for small bits of paper in the paper path. These may impede the proper flow of the checks.

If the paper feeds from the back, make sure that the power cord and interface cable aren't in the way. Tape them down with heavy duct tape if they are, and position the paper away from them.

If your printer can't start printing on the first sheet, you may need to get a forms leader, available from Intuit. (It is also available at many office and computer supply stores.) The forms leader uses a tacky surface to grab the paper so that it will feed properly. These are especially handy if your printer uses a paper bail roller that often gets in the way of the first check.

156

Using a Laser Printer

Laser printers aren't as prone to the same misalignment problems as daisywheel and dot matrix printers. Quicken makes it genuinely easy to print checks with a laser printer, but there are some tips and techniques you'll want to know about.

Most laser printers print on the top of the paper, as the paper is fed through the mechanism. If yours works this way, load the check stock into the paper tray face up. On Hewlett-Packard laser printers, as well as many other laser printer models, the checks should be loaded into the machine top first. That is, the top edge of the checks should feed through the machine first. If you insert the checks the other way, they'll print upside down.

You may wish to experiment with the orientation of your laser printer on a plain piece of paper. Quicken doesn't know the difference between plain paper and check stock. Make a sample print, as detailed earlier, and watch how the paper emerges.

By design, laser printers must print an entire page at a time. When using regular and wallet-size checks, you must print your checks in threes, or you'll waste those checks that are unprinted. This doesn't apply if your printer is Hewlett-Packard LaserJet compatible and is equipped with a manual paper feed tray. If your printer is so endowed, you can print one or two checks at a time. The full procedure is provided below in the "Printing Checks" section of this chapter.

Laser printers are as prone to jamming as dot matrix or daisywheel printers, but they jam for different reasons. If your printer jams on check stock, there may not be enough "cushion" of extra pages in the paper feed tray. Even if you are printing a small bundle of checks, load the rest of the tray with regular paper. If you're using continuous feed checks that have been torn off in threes, lay the checks flat and place a heavy book on top. Keep them there, preferably for several hours—or even overnight. This helps remove the crease.

157

Quicken lets you print additional copies of your checks when using a laser printer. You can choose 0 (the default), 1, 2, or 3. Why would you want to print extra copies of checks? Laser printers are not capable of making an impression on multipart forms. The top pages print, but the bottom ones are blank because they rely on impact to produce printed text.

However, you should not use the extra copies feature to make additional checks on check stock. Those checks are *negotiable,* and you probably don't want them floating around your office or home. Rather, you should order multipart laser checks, or at least, stack one or more blank sheets of plain paper under each sheet of check stock.

Printing Checks

With your sample checks now printing properly, you can use Quicken to print your real checks. Replace the sample check stock with your personalized checks. Be sure that the checks are inserted in the printer properly and that they are lined up with your previously identified alignment mark. Then, follow these simplified steps at the Write Checks screen.

Q Printing a Check

1. Press Ctrl-P. Chooses the Print Checks command. The window in Figure 8.4 appears.

2. Select printer and print options (see below).

3. Press the F8 key and indicate the type of checks you want to use. This step isn't required each time. Remembers your check selection for the next time you use the program.

4. Press Ctrl-Enter.

5. Indicate the number of the NEXT check in the printer. Type a new number or press the + and − keys to set a higher or lower number. Displays the check number window shown in Figure 8.5.

6. Press the F9 key or Enter. The F9 key prints the first check only (this helps you stop the printer in case of misalignment or misfeed). Enter prints all checks. □

158

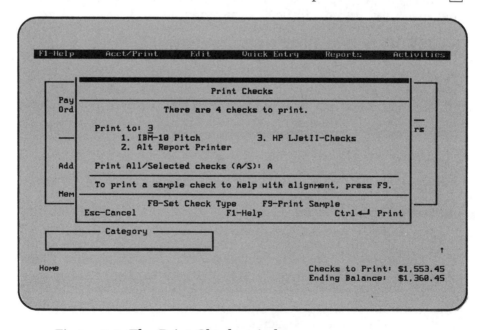

Figure 8.4. The Print Checks window.

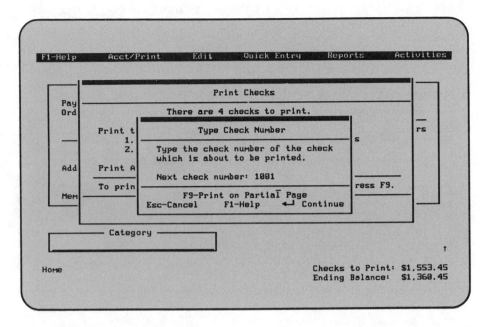

Figure 8.5. Enter the first check number to print in this window.

Quicken now initiates printing. After printing is done, Quicken asks if the checks were printed correctly. Answer yes or no accordingly.

If the checks printed correctly, you are done printing and can return to the Write Checks screen.

If one or more of the checks didn't print correctly, fix the problem (if any). In the window that appears, type the number of the first check that didn't print correctly. Quicken assumes all remaining checks also did not print properly and queues them up for reprinting. Press the Enter key to display the Type Check Number window. Enter the NEW number for the first incorrectly printed check and press the Enter key to start.

Selecting Checks to Print

One of the options in the Print Checks window is printing All or just Selected checks. When in the Print Checks window, enter A for All (the default) or S for Selected. When you've indicated Selected checks, pressing Ctrl-Enter displays the Select Checks to Print window, as shown in Figure 8.6.

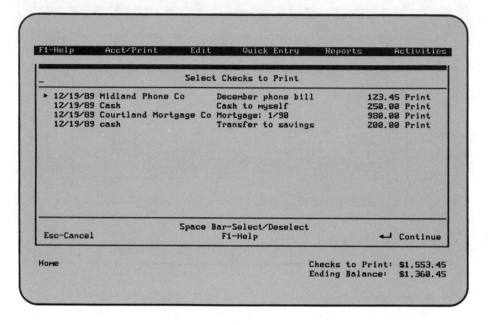

Figure 8.6. Indicate the checks to print in this window.

All of the checks that you've recorded but that have not yet been printed are listed, even checks that have been post-dated. (See the following section for more information on post-dated checks.) Quicken assumes that you want to print them all, so it initially places a Print indicator in the right-hand column. If you don't want to print a certain check, highlight it with the cursor keys and press the Spacebar to toggle the Print indicator on and off. With the Print indicator off, that check won't be printed. You can select and deselect any number of checks in this manner. Press the Enter key when you are done.

Working with Post-Dated Checks

When you have post-dated checks waiting to be printed, Quicken reminds you of this fact in the Print Checks window, as shown in Figure 8.7. The program initially displays the current date, not the date written on the post-dated checks. Alter this date if you want to print post-dated checks after the date indicated. Any check dated after the date you select will not be printed.

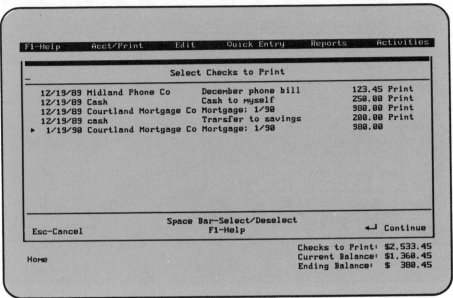

Figure 8.7. A sample list of checks, some post-dated.

Quicken also lets you select each post-dated check for printing. Using the list in the Select Checks to Print window, follow the same procedure for selecting and deselecting post-dated checks you would for any check.

Check Numbers in the Register

Once you've printed a check, Quicken appends the number next to it in the check register. You can tell that a check has been printed if there's a number beside it in the register, as shown in Figure 8.8.

If you need to reprint a check at some later date (the original was lost or you discovered a problem with the first one), you can force Quicken into thinking that the check hasn't been printed by typing an asterisk in the check number column. When you access the Print Checks menu, the check will be listed with all the other ones waiting to be printed.

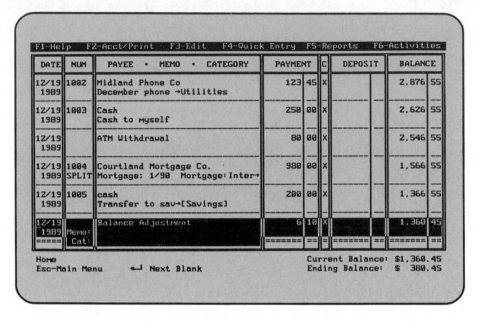

Figure 8.8. The check register, now with numbered checks.

Printing Single Checks with a Laser Printer

If you use a Hewlett-Packard LaserJet or compatible, and it is equipped with a manual feed tray, you can use it to print one or two checks at a time.

Let's assume that you have just one check to print. This check can be a regular, wallet, or voucher check. Place it sideways in the manual feed tray so that the check number and date feed into the printer first.

Follow these steps to set up Quicken to print on a partial page:

1. Choose the Print Checks command from the the Acct/Print menu.

2. Select the checks to print, as usual (or just press Ctrl-Enter if you've indicated that you want to print All checks).

3. At the Type Check Number window, press the F9 key, for Print On Partial Page. (This option appears only when using a laser printer.)

4. At the window shown in Figure 8.9, enter 1. (If you're printing two checks, enter 2.) Press the Enter key.

5. Indicate the next check number and press Enter.

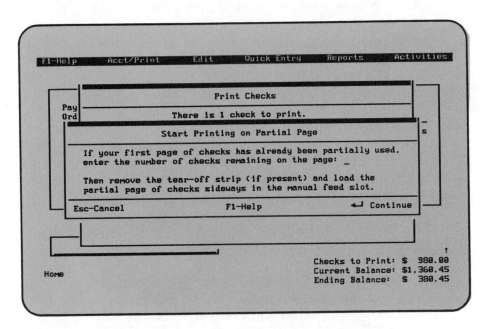

Figure 8.9. Quicken displays this message when you choose to feed checks manually using a Hewlett-Packard LaserJet printer.

What You Have Learned

This chapter concentrated on printing checks with Quicken. Here's what you have learned:

▶ For best results, use the checks offered by Intuit when printing checks with Quicken.

▶ You can use Quicken with three basic types of checks: regular, voucher, and wallet. These checks are available in either continuous-form or full-sheet laser formats.

▶ Unless you're using a "plain vanilla" printer, you will need to establish the type of printer you're using prior to producing checks.

▶ Before actually printing your checks, you should print one or more samples to ensure alignment and operation. Quicken comes with several sample checks you can use for this purpose.

▶ Most problems in printing will be due to alignment. You should also be sure that your printer is set to the proper print pitch and line height.

164

▶ To print checks, press Ctrl-P (from within the Write Checks screen). Select the checks to print and indicate the number of the check currently in the printer.

▶ You can select only those checks that you want printed. Indicate those checks you want to print in the Select Checks to Print window.

▶ The Select Checks to Print window shows all checks you've written but not yet printed, including post-dated checks. You can select these for printing, as well. When printed, post-dated checks will bear the date that you entered for them.

▶ To reprint a check at some later date, enter an asterisk in the check number column of the check register. The next time you print checks, Quicken will include it.

Chapter 9

Working with Other Quicken Accounts

In This Chapter

165

▶ *Overview of other account types*
▶ *Setting up a savings account*
▶ *Setting up a cash account*
▶ *Setting up a credit card account*
▶ *Maintaining asset and liability accounts*
▶ *Building special-purpose accounts*
▶ *Maintaining stocks, bonds, and other investments*

Throughout this book we've concentrated on using Quicken to maintain a standard checking account. While checking accounts are the type of account most often exploited by Quicken, they aren't the only kind the program can handle.

This chapter briefs you on applying Quicken to track various types of financial matters. You'll learn how to maintain savings, cash, credit card, and miscellaneous asset and liability, and investment accounts, plus how to follow almost any financial situation using one of Quicken's account types.

Other Account Types

Setting up a checkbook register account is just one option when starting a new account. As shown in Figure 9.1, you can set up any of the following accounts:

Bank account.

Cash.

Credit card.

Other asset.

Other liability.

Investment account.

166

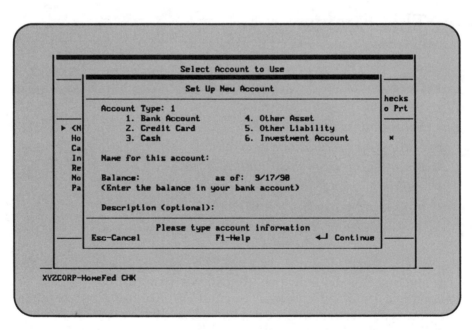

Figure 9.1. Account type options.

Quicken groups any account that deals with both credits and debits and allows you at least some free access to funds, as with a bank account. This includes, but is not limited to, checking accounts, savings accounts, money market savings accounts, IRAs, and CD accounts.

For the sake of simplicity, we'll differentiate between checking accounts and all other bank accounts, because—with few exceptions—only checking accounts allow you to write checks. With savings accounts, CD accounts, IRAs, and the like, credits and debits are entered directly into the register; no check is ever written or printed. This "rule" doesn't apply to unique checking-type accounts, like money market savings accounts that allow you to write checks to make withdrawals.

Setting Up a Savings Account

There are numerous types of savings accounts, from regular passbook savings accounts to money market accounts to CD accounts to IRAs. While these accounts vary in the interest that they pay and the regulations regarding withdrawal (especially early withdrawal), they have a similarity: you put money in for a period of time and withdraw it—generally by writing a voucher or counter-check at the bank. A checkbook is not issued, because the savings account is not designed to handle many transactions. In fact, most banks place a ceiling on withdrawals during a particular month or quarter.

167

Whatever type of savings account you have, you maintain it entirely from the register. The register looks exactly like the check register (in fact, it's the same), except that you don't have to worry about tracking check numbers or printing checks. When maintaining a savings account you are concerned about two types of transactions:

▶ *Credits*—money that goes *into* your account.
▶ *Debits*—money that goes *out* of your account.

Credits are typified by deposits and interest payments. Debits are typified by withdrawals, penalty fees, and service charges.

To set up a savings account, you should follow the same basic procedure outlined for checking accounts.

Q Setting Up a Savings Account

1. At the main menu, press 4.	Chooses the Select Account command.
2. Highlight the \<new account> option and press Enter.	Displays the Set Up New Account window.
3. Press 1 then Enter.	Indicates Bank Account as account type.
4. Type the account name and press Enter.	Names the account (e.g., Savings).
5. Enter balance and press Enter. You can always change the balance later.	Provides starting balance.
6. Enter date if different from today's date, and press Enter.	
7. Type description and press Enter. This is optional, but recommended since you may have more than one savings account.	Describes the account.

168

Select the newly created account in the Select Account window and press Enter. Quicken drops you into the register screen. You may now enter the various credit and debit transactions.

> ▶ **Tip:** Quicken lets you write checks for any type of bank account, whether it's a checking or savings account. If you prefer, you can enter savings account withdrawals as checks using the Write Checks screen. As usual, Quicken will record these as checks and will always prompt you that you have checks to print for the savings account. To avoid this, you can enter a transaction number instead of a check number beside each withdrawal, as shown in Figure 9.2. This will trick Quicken into thinking that the withdrawal check has been printed.

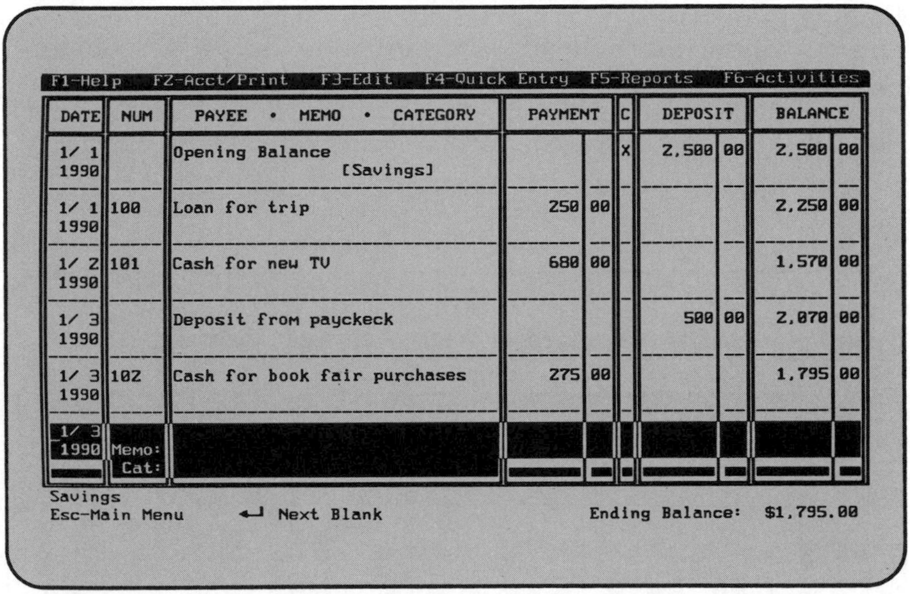

Figure 9.2. Transaction numbers for withdrawals.

Entering Deposits

You enter deposit information into the Savings Account register the same as you do into a Checking Account register. At the register screen, type the date of the transaction, a description (in the PAYEE column), and a dollar amount in the DEPOSIT column. You may furnish memo and category information if you like. When you've finished entering the information for the transaction, press Ctrl-Enter to record it.

Entering Withdrawals

Withdrawals are debits from your savings account, so instead of entering an amount in the DEPOSIT column, you enter it into the PAYMENT column. When you're done entering the information for the withdrawal, press Ctrl-Enter to record it.

Because withdrawals won't be the only type of debits you'll include in the register, as shown in Figure 9.3, you may wish to enter a transaction number or identifier in the NUM column. (You can also use this technique when entering deposits.) Make up your own codes for the transaction identifiers, such as D for deposit, I for interest payment, W for withdrawal, and S for service charge.

170

DATE	NUM	PAYEE • MEMO • CATEGORY	PAYMENT	C	DEPOSIT	BALANCE
1/ 1 1990		Opening Balance [Savings]		X	2,500 00	2,500 00
1/ 1 1990	W	Loan for trip	250 00			2,250 00
1/ 2 1990	W	Cash for new TV	680 00			1,570 00
1/ 3 1990	D	Deposit from payckeck			500 00	2,070 00
1/ 3 1990	W	Cash for book fair purchases	275 00			1,795 00
1/ 4 1990	I Memo: Cat:	Interest payment/December			23 98	1,818 98

F1-Help   F2-Acct/Print   F3-Edit   F4-Quick Entry   F5-Reports   F6-Activities

Savings
Esc-Main Menu   ↵ Next Blank

Current Balance: $1,795.00
Ending Balance: $1,818.98

Figure 9.3. Sample transaction identifiers in the NUM column.

Entering Other Credits and Debits

All other transactions in a savings account (indeed, any type of financial account) are handled either as a payment (debit) or as a deposit (credit). In most cases, these additional transactions will be added when you reconcile your account using the bank statement. To enter interest paid by your bank, enter the amount paid for the last period as a deposit. To enter a service fee charged by your bank, enter the amount charged as a payment. To enter a penalty (e.g., an early withdrawal penalty) charged by your bank, enter the amount charged as a payment.

Certain types of savings accounts will have other forms of debits and credits. For example, credit unions may pay share dividends in addition to (or instead of) interest. Enter these into the appropriate PAYMENT or DEPOSIT column.

Setting Up a Cash Account

You remember cash: it's that green stuff that always seems to disappear once you put it in your wallet. In this age of credit cards, debit cards, and push-button financial transactions, it can be easy to forget your cash expenditures, and the importance of keeping tabs on where the money goes. You can track your cash outlay in either of two ways:

▶ As transactions in a checking or savings account.
▶ As a separate account type.

171

Depending on your spending habits and requirements, you may want to use both systems. Each has its special application within Quicken.

Tracking Cash in a Bank Account

Assume that you deposit your $750 paycheck into the bank, but hold back $100 for spending loot. Quicken will record the paycheck deposit as $650; the $100 you received as cash is unaccounted for. When entering the deposit into the account, you should split the transaction as shown in Figure 9.4. (See Chapter 6, "Keeping Track of Transactions," for more details on splitting transactions.)

On the first line, enter the amount of the paycheck. On the second line, enter the amount of cash you received back at the bank. Record this as a negative number, so Quicken will know to subtract the cash, rather than add it. When the transaction is recorded, Quicken will enter a 650.00 in the DEPOSIT column.

With the split added, you will always know that your paycheck was really for $750 and that you received $100 back at the bank. The transaction reports, if you choose to print them, will also show the split.

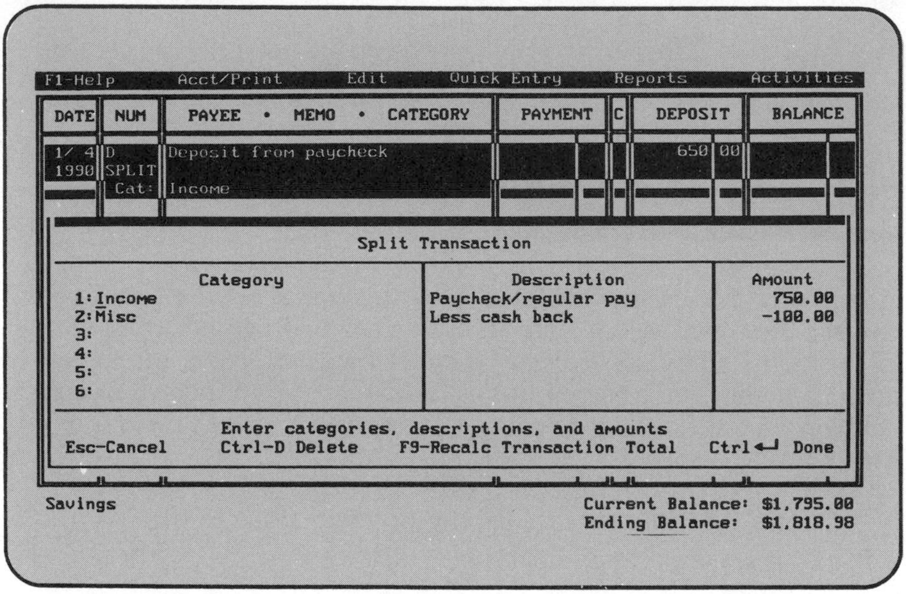

Figure 9.4. A sample split transaction—less cash back.

If you need to itemize your cash expenses, enter them separately in the Split Transaction window. How you enter the dollar amounts depends on whether the main transaction is a payment or deposit.

If the main transaction is a deposit (e.g., a check with cash back), enter the itemized split transactions as negative numbers, as shown in Figure 9.4.

If the main transaction is a payment (e.g., a check for cash or an ATM withdrawal), enter the itemized split transactions as positive numbers.

Figure 9.5 illustrates an example of a transaction using the payment approach. Here you write a payroll check to Sally Brown for $1200.55. As shown in Figure 9.5, four deductions are taken from that $1200.55.

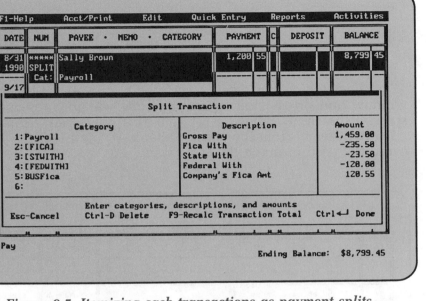

Figure 9.5. Itemizing cash transactions as payment splits.

Tracking Cash in a Cash Account

A separate cash account is ideal for those who prefer to deal with cash or who need to maintain a record of petty cash. Quicken uses a special account type for cash-only transactions. Follow these steps to create a cash account.

Setting Up a Cash Account

1. At the main menu, press 4.	Chooses the Select Account command.
2. Highlight the <new account> option and press Enter.	Displays the Set Up New Account window.
3. Press 3 then Enter.	Indicates Cash as account type.
4. Type the account name and press Enter.	Names the account (e.g., Cash).

173

5. Enter starting cash amount in dollars and press Enter. — Provides amount of cash you have to start.

6. Press Enter if date is correct.

7. Type description and press Enter. — Describes account (optional).

Select the newly created account in the Select Accounts window and press Enter. Quicken drops you into the register screen, shown in Figure 9.6. Note that the Cash register is slightly different from the check or Bank Account register. However, it is used in much the same way.

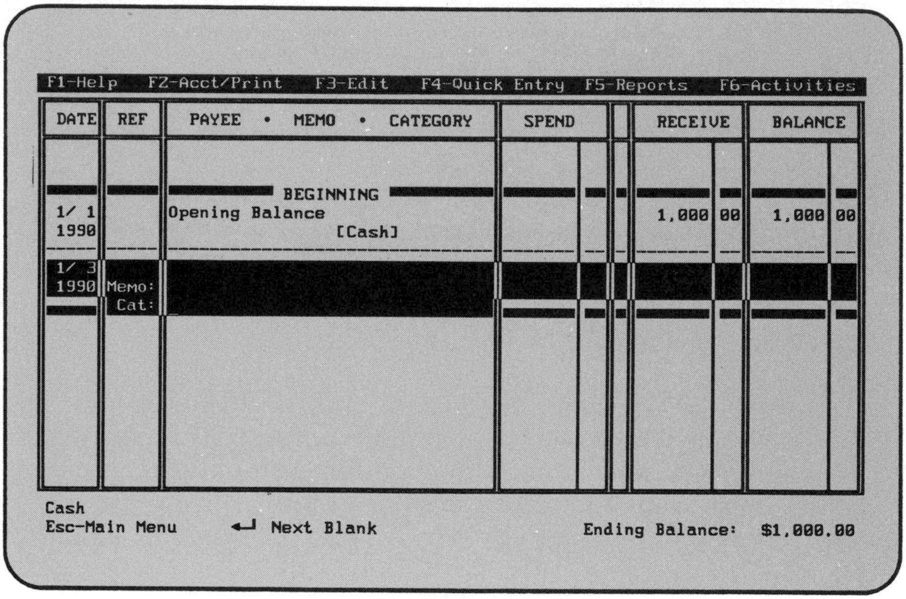

```
 F1-Help   F2-Acct/Print   F3-Edit   F4-Quick Entry   F5-Reports   F6-Activities

 DATE   REF   PAYEE  •  MEMO  •  CATEGORY   SPEND      RECEIVE    BALANCE

                        ████ BEGINNING ████
 1/ 1         Opening Balance                         1,000 00   1,000 00
 1990                            [Cash]

 1/ 3  Memo:
 1990  Cat:

 Cash
 Esc-Main Menu      ◄┘ Next Blank              Ending Balance:   $1,000.00
```

Figure 9.6. The Cash register.

Q Entering a Cash Transaction

1. Set cursor in first empty transaction line.

2. Enter date.

3. Enter reference (optional).

4. Enter data for payee, memo, and category.

5. If you are paying cash, enter the amount in the SPEND column.	Indicates a payment.
OR	
If you are receiving cash, enter the amount in the RECEIVE column.	Indicates a deposit.
6. Press Ctrl-Enter when done.	Records the cash transaction. ☐

The Cash register lets you split, transfer, and memorize transactions just like the check register. You use these features in the normal manner.

The level of detail you provide to your cash transactions is completely up to you. If you're interested in recording important cash transactions and leaving the rest unaccouted for, Quicken will automatically balance the ramainder and consider it as Miscellaneous Expenses.

175

To reconcile your cash account (while in the Cash register), press the F6 key and choose the Update Account Balances command from the Activities menu. Quicken then displays the window shown in Figure 9.7. In the "Update this account's balance to" entry field, enter the amount of cash you currently have on hand. You can optionally indicate a category for the balance adjustment. If you have less cash than Quicken's records indicate, the program will enter a deduction in the SPEND column. If you have more cash than Quicken's records indicate, the program will enter a credit in the RECEIVE column.

Transferring Money to a Cash Account

Rely on Quicken's transfer feature to transfer funds quickly and easily to and from your cash account. Suppose you have a checking account and you write a check to Cash. Assuming your cash account is named Cash, enter Cash in the category blank in the Write Checks screen. Quicken will automatically deduct the amount of the check from your checking account and credit it to your cash account. Of course, you can transfer money to and from other pre-existing Quicken accounts in the same manner. (For more details on account transfers, see Chapter 6, "Keeping Track of Transfers.")

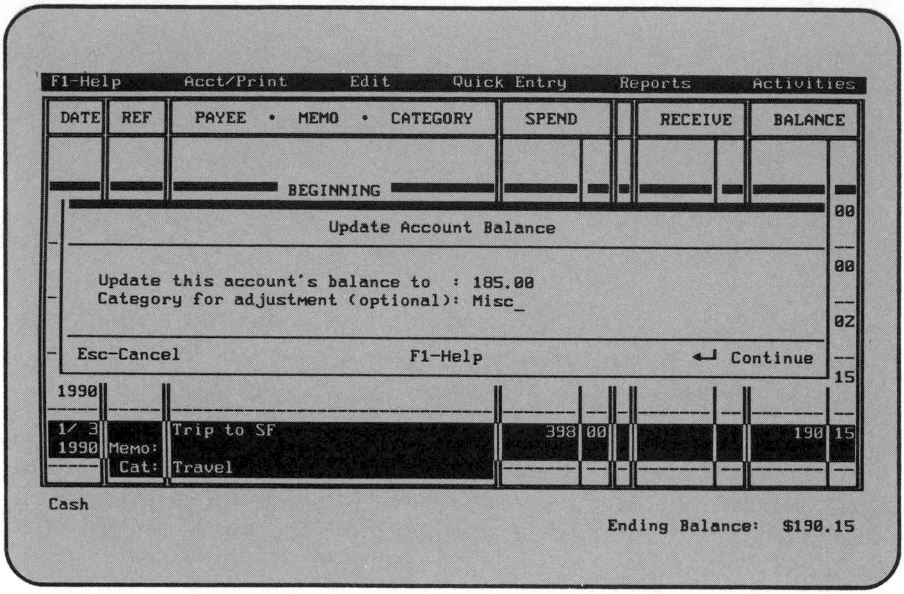

*Figure 9.7. Quicken displays this window when you want
to update the cash account balance.*

Setting Up a Credit Card Account

In an old Flintstone cartoon episode, the favorite refrain of Wilma
Flintstone and Betty Rubble was "Chaaaaarge it!!" That sentiment
goes far beyond animated TV shows. Each year, hundreds of bil-
lions of dollars worth of goods are charged to credit cards. These
cards allow you to "buy now, pay later." Even though the cash
outlay is deferred, you may still want to use Quicken to record and
maintain the purchases.

With judicious use of Quicken, you have a better overview
of your credit card accounts and know exactly how much your
"buy now, pay later" expenses are really costing you. Used in
this way, Quicken can help direct you to those credit cards that
are the least expensive for you to own. That saves you money in
the long run.

You will also want to keep track of credit card transactions if you often charge company expenses. Assuming that you enter the information to begin with, Quicken will provide detailed reports itemizing your credit card charges. That helps when being reimbursed by your company and avoids trouble with the IRS if you or your company are ever audited.

Types of Credit

Just because you have a credit card doesn't mean you need to set up a credit card account. Your payment schedule largely dictates whether you need to set up a credit card account. If you pay the card in full each month, there's hardly a reason to set up an account. Just treat the payment as an expense in your checking account. Cards you pay in full include American Express (certain account types), gas cards, and most open charge accounts at local businesses.

177

An exception to this rule can occur if you want to keep tabs on specific credit purchases. For example, suppose your small business regularly buys goods from a dozen local suppliers, all of whom have extended you credit. By using a Quicken credit card account, you can track your purchases and payments and know exactly what you bought and when you paid for it. You'd still use your checking account to write the check, but the individual credit card account would provide all the specific details. In this way, you use the credit card account as a record-keeping ledger.

Conversely, if you pay the balance of the credit over time, you'll want to keep tabs on the account with Quicken. This type of account likely represents the majority of credit cards you own and includes Visa, MasterCard, Discover, and most department store chains.

Note that some department stores (such as JCPenney) separate their credit purchases into two or more distinct categories, usually regular and major. *Major charges* are set aside for durable goods, like washing machines, TV sets, furniture, and other appliances. *Regular charges* encompass just about everything else.

As the monthly statement separates these two types of purchases—and sometimes assesses different credit limits and interest rates to them—you may wish to create two separate Quicken accounts for them. One account lists regular purchases and payments made against them, and the other account lists charges and payments for major purchases. You can, of course, group these two together and treat them as a single account.

Creating a Credit Card Account

You should set up a separate account for each credit card you use. Follow these steps to set up a new credit card account.

178

Q **Setting Up a Credit Card Account**

1. At the main menu, press 4.	Chooses the Select Account command.
2. Highlight the <new account> entry and press Enter.	Displays the Set Up New Account window.
3. Press 2 then Enter.	Indicates Credit Card as the account type.
4. Type name and press Enter.	Names the account (e.g., Visa or Diner's Club).
5. Enter a current balance owed and press Enter.	Provides the amount you currently owe on the card or charge account.
6. Press Enter if date is correct.	
7. Type description and press Enter. You can use a textual description (e.g., George's Visa) or a credit card account number (e.g., 5555-1111-444-3333).	Describes account.
8. Type credit limit (optional) and press Enter.	□

> ▶ **Note:** In a credit card account, this credit limit is best used as a warning that your balance is approaching the maximum amount of credit that is extended to you. Knowing that you're approaching the credit limit helps avoid those embarrassing moments when you try to pay your restaurant bill with your credit card, only to learn that your purchase has been declined.

Entering Transactions

The Credit Card register, shown in Figure 9.8, is similar to the register used to monitor cash expenses. The register provides blanks for:

179

Transaction date.

Transaction reference—This is an optional coded reference (e.g., D for dining, E for entertainment, or M for motel/hotel); you can fit up to five characters in the REF column.

Description of transaction, plus optional memo and category.

Amount of charge.

Amount of payment.

You can enter transaction information as you incur the charges, using the charge slips as receipts. Or you can wait until the credit card statement arrives and use it for entering charges and payments. In either case, you'll probably want to keep your own charge slips and compare them against the monthly statement. Any deviations should be reported to the credit card company immediately.

 Entering a Credit Card Transaction

1. At the register, enter the transaction date.
2. Enter the reference.   Identifies the transaction.

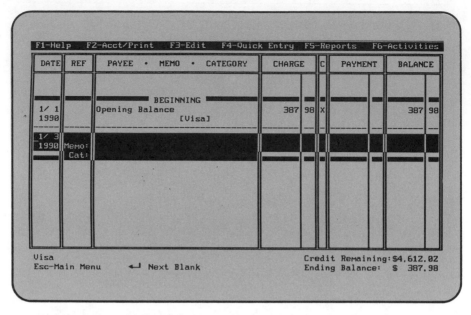

Figure 9.8. The Credit Card register.

3. Enter the description in PAYEE column.

Provides description of charge or payment.

4. For a charge, enter the amount in the CHARGE column.
OR
For a payment, enter the amount in the PAYMENT column. In credit card accounts, the PAYMENT column is used for payments made *to* the credit card company.

Indicates a charge.

Indicates a payment.

5. Press Ctrl-Enter when done.

Records the transaction. ☐

180

Transferring Funds

When paying your credit card bills each month, you can use Quicken's transfer feature to apply your payment to each of your credit card accounts automatically.

1. In the Write Checks screen, fill out the check to the credit card company in the usual manner.

2. In the Category blank, enter the name of the credit card account (e.g., Visa or MasterCard). This is the name you gave the credit card account when you created it. If you don't remember the names of your credit card accounts, enter a left bracket ([) in the Category blank and press Ctrl-C. Quicken will display the available account names at the end of the Category List window.

3. Record the check (press Ctrl-Enter), and Quicken will automatically enter the amount of the check as a PAYMENT to your credit card account.

181

As shown in Figure 9.9, your check register will indicate those transactions that have been transferred to other Quicken accounts. Transfers are always indicated in the Cat: blank with the account name enclosed in brackets.

Conversely, you can transfer money from a credit card account into a checking or savings account. Use this method when you write yourself a cash advance from your credit card.

1. In the Credit Card register, enter the name of the checking or savings account (Checking, Savings, or whatever) in the Cat: blank.

2. Enter the amount of the transfer as a CHARGE.

3. Press Ctrl-Enter to record the transaction.

Quicken will deposit those funds into the appropriate account.

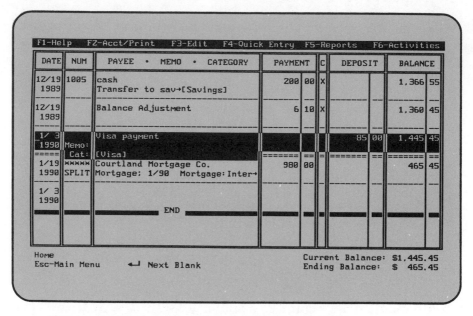

Figure 9.9. You can easily transfer deposits and payments between credit card accounts (and all other Quicken accounts, for that matter) and your checking account.

Reconciling Your Credit Card Accounts

Once a month you should reconcile your credit card accounts to make sure your records coincide with those of the credit card company.

Before reconciling the account, use your monthly statement to make sure all the transactions listed are included in the Credit Card register. Include previous payments, interest charges, new charges, credits, and so forth. Make sure that each transaction is posted in the proper column. For example, don't put an interest charge in the PAYMENT column or a credit in the CHARGE column. Above all, don't enter the payment you're about to make; save that for Quicken.

With all the transactions entered (while at the Credit Card register):

1. Choose the Pay Credit Card Bill from the Activities menu. The window in Figure 9.10 appears.

2. Enter the total for all charges, cash advances, and other debits, minus finance charges (if any).

3. Enter recent payments or credits listed on the statement.

4. Provide a new balance, as indicated on the credit card statement.

5. Enter the total finance charges, as indicated in the statement. You can optionally assign the finance charges to a Quicken category. The program will automatically create a separate transaction for finance charges, as a means to track them later.

6. Press the Enter key after filling in the finance charges and (optional) category. Quicken displays a window showing Uncleared Items in the Register, as illustrated in Figure 9.11.

7. If an item in the list is included on your statement, highlight it and press the Spacebar. If you need to display the Credit Card register (e.g., to make a correction or adjustment or to add items to the register that are shown in the statement), press the F9 key. When you're done, press the F9 key again to return to the Uncleared Items window. Any difference between Quicken's register and the credit card statement are shown in the lower right-hand corner of the Uncleared Items window. After marking all cleared items and adjusting missing transactions, the difference should be 0.00.

8. When you are finished marking cleared items, press Ctrl-F10.

9. If the difference between Quicken's register and the credit card statement is 0.00, you can go to step 10. If not, you'll be asked to enter an adjustment to your account. You also have the option of suspending reconciliation and looking for the difference yourself. Quicken will indicate the nature of the adjustment(s) and will tell you the amount of the disparity, as shown in Figure 9.12. If desired, enter a category for each adjustment. Press Enter when finished.

10. When Quicken is satisfied that the dollar amounts in its register and the bank statement agree, it displays the Make Credit Card Payment window, shown in Figure 9.13. If you don't want to pay the bill now, press Esc to cancel. Otherwise, enter the name of one of your checking accounts to pay the bill and indicate whether you want to make out a Quicken or hand-written check.

183

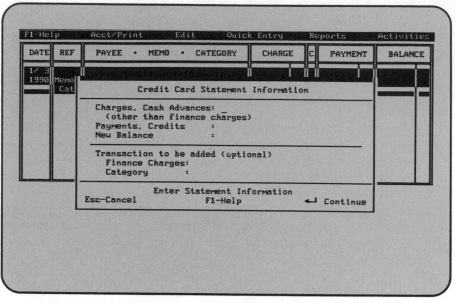

Figure 9.10. The Credit Card Statement Information window.

184

```
F1-Help      Acct/Print       Edit      Quick Entry      Reports        Activities

 REF  │C│    AMOUNT    │   DATE   │          PAYEE          │           MEMO
      │×│      198.00  │ 1/ 1/90  │ Bill's Lumber           │
      │×│      187.54  │ 1/ 2/90  │ BBQs R Us               │
      │×│       85.00  │ 1/ 3/90  │ Visa payment            │
▶     │ │    1,008.34  │ 1/ 3/90  │ Trust Us Airways        │
      │×│       10.00  │ 1/ 3/90  │ Finance Charges         │



■ To Mark Cleared Items, press Space Bar   ■ To Add or Change Items, press F9

                         RECONCILIATION SUMMARY
     Items You Have Marked Cleared (×)
    ──────────────────────────────────── Cleared (X,×) Balance      868.52
     4    Charges, Debits       480.54   Statement Balance        1,866.86
     0    Payments, Credits       0.00   Difference                -998.34

F1-Help          F8-Mark Range        F9-View as Register       Ctrl-End Done
```

Figure 9.11. Uncleared items in the Credit Card register mean that the bank hasn't posted those transactions to your account.

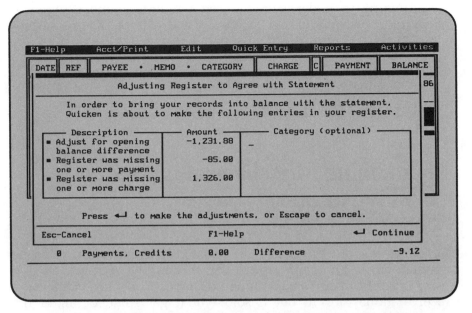

Figure 9.12. Quicken displays any disparity between the Credit Card register and the bank statement.

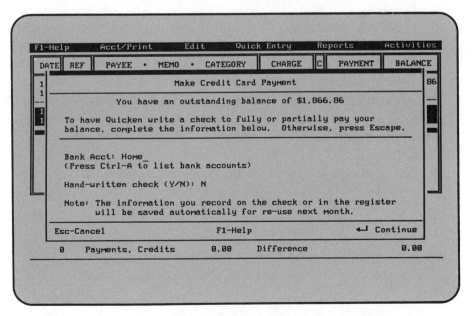

Figure 9.13. The Make Credit Card Payment window.

Electing to make a credit card payment using a Quicken checking account cuts down on a few extra steps. Not only does Quicken write the check for you, but it also pops you into the Write Checks or check register screen, where you can edit the check or print it, as desired. If you complete the check with a payee, memo, and address, Quicken will remember that information the next time.

Maintaining Miscellaneous Asset and Liability Accounts

186

Financial matters that don't entail bank statements can often be maintained as an other asset or other liability account. Use an *asset account* to track something you own. You may or may not receive money for it, but if sold, you'd get some or all of the money for it.

Examples of Assets

Investments—includes IRAs, Keogh plans, and whole-life insurance policies. (Stocks and bonds, another type of investment, should be handled with the investment account type, detailed later in this chapter.)

Your house—an equity investment.

Accounts receivable—money you expect to get in the future.

Personal belongings—includes jewelry, clothing, and electronic equipment, whether or not they are completely paid for.

Home tax basis—includes improvements and repairs made to your home or real estate property that you can deduct from your taxes when you sell the home.

Use a *liability account* to track something you owe and generally make monthly or periodic payments for.

Examples of Liabilities

Your car, house, or boat payment.
Debts to others.
Lines of credit.
Accrued business expenses—includes payroll taxes and social security for employees.

Quicken tracks miscellaneous assets in an other asset account; miscellaneous liabilities are maintained in an other liability account.

You can either create individual Quicken accounts for each major asset and liability or group similar items into one account. For instance, you can group all debts into one other asset account, or you can put them into separate accounts. For most individuals and businesses, a logical grouping is adequate and easier to work with.

187

Setting Up an Account

You set up other asset and other liability accounts the same as you do a Quicken bank account or cash account.

Q Setting Up an Other Asset or Other Liability Account

1.	At the main menu, press 4.	Chooses the Select Account command.
2.	Highlight the <new account> option and press Enter.	Displays the Set Up New Account window.
3.	Press 4 to create an other asset account. OR Press 5 to create an other liability account.	
4.	Type name, and press Enter.	Names the account.
5.	Enter the total amount of the asset or liability and press Enter.	

6. Type a description
   (optional), and press Enter.   ☐

The Other Asset and Other Liability registers are almost identical (the asset window is shown in Figure 9.14), and you use them in the same manner. Their design is consistent with the registers for Bank Accounts, Cash, and Credit Cards. The difference is in the DECREASE and INCREASE columns.

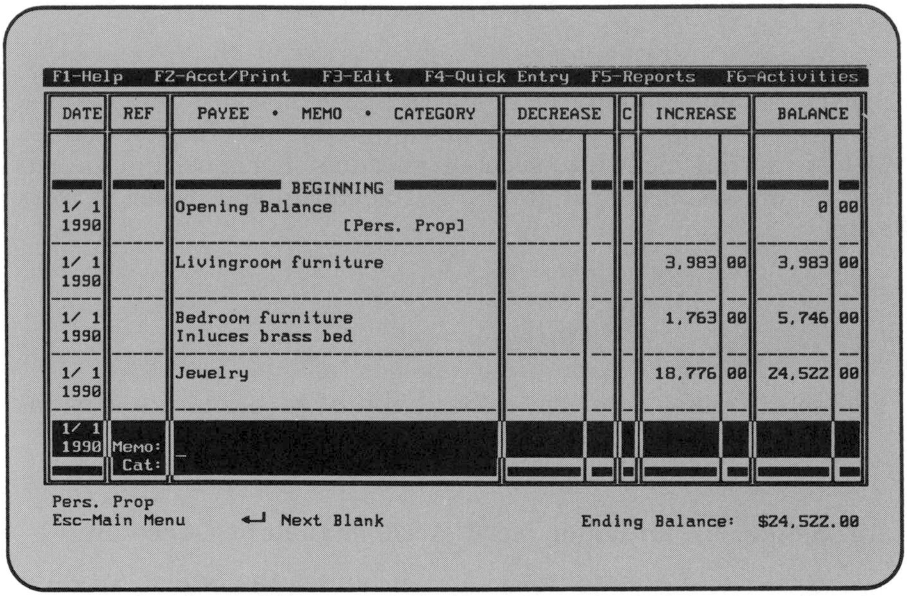

188

```
 F1-Help   F2-Acct/Print   F3-Edit   F4-Quick Entry  F5-Reports   F6-Activities

 DATE  REF      PAYEE  •  MEMO  •  CATEGORY    DECREASE  C  INCREASE    BALANCE

                        ▬▬▬ BEGINNING ▬▬▬
 1/ 1       Opening Balance                                              0  00
 1990                        [Pers. Prop]

 1/ 1       Livingroom furniture                           3,983  00  3,983  00
 1990

 1/ 1       Bedroom furniture                              1,763  00  5,746  00
 1990       Inluces brass bed

 1/ 1       Jewelry                                       18,776  00 24,522  00
 1990

 1/ 1 Memo:
 1990 Cat:  _

 Pers. Prop
 Esc-Main Menu      ↵  Next Blank            Ending Balance:  $24,522.00
```

Figure 9.14. A sample Other Asset register window.

An entry in the DECREASE column decreases the balance, just as an entry in the PAYMENT column of a checkbook register decreases the amount in your checking account.

The INCREASE column functions in the same manner as the DEPOSIT column in the checkbook register. It increases the balance.

Clearing and Updating Your Account Transactions

You should use the C (CLEAR) column to mark those assets and liabilities you no longer have. For instance, if you're tracking your personal assets (e.g., antique furniture or jewelry), you'd use the C column to mark those assets you sell. To clear an item, position the cursor in the C column, and enter an asterisk.

Every once in a while, you'll want to update the value of your other assets and other liabilities. Follow these steps to ensure that Quicken has an accurate record of your financial picture:

1. From the Other Asset or Other Liability register, choose the Update Account Balance command from the Activities menu.

2. Enter the balance you should have (based on a IRA bank statement, for instance) and press the Enter key.

3. If the balance you entered doesn't agree with the ending balance in the register, Quicken will alert you to this fact and ask if you want to make an adjustment. Provide an optional category for the adjustment transaction and press the Enter key.

189

If you'd like, you can make the adjustment to the account yourself. You may prefer to review the register if the difference is great.

Creating Investment Accounts

New to Quicken version 4.0 is a sixth account type for tracking investments. The investment account is primarily designed to track stocks, bonds, CDs, and mutual funds. However, you can also use an investment account to monitor entire brokerage portfolios, real estate investment trusts, unit trusts, IRAs, and Keogh plans.

Additional forms investments, like CDs, collections (records, dolls, antiques, and so forth), employer retirement funds, and money market funds, can also be tracked using an investment account, but most users will find Quicken's other asset account type more reliable and efficient.

Quicken performs three basic functions for tracking investments: You use Quicken to:

Record investment transactions in a register. This register is similar to the others Quicken uses, but it employs some unique transaction "codes" (we'll get to these in a bit).

Update prices of your investments so you always know what they are worth. When you update the price for an investment, all transactions that use that investment are automatically changed. That way, you don't need to go through the register manually, changing the value of each investment.

Produce reports so you can readily see how your investments are performing. The reports can also be used at tax time for calculating your tax liability to Uncle Sam.

Quicken understands the basics of investments and doesn't get involved with trends, fundamental analysis, technical analysis, profit-to-earnings ratios, return on investment, and other complex aspects of the Wall Street game.

190

With Quicken, you simply enter the value of the securities plus the number of shares you own. The total (which is number of shares times cost per share) is the current market value (10 shares at $100/share is $10,000). If a security increases in value at some later date, and you update the value using the program's Update Prices feature, the transaction is shown as a percent of gain. Conversely, a security that loses money is shown as a negative "gain."

So while Quicken makes it fairly easy to handle investments, note that the program is designed for the individual investor, particularly one who deals in securities on a part-time basis, and not for a broker or business. If you need to keep closer tabs on your investments, monitor your company's financial picture, or calculate all sorts of meaningful data to assist you in your buying and selling, you should use another program.

Some Important Words on Investment Accounts

Quicken actually creates two forms of investment accounts: standard and mutual fund.

You can mix and match securities in a *standard account*. A standard account is like a portfolio, combining a little bit of this with a pinch of that. A brokerage account is a common form of Quicken's standard account.

A *mutual fund* contains just one security.

The process for creating either type of account is basically the same. If you're just starting out with investment accounts, you may want to first create a mutual fund account, as these entail fewer steps and options.

About Cash Balances

A regular investment account can contain two types of balances: an amount for the value of the securities and cash. In this case, cash doesn't necessarily means greenbacks tucked in a mattress, but rather money available for investing. If you have an account with a broker, you have most likely deposited money with that broker for future purchases of securities. Rather than writing a check each time you want to buy stocks, for example, you merely contact the broker and place your order. The cost of the securities is deducted from your cash balance.

191

In a standard investment account, you can indicate a cash balance, if you desire, and use the money from this balance to "pay" for your securities. Conversely, when you sell a security, you can convert the money to cash and keep it in the Investment register. You can use this feature whether or not you buy and sell through a broker. This is merely an optional convenience Quicken offers.

Note that mutual fund investment accounts do not allow for cash balances. If you require, you can set up a separate cash account if you buy and sell individual securities through a broker. Name the account Broker, for instance, and use Quicken's transfer feature. We'll provide an example of this type of transaction later.

Setting Up a Standard Investment Account

Follow these steps to set up a standard investment account:

1. At the main menu, choose 4 for Select Account.
2. Highlight the <new account> entry and press Enter.
3. At the new account screen, type 6 for Investment account.
4. Enter a name for the account and press Enter.
5. Answer N to the prompt that asks if this account is a mutual fund.

6. Enter an optional description for the account and press Enter.

7. Highlight the newly created account in the sSlect Account screen and press Enter.

8. Quicken displays a note for first-time setup of the standard investment account. In short, you need to enter at least one security transaction. Logically, this transaction is adding one or more shares for a security. Press Enter when you are done reading the note and follow the directions below.

9. Place the cursor in the ACTION column and type ShrsIn, for "shares in." This indicates that you want to add a security to the Investment register. Press Enter when done.

10. Place the cursor in the SECURITY column, type the name of the security and press Enter. Quicken won't recognize it at first, and will ask you if you want to add it to the securities list and press Enter. Answer yes to go on and, in the Set Up Security window, fill in the type of security (either Bond, CD, Mutual Fund, or Stock). Press Enter to go on.

11. Type the price *per share* for the security and press Enter.

12. Type the number of shares you want to add and press Enter.

13. Quicken allows you to alter the calculated Amount figure in the Investment register, for example, to adjust the cost with commissions and other fees. Press Enter if you don't want to change the amount.

14. Enter a memo for the security, if any. The memo entry will appear in Quicken's other registers if you transfer funds from an investment account.

15. Press Ctrl-Enter to record the transaction. You are now ready to enter another transaction into the register, if desired.

If you wish, you can enter a cash balance for this account. Within the register:

1. Press the F6 key for Activities.

2. Press 2 for Adjust Balance.

3. Press 1 for Adjust Cash Balance.

4. Enter a date for the transaction (or skip if the current date is acceptable) and type a cash amount.

5. Press Enter when done. Quicken will record the cash balance as a separate transaction.

192

Setting Up a Mutual Fund Investment Account

Follow these steps to set up a mutual func investment account:

1. At the main menu, choose 4 for Select Account.
2. Highlight the <new account> entry and press Enter.
3. At the New Account screen, type 6 for Investment account.
4. Enter a name for the account and press Enter.
5. Answer Y to the prompt that asks if this account is a mutual fund. Remember, mutual funds contain only one security (of course, you can enter any number of transactions for that one security as you wish).
6. Enter an optional description for the account and press Enter.
7. Fill in the Set Up Mutual Fund Security screen and press Enter.
8. Highlight the newly created account in the Select Account screen and press Enter.
9. Quicken displays a Create Opening Share Balance screen and requires that you enter the opening balance for the security. In the appropriate entry fields, provide the date, number of shares, and price per share. Press Enter when done, and Quicken automatically creates the first transaction for you. You are now ready to add more transactions to the register, if you wish.

193

Anatomy of the Investment Register

As with other Quicken registers, the Investment register consists of numerous columns for data entry. Figure 9.15 shows the register for a standard investment account.

> *DATE column*—contains the date of the transaction. Quicken initially proposes today's date (or more accurately, the date as set by the DOS clock in your computer). You can always change that date, if desired.

ACTION column—describes the type of transaction. Quicken understands 23 investment actions. You are already familiar with ShrsIn, for "shares in." There is also ShrsOut, Buy, BuyX, MiscExp, and several others. See Table 9.1 for a complete list of investment actions and what they do. Table 9.2 shows the investment actions available in mutual fund accounts; note that those actions that rely on using cash within the account are unavailable. You can always view and select the available investment actions by pressing Ctrl-L while in the Investment register. Once you get used to Quicken and its investment accounts, you can type the investment actions into the ACTION column directly.

194

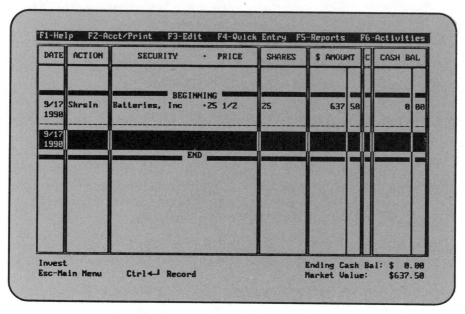

Figure 9.15. Register for a standard investment account.

PRICE column—lists the single-unit price of the investment.

SHARES column—lists the number of shares involved in the transaction.

$ AMOUNT column—shows the total amount spent on the security. Normally, this amount reflects the price of the shares times the number of shares, but it can also include commissions, fees, and other costs.

C column—shows those transactions that have cleared. It is used when reconciling the account. An X shows cleared transactions.

CASH BAL (cash balance) column—shows the amount of cash on hand. It is available only in standard investment accounts.

Table 9.1.   List of Investment Actions.

Action Symbol	Description
	Add/Remove Shares
ShrsIn	Transfer shares into account
ShrsOut	Transfer shares out of account
	Buy Shares
Buy	Buy a security with cash in account
BuyX	But a security with cash transferred from another Quicken account
	Capital Gains Distribution
CGLong	Receive cash from long-term capital gains distribution
CGLongX	Transfer cash from long-term capital gains distribution out of account
CGShort	Receive cash from short-term capital gains distribution
CGShortX	Transfer cash from short-term capital gains distribution out of account
	Dividend
Div	Receive cash from dividend
Div	Transfer cash from interest or dividend out of account
	Interest
IntInc	Receive cash from interest income
MargInt	Pay for interest on margin loan by using cash from account

Continued

195

Table 9.1   continued

Action Symbol	Description
	Other Transactions
MiscExp	Pay for miscellaneous expense with cash from account
Reminder	Using the Billminder program, remind of some pending event with investment account
RtrnCap	Receive cash from return of capital
StkSplit	Split a stock
	Reinvest
ReinvDiv	Reinvest in additional shares of security with money from dividend or interest
ReinvLg	Reinvest in additional shares of security with money from long-term capitals gains distribution
ReinvSh	Reinvest in additional shares of security with money from short-term capital gains distribution
	Sell Shares
Sell	Sell security and leave cash in account
SellX	Sell security and transfer cash out of account
	Transfer Cash
XIn	Transfer cash into account
XOut	Transfer cash out of account

Table 9.2.   Investment Actions in Mutual Fund Accounts.

Action Symbol	Available in Mutual Fund Account
ShrsIn	X
ShrsOut	X
Buy BuyX	X
CGLong CGLongX	X
CGShort CGShortX	X

Continued

196

Action Symbol	Available in Mutual Fund Account
Div	X
DivX	
IntInt	
MargInt	
MiscExp	
Reminder	X
RtrnCap	X
StkSplit	
ReinvDiv	X
Reinvg	X
ReinvSh	X
SellSellX	X
XIn	
XOut	

197

About Security Types

Quicken initially knows about four types of securities:

▶ Bonds.

▶ CDs.

▶ Mutual funds.

▶ Stocks.

You indicate the type of security when setting up the securities list or when entering transactions. Every security you define in Quicken has a name and a type. Optional attributes are a symbol for the security (the NYSE symbol, for example, but you can use up to 12 characters) and an investment goal. Quicken supplies four typical investment goals: college fund, growth, growth and income, and income. Or you can provide your own unique goal if you wish, such as "plant expansion."

If you already know the securities you want to track, you can enter them all at once in the Security List window, as shown in Figure 9.16. From anywhere in the register, choose the Security List command from the Quick Entry menu or press Ctrl-Y. Then:

1. Highlight <New Security> and press Enter.

2. Type the name of the security (up to 18 characters) and press Enter.

3. Type an optional symbol and press Enter.

4. Enter the type of security such as Bond, CD, Mutual Fund, or Stock. If you don't enter anything at this blank, Quicken will display a list of possible choices or allow you to enter a security type of your own. Press Enter when done.

5. Type an optional goal and press Enter to continue.

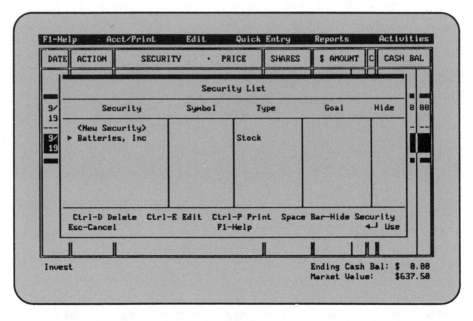

Figure 9.16. Security List window.

You can add as many new securities as you wish. You can also edit or delete securities from the list by highlighting them, then pressing Ctrl-E or Ctrl-D, respectively.

When entering transactions, you can also establish securities one at a time. If you enter a security (in the SECURITY column) that Quicken doesn't recognize, you have your choice of creating a new security or selecting from among the items in the list. Follow the steps already outlined when creating securities during transaction entry.

Q Entering Investment Transactions

1. Position the cursor at the bottom of the register.

2. Enter the date for the transaction (or skip to step 3 if the current date is OK).

3. Type an action in the ACTION column and press Enter.

   Identifies the type of transaction.

4. Type the name of the security. If you've never entered that security before, Quicken will ask you to add it to the securities list, as detailed above. Press Enter when done.

   Describes the security.

5. Indicate the unit price or price per share and press Enter.

6. Enter the number of shares (or 1 if the price denotes the entire amount of the security).

7. Press Enter twice to move the cursor to the memo field. Enter a memo, if desired, and press Enter when done.

199

Depending on the type of investment action you've selected, provide the following additional information:

▶ Commission/fee.
▶ Account for transfer in/out.
▶ The amount of the transfer.
▶ Name of category for miscellaneous expenses.
▶ Number of splits and amount for stock splits.

Figure 9.17 shows an example of entering a transaction that requires additional information.

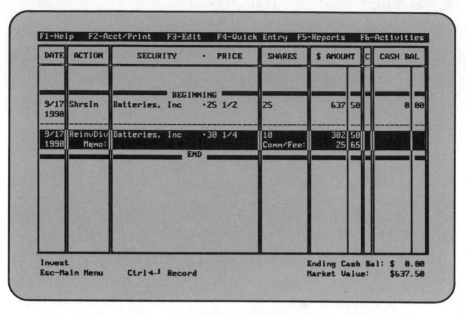

Figure 9.17. Transaction with additional information.

Transferring Cash to/from an Investment Account

Often you will want to transfer cash to or from an investment account. Quicken provides the same easy transfers between accounts that you learned about earlier in this book. Transfers can be made between both standard and mutual fund accounts.

To enter a transfer, type the name of the other Quicken account in the Account field. Enclose the account name in brackets, as in:

[Checking]   Transfer to/from account named
                Checking
[Cash]   Transfer to/from account named Cash
[Broker]   Transfer to/from account named
                Broker

As usual, the account for the transfer must already exist. If it does not, Quicken will indicate that it can't find the account you want. Select another account or take the time to create the account. The following investment actions deal with transfers to or from other Quicken accounts:

Action	Transfer to/from Investment Account
BuyX	To
CGLongX	From
CGShortX	From
DivX	From
SellX	From
XIn	To
XOut	From

Updating Prices

201

Suppose you've entered a month's worth of transactions. Invariably, the value of stocks, bonds, and similar investments will have changed. If that change is for the better, your investment portfolio is actually doing better than what Quicken shows. Or, if your investments have declined in value, the balance will be an inflated amount. Either way, you'll want to update the prices of your investments to reflect their current value.

Q Updating Prices

1. From anywhere within the register, choose the Update Prices command from the Activities menu or press Ctrl-U.

   The Update Prices and Market Value window appears (see Figure 9.18) showing all securities in the account. (You can choose to view just one account by pressing the F9 key; press the F9 key again to view all accounts.)

2. Highlight the security you want to update.

3. Change the price in the MKT PRICE column and press Enter.

   The price for the security is updated.

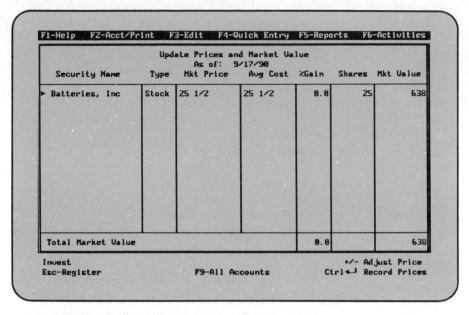

| F1-Help | F2-Acct/Print | F3-Edit | F4-Quick Entry | F5-Reports | F6-Activities |

```
                      Update Prices and Market Value
                            As of:  9/17/90
       Security Name      Type  Mkt Price    Avg Cost  %Gain   Shares  Mkt Value

  ▶ Batteries, Inc       Stock  25 1/2       25 1/2     0.0       25        638
```

| Total Market Value | | | | 0.0 | | 638 |

```
Invest                                                     +/-  Adjust Price
Esc-Register                    F9-All Accounts            Ctrl◄┘ Record Prices
```

Figure 9.18. Update prices window.

4. Repeat steps 2 and 3 for all securities you wish to change.

5. Press Ctrl-Enter when done with all price updates. ☐

All price changes within the same day are considered as mere edits to the transaction, and Quicken doesn't treat them as true updates. For example, if you enter a transaction for a security, then later in that day update its price, Quicken will assume you merely edited the transaction.

Update the price on a different day, however, and Quicken will assume the value of the security rose or fell. If the price went up, Quicken will display an up arrow beside the market price and show a percent of gain in the %GAIN column. If the price went down, Quicken will display a down arrow beside the market price and show a loss in the %GAIN column. Quicken will also estimate the average original cost of the shares in the column before the gain or loss. An asterisk (*) appears next in the market price column if Quicken is estimating the share price.

If necessary, you can update the price of a security as of a particular day. While in the Update Prices and Market Value

202

window, press Ctrl-G and type in the date for the change. Or, press one of the following quick function keys to enter a different date:

Press	To change date to
Ctrl- −	Previous day
Ctrl- +	Next day
Ctrl-Page Down	Previous month
Ctrl-Page Up	Next month

Creating Special-Purpose Accounts

You can apply one of Quicken's six account types to a variety of personal and business requirements. Here are some examples:

203

Create another assets account for handling real inventory — Use this account to keep track of office supplies, such as pens and pencils, fax paper, and copier paper. Enter the number of items of each in stock, as well as a purchse price. Quicken will maintain a running tally of the worth of the inventory and provide a balance indicating what you've paid to build your storehouse. Regularly add and delete items as they are used. Of course, you can use this technique to track any type of inventory.

Create a bank account to handle employee payroll — You record and print checks from the payroll account, even though you use the same checks as your other transactions. You may want to use this technique of keeping payroll separate if you have more than a few dozen employees.

Provide a separate other liability account — You can use this account for withheld employee taxes, insurance, and social security. By maintaining these items in a separate account, you are less likely to consider the money part of the general operating fund. The IRS takes a dim view of employers spending their employee's tax withholding.

Build numerous other asset subaccounts under your main bank accounts — These subaccounts track unique personal or business financial matters (e.g., vacation and college funds). The money is all in one pool (e.g., your savings or checking account), but your subaccounts help you to remember how you want the funds divided. Using subaccounts helps you to set aside money for special purposes, to "squirrel" it away for a rainy day.

Use an other asset account to keep track of the various improvements and repairs you make to your home —Generally, these costs are for the home you live in, as opposed to a house you own as income property. Not only does this help you track the costs of home ownership, but it's also helpful when it's time to sell the house. You can apply the improvements and repairs to the tax basis of your home (and therefore reduce the income taxes you might have to pay on the capital gains on the sale of your house). You can also defend a higher selling price, apart from the value set by an appraiser.

Schools and other nonprofit organizations will want to keep track of charitable donations and their amounts—This is especially true if your school or organization is also funded with public money (grants, taxes, and whatnot).

What You Have Learned

This chapter discussed additional forms of Quicken accounts: cash, credit card, other asset, other liability, and investment. Here's what you have learned:

▶ Savings, cash, credit card, asset/liability, and investment accounts are maintained entirely from the register. You don't use the Write Checks window to enter payment transactions.

▶ Savings accounts have two general types of transactions: credits (e.g., deposits and interest) and debits (e.g., withdrawals and service charges).

▶ Cash accounts let you track your loose change or monitor expenditures from a petty cash fund.

▶ You can track your cash outlay either as transactions in a checking or savings account or as a separate account type.

▶ As with all Quicken account types, you can split cash transactions to indicate the origin or destination of a lump sum.

▶ Credit card accounts let you track any financial dealings (e.g., a loan) where you owe money and must regularly pay back the loan in installments.

▶ You should create a separate credit card account for each credit card (or other consumer/business credit) you own. Identify the card by its name and/or account number.

▶ Quicken will reconcile your Credit Card registers automatically.

▶ You should use an other asset account to track something you own and an other liability account to track something you owe and generally make monthly or periodic payments for.

▶ You should use an investment account to track stocks, bonds, IRAs, Keough plans, and other types of "paper" investments.

205

206

Creating and Printing Reports

In This Chapter

- ▶ *About Quicken's reports*
- ▶ *Building a standard report*
- ▶ *Examples of personal, business, and investment reports*
- ▶ *Producing custom reports*
- ▶ *Transaction filtering with text matching*

Dragnet fans remember the immortal words of Sergeant Joe Friday: "Just the facts, ma'am." As a Quicken user, you can ask the program to provide you with just the facts, and it will spit out reams of digested information and reports on your spending habits, your budget, even the exact dollar amount of your financial worth. Quicken's reports feature is nearly automatic; you just select the type of report you want to review, and Quicken will build it. If needed, you can fine-tune the design of reports to include the information you want, organized as you want.

This chapter deals with creating and printing reports in Quicken. You'll learn how to print Quicken's preset personal, business, and investment reports quickly, as well as how to build customized reports that contain just the data you're interested in.

An Overview of Quicken Reports

Although Quicken can display its reports on screen, you'll probably want to print them so you can refer to them readily at a later date. After printing, place your reports in a binder or notebook for safekeeping. If you print reports often, you may want to separate them into categories. For example, Quicken offers five types of preset personal reports, including cash flow, monthly budget, and itemized categories. If you regularly print these reports, say, each month or each quarter, store them separately in your reports notebook.

Quicken divides its report-making facility into four major components: personal reports, business reports, investment reports, and custom reports. You can use any report regardless of your application; just because you use Quicken for business doesn't mean that you can't produce a personal report. Personal reports are geared primarily to the needs and requirements of individuals, while business reports are specifically enhanced to take care of business accounting needs.

208

Personal Reports

You can choose from among the following five predesigned personal reports. If desired, you can add customizing touches to these reports; customizing options are detailed later in this chapter.

> *Cash flow report*—shows the amount of incoming money compared to outgoing money. Quicken cash flow reports cover bank, cash, and credit card accounts.

> *Monthly budget report*—compares what you spent during a month with what you wanted to spend. You can indicate the exact categories to compare (e.g., utilities and housing); you can also vary the budget on a month-to-month basis. Quicken gives you a monthly budget for all bank, cash, and credit card accounts.

Itemized categories report—itemizes transactions, grouped and subtotaled by category. This report covers all account types.

Tax summary report—summarizes all those transactions that have been categorized as tax related. This report covers all account types.

Net worth report—summarizes the ending balance from all your accounts, providing you with a net worth statement current up to the day it was produced.

Business Reports

You can choose from among the following seven predesigned business reports. As with personal reports, you can add customizing touches to these reports. Customizing options are detailed later in this chapter.

209

P&L statement report—totals your income and expenses for each category, by month. This is the standard profit and loss statement used in business. It covers all account types.

Cash flow report—shows the amount of incoming money to outgoing money. Quicken cash flow reports cover bank, cash, and credit card accounts.

A/P by vendor report—lists checks you've written but not yet printed, grouped and subtotaled by payee. This report includes transactions from bank, cash, and credit card accounts.

A/R by customer report—lists outstanding balances by customer, by each month. This report applies only to select other asset accounts.

Job/project report—totals income and expenses for each class, assuming you've classified your job and projects in this manner. This report covers all account types.

Payroll report—totals income and expenses for each employee, subtotaled by category. This report uses only those transactions categorized as Payroll (from any account type).

Balance sheet report—shows the net worth of your business, using the ending balances from all your accounts.

Investment Reports

The investment reports provide details on your investment portfolio. Quicken can differentiate between real gains and losses as you actually buy and sell stocks as well as unrealized gains and losses, money you make or lose on paper.

Portfolio value report—shows the value of your investments as of a particular date. Included in the report are the number of shares, most recent known price, cost basis, unrealized gains or losses, and market value.

Investment performance report—shows the average annual total return of your investments during a specified time period.

Capital gains report—shows the capital gains for securities sold during a specified period of time.

210

Investment income report—displays taxable and nontaxable interest income, taxable and nontaxable dividend income, and margin interest income.

Investment transactions report—shows how transactions investments over a specified period of time have affected your financial picture.

Custom Reports

In addition to Quicken's 12 preset personal and business reports, you can create customized reports to fit your specific needs. Quicken provides the basic framework for each custom report; you fill in the blanks by telling the program what you want included and how you want it to appear in the final report. Quicken offers the following four custom reports:

Transaction report—creates a report listing specific transactions. You indicate how the report is sorted and subtotaled.

Summary report—creates a report summarizing your transactions, but it does not include the actual transactions. You can include category, class, payee, or account information.

Budget report—creates a report itemizing selected transactions, comparing them with preset budget limits.

Account balances report—summarizes and totals the ending balance from all your accounts, at specified intervals.

Memorizing Reports

Quicken allows you to memorize often-used reports so you can access them more quickly in the future. At any report screen, press Ctrl-M and provide a unique name for that report. Press Enter, and the report is memorized for future use.

To access the memorized report, choose the Memorized Report option from the Report menu. Use the cursor keys to select the report you want to use and press Enter. At the memorized report window, you can edit any memorized report by selecting it, then pressing Ctrl-E. Or, if you choose to delete a memorized report, select it then press Ctrl-D.

Producing a Standard Report   211

The preset personal and business reports are the easiest to produce. You can elect to view the report on screen (using cursor keys to move around the report if it's larger than one screen) or to print it on paper.

Q **Producing a Standard Report**

1. From any register, choose the Personal Reports, Business Reports, or Investment Reports command from the Reports menu.

   The Reports List window appears as shown in Figure 10.1. (This screen shows the available personal reports.)

2. Select the report to use.

   The report window appears, such as the one in Figure 10.2. Some reports require slightly different information, but the contents of the report window are fairly self-explanatory.

3. Fill in the blanks in the report window; press Enter when done.

4. View the report, using cursor keys to move around.
OR
Print the report by pressing the F8 key.

Displays the Print Report window, shown in Figure 10.3.

5. When printing reports, Quicken asks you to select a destination printer. Select a printer and press Enter.

□

212

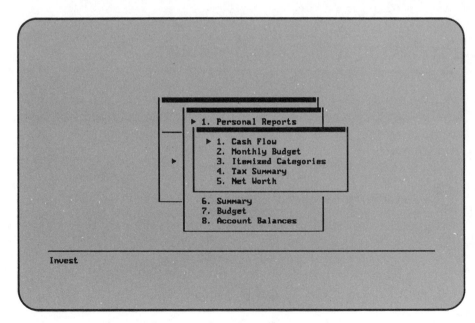

Figure 10.1. Quicken's five personal reports.

Viewing Reports on Screen

Quicken always displays its reports on screen before they are printed. You can use this feature in lieu of printing or to check that the information you want to print is included in the report. Most likely, the entire report will extend beyond the boundaries of your computer screen. Use the cursor keys, as detailed in Table 10.1, to see more of the report.

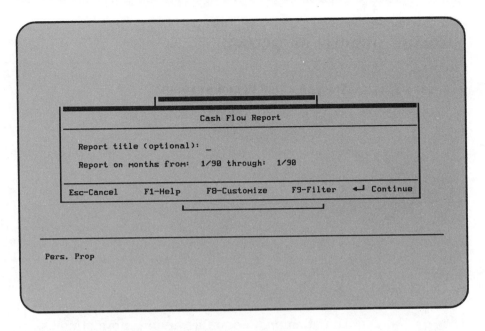

Figure 10.2. A sample report window.

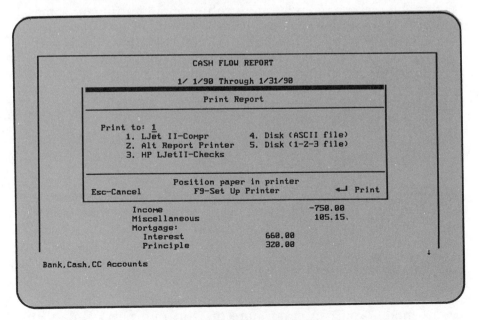

*Figure 10.3. Print any report by indicating the printer
(you can also change printer selections).*

213

Table 10.1. Moving Within the Reports on Screen.

To Move	Press
Down one screen	Page Down
Up one screen	Page Up
Right one screen	Tab or Ctrl-right arrow
Left one screen	Shift-Tab or Ctrl-left arrow
To the upper left corner of report	Home
To the bottom right corner of report	End

Note that while previewing a report, Quicken displays a border around the text. This border, shown in Figure 10.4, represents the edge of the paper and shows you the extent of the report.

▶ **Tip:** Quicken attempts to cram as much information as possible onto the screen at once. If your report includes transactions, some of the columns may be set to half-width, thereby making room for more columns but cutting off some of the transaction text. To view the report in its full width, press the F9 key and increase the total width of the report from 80 to 132 characters. Likewise, you'll want to print this report in compressed mode, as detailed in the next section.

Printing Wide Reports

Reports that are too wide to fit on a single width of paper are automatically printed in strips. After printing, you can tape the strips together to make one large report. In this fashion, Quicken can produce a report of almost unlimited width (as well as length), although it's a rare report that's wider than about two or three pages.

If your printer can print in compressed (17 characters per inch) mode, you can cram more text on one page. Unless the report is very wide, you may be able to print it on a single width of paper. To set up the printer for compressed mode:

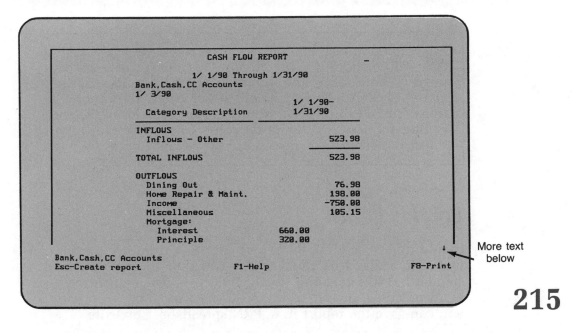

```
                    CASH FLOW REPORT              _

                  1/ 1/90 Through 1/31/90
           Bank,Cash,CC Accounts
           1/ 3/90
                                         1/ 1/90-
               Category Description      1/31/90

           INFLOWS
               Inflows - Other               523.98

           TOTAL INFLOWS                     523.98

           OUTFLOWS
               Dining Out                     76.98
               Home Repair & Maint.          198.00
               Income                        -750.00
               Miscellaneous                 105.15
               Mortgage:
                 Interest          660.00
                 Principle         320.00

           Bank,Cash,CC Accounts
           Esc-Create report            F1-Help              F8-Print
```

More text below

215

Figure 10.4. The border around the on-screen report shows the edges of the "paper."

1. Press the F9 key at the Print Report window.
2. Select Report Printer Settings.
3. Find your printer in the list, and select the 17 pitch option. Refer to Chapter 2, "Getting Started with Quicken," if your printer isn't listed.
4. If your printer lacks a 17 pitch option, select your printer. (Be sure to choose Portrait or Landscape to indicate whether to print vertically or horizontally on the page, respectively.) Press the F8 key.
5. Enter the control codes to place your printer in 17 pitch mode in the Before Printing blank. Press Enter until the Report Printer Settings window appears.
6. Fill in the Report Printer Settings menu, as required; press Ctrl-Enter when done.
7. When you're back at the Print Report screen, press Enter to initiate printing.

> ▶ **Tip:** If you seldom print wide reports, you may wish to define the Alternate Report Settings printer to compressed and leave the standard Report Printer Settings alone. In Step 2 above, merely select Alternate Report Settings. In the Print Report window (Step 7), select Alt Report Printer (option 2). When you print a normal-width report, select Report Printer (option 1) at the Print Report window.

Printing to Disk

In addition to sending the report data to a printer, you can capture it in a disk file. Quicken lets you save the report data as a standard ASCII text file, which you can use with almost any word processor or electronic spreadsheet program. Alternatively, you can save the report in a .PRN spreadsheet text file.

To save the report in ASCII format, choose option 4, Disk (ASCII file) at the Print Report window. Provide a name for the file. You may include an optional file extension. Indicate the maximum width of the lines and the total number of lines per page. The defaults are 80 character per line and 66 lines per page. These values include space for margins.

To use the file, start your word processor and edit the document. You may need to adjust the margins in your word processor to accommodate the format of the report. Depending on the capabilities of your word processor, you can change such features as the type style (or font), type size, and boldfacing.

To save the report as a spreadsheet text file, choose option 5, Disk (1-2-3 file). Enter a file name, without an extension. Quicken automatically adds the .PRN extension to the file. After saving the file, Quicken displays a help message telling you how to import the file into 1-2-3.

Note that most spreadsheet programs for the PC, including Microsoft Works, can also read .PRN files. If you're using Microsoft Works, for example, select the saved .PRN file, then indicate that you want it opened as a Spreadsheet file (as opposed to a Word Processor or Database file). The program will format the text automatically to fit into the cells of the spreadsheet. Enlarge the columns of the spreadsheet so you can view and print all the text contained within them. Figure 10.5 shows an example of a cash flow report imported as a .PRN file into Microsoft Works.

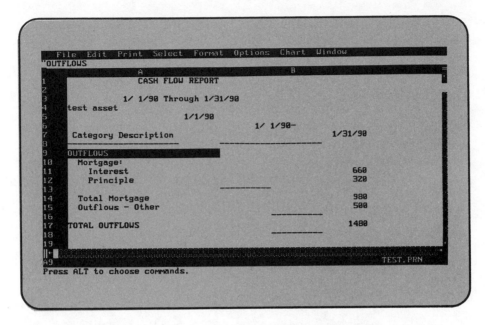

Figure 10.5. A sample imported .PRN file in Microsoft Works.

Customizing Standard Reports

You can elect to customize any of the five preset personal reports. At the Report window, press the F8 key to customize the report (e.g., determine exact report dates, subtotal formats, and sort formats) or the F9 key to indicate the transactions you want, based on text-search information. For instance, you can include only those transactions to a particular payee, restrict the reports to include only tax-related transactions, or include transactions that match certain categories, classes, or memos.

The section entitled "Producing Custom Reports," later in this chapter, details the use of these two options.

Examples of Personal Reports

The following are examples of Quicken's five preset personal reports.

Cash Flow

The cash flow report (see Figure 10.6) lists money that comes in as INFLOWS and money that goes out as OUTFLOWS. The difference, or the OVERALL total, shows whether you have a surplus or a deficit. To keep on top of your finances, obviously, you'll want to make sure you have a surplus—however small —for all or most of the months in the year.

218

```
                              Cash Flow
                      12/ 1/89 Through 1/31/90
Bank,Cash,CC Accounts                                        Page 1
1/ 3/90
                                         12/ 1/89-
                Category Description        1/31/90
         --------------------------    ---------------------
         INFLOWS
            Inflows - Other                 1,023.98
                                          -----------
         TOTAL INFLOWS                      1,023.98

         OUTFLOWS
            Dining Out                          76.98
            Home Repair & Maint.               198.00
            Income                            -750.00
            Miscellaneous                      105.15
            Mortgage:
               Interest          1,320.00
               Principle           640.00
                                -----------
            Total Mortgage                    1,960.00
            Travel                              398.00
            Water, Gas, Electric               123.45
            Outflows - Other                 3,081.85
                                          -----------
         TOTAL OUTFLOWS                      5,193.43

                                          -----------
         OVERALL TOTAL                     -4,169.45
                                          ===========
```

Figure 10.6. A sample personal cash flow report.

Included as entries under INFLOWS and OUTFLOWS are categories within your bank, cash, and credit card accounts. If you've used subcategories, these are itemized separately.

Monthly Budget

The monthly budget report, illustrated in Figure 10.7, compares what you've spent during a particular month with what you planned to spend. For example, if you planned to spend $100 per month for clothing for your family, and you spent $150, you know you're over budget for that category. The monthly budget report contains only those categories from bank, cash, and credit card accounts that you specify. You can set a standard monthly budget or vary the budget every month for the entire year (e.g., you're more likely to spend more money in August and September for clothes than during other times of the year).

```
                              Monthly                            -
                         1/ 1/90 Through 1/31/90
            Bank,Cash,CC Accounts
            1/ 9/90
                                  1/ 1/90       -      1/31/90
                 Category Description  Actual    Budget     Diff

            OUTFLOWS
              Clothing               43.98    100.00     -56.02
              Dining Out             76.98     75.00       1.98
              Groceries               0.00    350.00    -350.00
              Home Repair & Maint.   198.00    100.00      98.00
              Household Misc. Exp    134.05     75.00      59.05
              Housing                 0.00  1,250.00  -1,250.00
              Medical & Dental        0.00     75.00     -75.00
              Telephone Expense       0.00     50.00     -50.00

            TOTAL OUTFLOWS          453.01  2,075.00  -1,621.99


   Bank,Cash,CC Accounts
   Esc-Create report              F1-Help                    F8-Print
```

Figure 10.7. This monthly budget report helps you spot if you're spending too much in one category.

To enter or change monthly budget values when viewing the report, press the F7 key from the Monthly Budget Report window. (You must set up the monthly budgets for at least one category before you can view or print a monthly budget report.) The Specify Budget Amounts window appears, as shown in Figure 10.8.

```
                        Specify Budget Amounts
                                                      Budget      Monthly
           Category        Type       Description     Amount      Detail

         Invest Inc       Inc  Investment Income
         Oldage Pen       Inc  Old Age Pension
         Other Inc        Inc  Other Income
         Paycheck         Inc
       ▶ Auto Fuel        Expns Automobile Fuel        65_
         Auto Other       Expns Automobile Expense
         Bank Chrg        Expns Bank Charge
         Canada Pension   Expns Canadian Pension Plan
         Charity          Expns Charitable Donations
         Childcare        Expns Childcare Expense
         Christmas        Expns Christmas Expenses
         Clothing         Expns Clothing              100.00

                                  ↑,↓ Select
    Esc-Cancel        F1-Help   Ctrl-E Edit Monthly Detail    Ctrl↵  Done


    Home
```

Figure 10.8. Specify budgeted amounts for each category here.

1. Use the cursor keys to select a category to include. Those categories without a monthly budget amount are not included in the report.
2. Type the monthly budget. If you don't want to enter a budget amount, but want the category listed in the monthly budget report, enter a 0 (zero).
3. If you'd like to enter a different budget amount for each month of the year, select the desired category and press Ctrl-E. In the window that appears (shown in Figure 10.9), enter a budget amount for each month, as desired. As a shortcut, press the F9 key to copy the last entered amount to all months to the end of the year. Press Enter when done.
4. When you're done entering the budget amounts, press Ctrl-Enter. You can now view and print the monthly budget report.

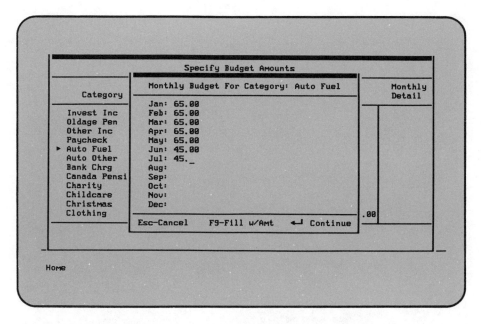

Figure 10.9. You can optionally assign a different budgeted amount for each month of the year.

> ▶ **Tip:** Quicken omits the category when there's no entry in the Budget Amount column. To delete a category from your monthly budget report, select it with the cursor keys and press the Spacebar until the old budget amount is deleted. If you want to change the budget amount for a particular category, simply type a new number in the Budget Amount column.

Itemized Category

The itemized category report shows your account transactions grouped and subtotaled by category. The itemized category report, as depicted in Figure 10.10, lists transactions from all Quicken accounts. Included in the report is all the information provided in the account register, including payee, memo, category, and clear status.

```
                              Itemized
                       1/ 1/90 Through 1/31/90
 All Accounts                                                    Page 1
 1/ 9/90

   Date    Acct      Num         Payee        Memo       Category    Clr   Amount
   -----  --------  ------  -----------------  -----------  ---------------  -  ----------

                            INCOME/EXPENSE
                            INCOME
                              Income - Other
                              --------------
   1/ 3  Savings  D          Deposit from pay                                     500.00
   1/ 4  Savings  I          Interest payment                                      23.98
   1/ 1  Pers. Pr            Livingroom furni                                   3,983.00
   1/ 1  Pers. Pr            Bedroom furnitur Inluces bra                       1,763.00
   1/ 1  Pers. Pr            Jewelry                                           18,776.00
                                                                              ----------
                            Total Income - Other                              25,045.98
                                                                              ----------
                            TOTAL INCOME                                      25,045.98


                            EXPENSES
                              Clothing
                              --------
   1/ 5  Home     *****  Jackets Etc.                     Clothing              -43.98
                                                                              ----------
                            Total Clothing                                     -43.98

                              Dining Out
                              ----------
   1/ 2  Cash                El Taco Palance               Dining               -76.98
                                                                              ----------
                            Total Dining Out                                   -76.98

                              Home Repair & Maint.
                              --------------------
   1/ 1  Visa                Bill's Lumber                 Home Rpair    X     -198.00
                                                                              ----------
                            Total Home Repair & Maint.                        -198.00

                              Household Misc. Exp
                              -------------------
   1/ 5  Home     *****  Fred's TV & Appl                  Household          -134.05
                                                                              ----------
                            Total Household Misc. Exp                         -134.05

                              Income
                              ------
   1/ 4  Savings  D       S Deposit from pay Paycheck/re Income                750.00
                                                                              ----------
                            Total Income                                       750.00
```

Figure 10.10. Sample personal itemized category report.

Normally, the report shows all your transactions. Most likely, you'll want to narrow the transactions to include only those transactions that are most important to you. This requires that you "filter" the report before viewing or printing it. Filtering is more fully discussed in the section entitled "Producing Custom Reports," later in this chapter.

Tax Summary

The tax summary report (see Figure 10.11) lists all those transactions that have been categorized as tax related. (The tax-related stamp can be turned on and off for specific categories, as detailed in Chapter 6, "Keeping Track of Transactions.") The report lists transactions from all your accounts.

222

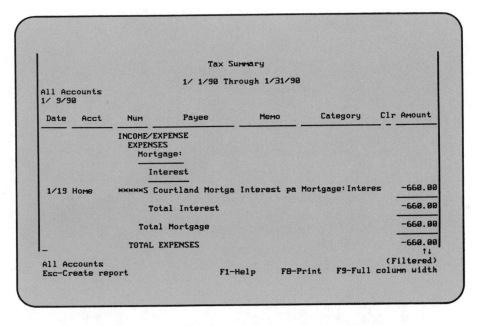

Figure 10.11. Use this tax summary report at tax time.

Net Worth

How many times have you wanted to know the total amount of cash you have in all of your bank accounts? The net worth report, illustrated in Figure 10.12, provides you with this information, plus the balance from your cash, credit card, other asset, and other liability accounts. In this way, the account balances report furnishes you with a statement of net worth. Money listed in bank, cash, and other asset accounts increases your net worth; debts listed in credit card and other liability accounts reduce that net worth.

Examples of Business Reports

The following are examples of Quicken's seven preset business reports.

223

```
                            Balances
                          As of 1/ 9/90
     All Accounts
     1/ 9/90

                                            1/ 9/90
                        Account                 Balance
     -----------------------------------    --------------------
     ASSETS
       Cash and Bank Accounts
         Cash                                         185.00
         Home
           Ending Balance               1,200.33
           plus: Checks Payable           245.12
                                        -----------
         Total Home                                 1,445.45
         Savings-Main savings account             2,668.98
                                                  -----------
       Total Cash and Bank Accounts                4,299.43

       Other Assets
         Pers. Prop-Personal property             24,522.00
                                                  -----------
       Total Other Assets                         24,522.00

                                                  -----------
     TOTAL ASSETS                                 28,821.43

     LIABILITIES
       Checks Payable                                245.12

       Credit Cards
         Visa-11234-123-123-123                    1,876.86
                                                  -----------
       Total Credit Cards                          1,876.86

                                                  -----------
     TOTAL LIABILITIES                             2,121.98

                                                  -----------
     OVERALL TOTAL                                26,699.45
                                                  ===========
```

Figure 10.12. A net worth report.

P&L Statement

A P&L (profit and loss) statement shows your profit and loss, by category. Income categories are grouped together at the top of the report; expenses categories follow. Figure 10.13 shows a sample P&L statement produced by Quicken.

Cash Flow

The cash flow report (see Figure 10.14) lists money that comes in as INFLOWS and money that goes out as OUTFLOWS. The difference, stated as the OVERALL total, shows whether you have a surplus or a deficit. The business cash flow report is the same as the personal cash flow report, detailed above.

```
                        P&L

            12/ 1/89 Through 1/31/90
        BUSS-Business
        1/ 9/90
                            12/ 1/89-
            Category Description    1/31/90

              Income - Other      2,500.00

            TOTAL INCOME           2,500.00

            EXPENSES
              Bank Charge            34.76
              Office Expenses     1,543.98
              Rent Paid             657.00

            TOTAL EXPENSES         2,235.74


            TOTAL INCOME/EXPENSE    264.26
                                                    ↑↓
        BUSS-Business
        Esc-Create report          F1-Help        F8-Print
```

Figure 10.13. A sample profit and loss statement, ideal for small businesses.

A/P by Vendor

The A/P (accounts payable) by vendor report provides an overview of your upcoming debts. The report, shown in Figure 10.15, lists checks by payee, separated into monthly columns. It's unlikely that you'll have more than one or two columns for each payee, unless you are in arrears in your payments. Note that the A/P by vendor report lists only those checks you've written, but not yet printed. This can include regular dated checks that you've not printed yet or post-dated checks.

A/R by Customer

The A/R (accounts receivable) by customer report (see Figure 10.16) lists money you expect to receive in the near future. In order to use this report, you must set up an other asset account where you enter your accounts receivable invoices. In the Accounts Receivable register, as shown in Figure 10.17, you

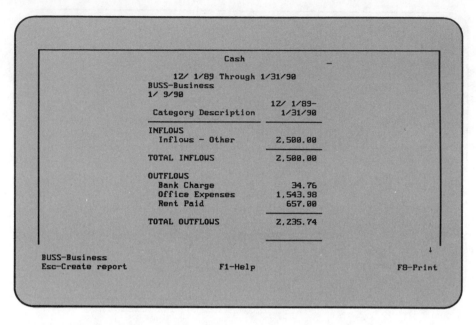

Figure 10.14. Business cash flow report.

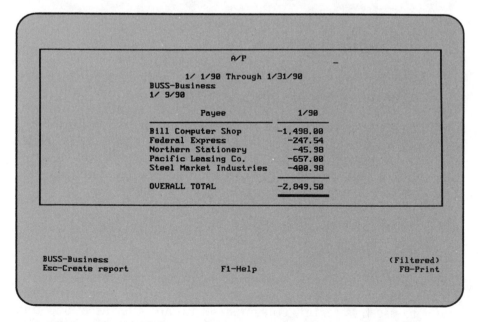

Figure 10.15. This report itemizes accounts payable (bills you need to pay).

enter the invoice date, invoice number (if any), and the payee. You can also include a category, class, and memo, if desired. The amount of the invoice is posted in the INCREASE column. As your invoices are paid, they are marked off in the DECREASE column.

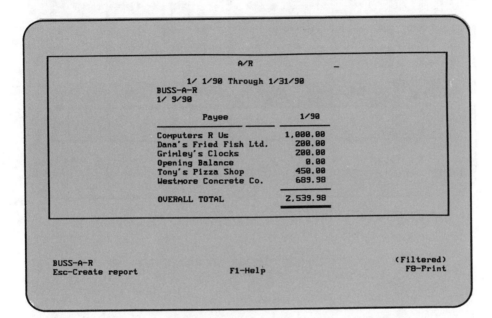

```
                              A/R                      -

                    1/ 1/90 Through 1/31/90
            BUSS-A-R
            1/ 9/90

                         Payee              1/90
                    _____    _____
            Computers R Us            1,000.00
            Dana's Fried Fish Ltd.      200.00
            Grimley's Clocks            200.00
            Opening Balance               0.00
            Tony's Pizza Shop           450.00
            Westmore Concrete Co.       689.98
                                       _____
            OVERALL TOTAL             2,539.98


     BUSS-A-R                                              (Filtered)
     Esc-Create report            F1-Help                 F8-Print
```

Figure 10.16. This report itemizes accounts receivable (money you're getting in).

227

Before printing the A/R by customer report, Quicken preselects all other asset accounts. You'll want to deselect those you don't want included in the report. (Deselect by highlighting the account and pressing the Spacebar.)

Job/Project

The job/project report (see Figure 10.18) helps you track income and expenses by job, project, property, date, department, and other criteria you've entered as class information. (See Chapter 6, "Keeping Track of Transactions," for more details on creating and using classes.) In order to use this report, you must first assign classes to those income and expense categories you want included.

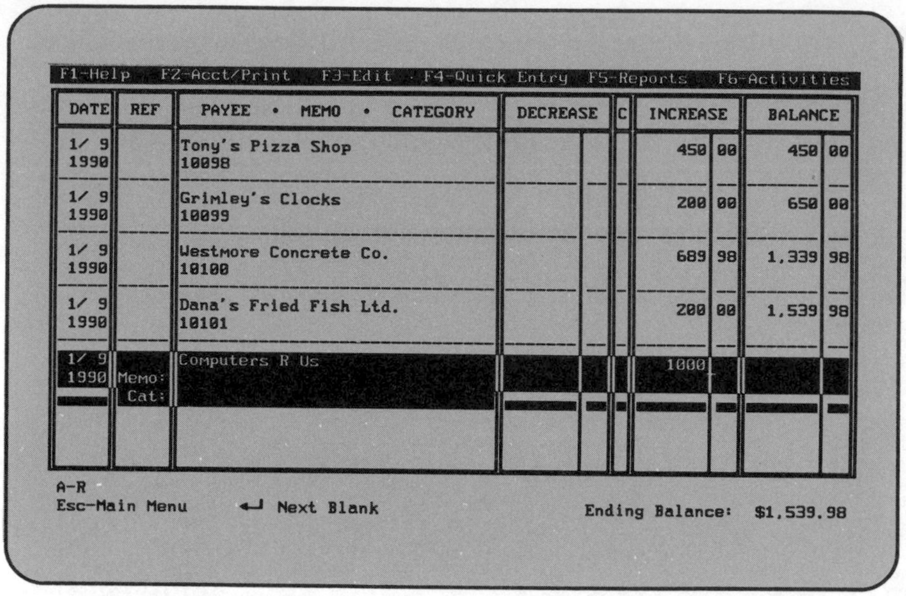

Figure 10.17. Entries in a sample Accounts Receivable register.

Job/Project
1/ 1/90 Through 1/31/90

Category Description	Prod 100A	Prod 100B	Other	OVERALL TOTAL
INCOME/EXPENSE				
INCOME				
Income - Other	45.98	103.00	5,039.98	5,188.96
TOTAL INCOME	45.98	103.00	5,039.98	5,188.96
EXPENSES				
Bank Charge	0.00	0.00	34.76	34.76
Freight	0.00	0.00	247.54	247.54
Office Expenses	0.00	0.00	1,543.98	1,543.98
Rent Paid	0.00	0.00	657.00	657.00
Expenses - Other	601.71	819.05	400.98	1,821.74
TOTAL EXPENSES	601.71	819.05	2,884.26	4,305.02
TOTAL INCOME/EXPENSE	-555.73	-716.05	2,155.72	883.94
BALANCE FORWARD				
A-R	0.00	0.00	0.00	0.00
Business	0.00	0.00	5,000.00	5,000.00
Job	0.00	0.00	0.00	0.00
TOTAL BALANCE FORWARD	0.00	0.00	5,000.00	5,000.00
OVERALL TOTAL	-555.73	-716.05	7,155.72	5,883.94

Figure 10.18. Job/project report.

Payroll Report

The payroll report, as illustrated in Figure 10.19, lists your employees and the various payroll-related expenses during a given time period. To use the report, you must use the Payroll category in the Category blank for each payroll check you write. If you want to itemize the payroll deductions (a good idea) and have them show up in the payroll report, you must split the check as shown in Figure 10.20. Deductions will most often be posted into other liability accounts, so you can keep track of them. Therefore, when you enter the Payroll category, you'll actually be entering a transfer to another Quicken account.

Payroll
1/ 1/90 Through 1/31/90

Payee	INC/EXP EXPENSES Payroll Gross	INC/EXP EXPENSES Payroll TOTAL	INC/EXP EXPENSES Payroll-Dues	INC/EXP EXPENSES Payroll-Fed	INC/EXP EXPENSES Payroll-FICA	INC/EXP EXPENSES Payroll-Ins	INC/EXP EXPENSES TOTAL
Arnold Gross	-676.90	-676.90	250.00	157.00	56.98	83.00	-129.92
Bill Smithers	-500.00	-500.00	25.00	128.00	45.00	-78.76	-380.76
George Stout	-750.00	-750.00	0.00	166.87	75.98	98.00	-409.15
Tony Abalone	-500.00	-500.00	25.00	128.00	45.00	-78.70	-380.70
OVERALL TOTAL	-2,426.90	-2,426.90	300.00	579.87	222.96	23.54	-1,300.53

Figure 10.19. Sample business payroll report.

Balance Sheet

The balance sheet, shown in Figure 10.21, lists the balances from all your accounts: bank, cash, credit card, other asset, and other liability. Each balance is listed separately, under the main headings of ASSETS and LIABILITIES.

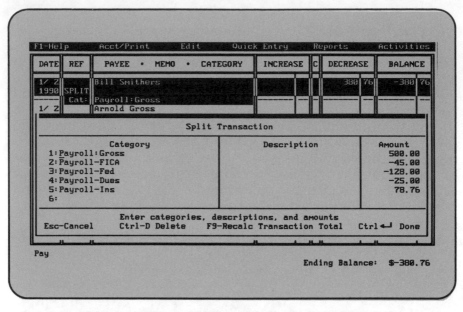

Figure 10.20. Payroll checks must often use split
transactions to show the gross pay and all deductions.

```
                          Balance
                        As of 1/ 9/90
BUSS-All Accounts                                          Page 1
1/ 9/90
                                          1/ 9/90
                    Account                Balance
       ------------------------------------- ------------------
       ASSETS
         Cash and Bank Accounts
           Business-Business acct
             Ending Balance             4,615.74
             plus: Checks Payable       2,849.50
                                        -----------
             Total Business-Business acct          7,465.24
             Job-Job/project accountin            -1,271.78
                                                   -----------
         Total Cash and Bank Accounts              6,193.46

         Other Assets
           A-R-Accounts Receivable                 2,539.98
                                                   -----------
         Total Other Assets                        2,539.98

                                                   -----------
       TOTAL ASSETS                                8,733.44

       LIABILITIES
         Checks Payable                            2,849.50

         Other Liabilities
           Pay-Payroll account                    -1,400.53
                                                   -----------
         Total Other Liabilities                  -1,400.53

                                                   -----------
       TOTAL LIABILITIES                           1,448.97

                                                   -----------
       OVERALL TOTAL                               7,284.47
                                                   ===========
```

Figure 10.21. The balance sheet for business.

Producing Investment Reports

Quicken comes with five preset reports for analyzing your investment accounts. These reports are:

▶ Portfolio value.
▶ Investment performance.
▶ Capital gains (Schedule D).
▶ Investment income.
▶ Investment transactions.

Portfolio Value

231

The portfolio value report shows the value of each of your securities on a specified date (usually the current date). The report includes the number of shares, the most recent price per share (as known by Quicken), your cost basis for the security, unrealized (paper) gain or loss in dollars, and the market value on the specified date.

Figure 10.22 shows a sample portfolio value report.

Investment Performance

The investment performance report displays the average annual total return on your investment during a specified time period. For example, if you are looking at the months June, July, and August, Quicken analyzes the results and applies the numbers to an annual figure. As an option, the investment performance report allows you to subtotal by month, quarter, year, account, security, security type, or investment goal.

Figure 10.23 shows a sample investment performance report.

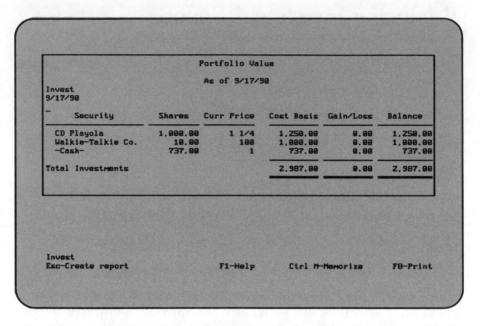

Figure 10.22. Sample portfolio value report.

Capital Gains

Capital gains shows long-term and short-term capital gains for your securities sold during a specified period of time. To use the capital gains report, you should tell Quicken the dates you bought and sold your securities and the actual cost basis for the investments. You can use the capital gains report to complete your Schedule D IRS form.

Figure 10.24 shows a sample capital gains report.

Investment Income

The investment income report shows interest as income (both taxable and nontaxable), dividend income, capital gains distributions, and margin interest expense during a specified time period. You can use this report to analyze the often hidden costs and return on your investments.

Figure 10.25 shows a sample investment income report.

```
                    PERFORMANCE REPORT BY SECURITY
                       1/ 1/90 Through 9/17/90
Invest                                                              Page 1
9/17/90
                                                            Avg. Annual
    Date Action        Description      Investments   Returns  Tot. Return
    ----- ------  --------------------------- ------------ ----------- -----------

         Batteries, Inc
         --------------
    12/31       Beg Mkt Value                0.00
    9/ 1 ShrsIn 25 Batteries, Inc          637.50.
    9/17 Sell   25 Batteries, Inc                         715.00
    9/17        End Mkt Value                              0.00
                                      ------------ ----------- -----------
         Total Batteries, Inc              637.50       715.00    1,269.7%

         CD Playola
         ----------
    12/31       Beg Mkt Value                0.00
    9/ 5 ShrsIn 1,000 CD Playola        1,250.00
    9/17 IntInc CD Playola                                22.00
    9/17        End Mkt Value                           1,250.00
                                      ------------ ----------- -----------
         Total CD Playola              1,250.00     1,272.00      70.0%

         Walkie-Talkie Co.
         -----------------
    12/31       Beg Mkt Value                0.00
    9/ 2 ShrsIn 20 Walkie-Talkie Co.    2,000.00
    9/10 ShrsOu 10 Walkie-Talkie Co.                    1,000.00
    9/17        End Mkt Value                           1,000.00
                                      ------------ ----------- -----------
         Total Walkie-Talkie Co.       2,000.00     2,000.00       0.0%
```

233

Figure 10.23. Sample investment performance report.

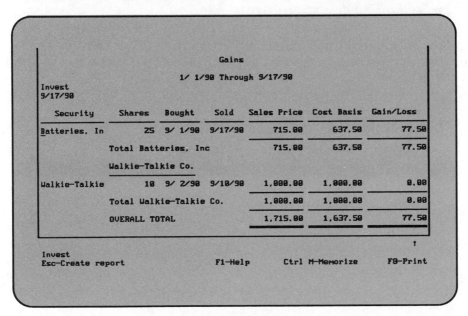

Figure 10.24. Sample capital gains report.

```
                    Investment Income                    _
                 1/ 1/90 Through 9/17/90
          Invest
          9/17/90
                                                OVERALL
                Category Description   Batterie CD Playo   TOTAL

          INCOME/EXPENSE
            INCOME
              Investment Interest Inc   0.00    22.00    22.00
              Realized Gain/Loss       77.50     0.00    77.50

            TOTAL INCOME               77.50    22.00    99.50


          TOTAL INCOME/EXPENSE         77.50    22.00    99.50




                                                          ↓
          Invest
          Esc-Create report            F1-Help     Ctrl M-Memorize    F8-Print
```

234

Figure 10.25. Sample investment income report.

Investment Transactions

The investment transactions report itemizes all or selected transactions from one or more Investment registers. You are provided
with the:

> *Date of transaction.*
> *Investment account name.*
> *Action type (such as ShrsIn or BuyX).*
> *Name of security.*
> *Category for transaction, if any.*
> *Price for security.*
> *Number of shares in transaction.*
> *Cost of commissions and fees.*

Available cash.

Current investment value for security.

Total cash plus investment value.

You can limit the investment transaction report to reflect transactions made during any specified time period. As an option, you may subtotal by month, quarter, year, account, category, security, security type, or investment goal.

You may also, as desired, show or hide unrealized (paper) gains and losses. If you show unrealized gains and losses, the report shows the actual value of your investments at the beginning and end of the specified period. If you select to hide unrealized gains and losses, the report shows the change in the cost basis of your investments between the beginning and end of the specified period.

Figure 10.26 shows a sample investment transactions report.

235

Producing Custom Reports

Quicken lets you create four unique forms of custom reports—transaction, summary, budget, and account balances—as well as customize any of the 12 preset personal and business reports. The process is the same whether you are designing a custom report or customizing a preset report.

Q Creating a Custom Report

1. From the main menu, choose the Reports command.

2. Select the report you want to produce. The exact content of the window varies depending on the report type you select. Note: If you are currently at a register or a Write Checks screen, choose one of the report types from the Reports pull-down menu.

   If you selected a custom report, the Create Transaction Report window appears. A transaction is shown in Figure 10.27.

```
                        Investment Transactions
                        1/ 1/90 Through 9/17/90


                                                        Invest.    Cash +
  Date  Action  Secur      Categ     Price    Shares  Commssn    Cash    Value     Invest.
  ----- ------- ----------- --------- -------- ------- --------- -------- --------- -----------

          Batteries, Inc
          --------------
  9/ 1 ShrsIn  Batteries,            25 1/2     25              -637.50   637.50
                         [Invest]                                637.50               637.50

  9/17 Sell    Batteries,               30      25     35.00    637.50  -637.50
                         Realized Gain/Loss                       77.50                77.50

                                                               --------- --------- -----------
          Total Batteries, Inc                                  715.00     0.00     715.00

          CD Playola
          ----------
  9/ 5 ShrsIn  CD Playola            1 1/4    1,000           -1,250.00 1,250.00
                         [Invest]                              1,250.00             1,250.00

  9/17 IntInc  CD Playola  Investment Interest Inc              22.00                 22.00
                                                               --------- --------- -----------
          Total CD Playola                                      22.00   1,250.00   1,272.00

          Walkie-Talkie Co.
          -----------------
  9/ 2 ShrsIn  Walkie-Talk            100       20           -2,000.00 2,000.00
                         [Invest]                              2,000.00             2,000.00

  9/10 ShrsOut Walkie-Talk                      10            1,000.00 -1,000.00
                         [Invest]                             -1,000.00            -1,000.00

                                                               --------- --------- -----------
          Total Walkie-Talkie Co.                               0.00   1,000.00   1,000.00
```

```
                        Investment Transactions
                        1/ 1/90 Through 9/17/90


                                                        Invest.    Cash +
  Date  Action  Secur      Categ     Price    Shares  Commssn    Cash    Value     Invest.
  ----- ------- ----------- --------- -------- ------- --------- -------- --------- -----------
                                                               --------- --------- -----------
          OVERALL TOTAL                                         737.00  2,250.00   2,987.00
                                                               ========= ========= ===========
```

Figure 10.26. Sample investment transactions report.

3. Press the F8 key, if you   The Create Report window
   selected a preset personal   appears.
   or business report.   ☐

The exact contents of the window varies depending on the exact
report type you selected.

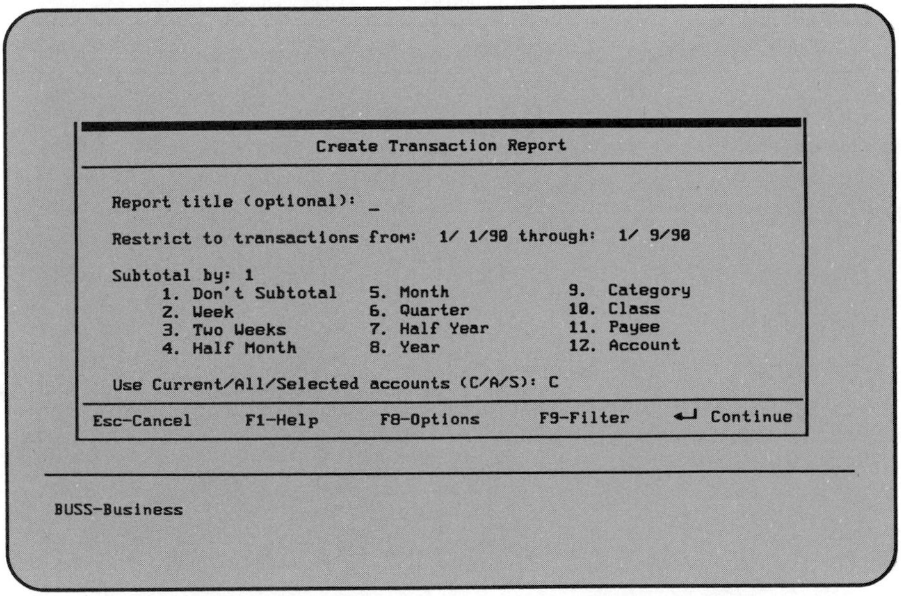

```
                      Create Transaction Report


 Report title (optional): _

 Restrict to transactions from:  1/ 1/90 through:  1/ 9/90

 Subtotal by: 1
      1. Don't Subtotal   5. Month        9.  Category
      2. Week             6. Quarter      10.  Class
      3. Two Weeks        7. Half Year    11.  Payee
      4. Half Month       8. Year         12.  Account

 Use Current/All/Selected accounts (C/A/S): C

 Esc-Cancel      F1-Help       F8-Options      F9-Filter    ↵ Continue


 BUSS-Business
```

Figure 10.27. The Create Transaction Report window.

▶ **Important Note:** All of Quicken's preset personal and
business reports are really custom reports that have
already been defined for you. (The investment reports are
unique and use special formatting.) That's why you can further customize them, if you desire. The 12 preset personal
and business reports belong to one of Quicken's four custom report types, as shown in Table 10.2.

Table 10.2. Preset Report Types.

Personal Report	Custom Form
Cash flow	Summary
Monthly budget	Budget

Continued

237

Table 10.2   continued

Personal Report	Custom Form
Itemized category	Transaction
Tax summary	Transaction
Net worth	Account balances

Business Report	Custom Form
P&L statement	Summary
Cash flow	Summary
A/P by vendor	Summary
A/R by customer	Summary
Job/project summary	Summary
Payroll	Summary
Balance sheet	Account balances

Filling in the Create Report Window

At a minimum, the Create Report window allows you to enter:

A name for the report—Enter a name for the report. If you leave this blank, Quicken will provide a name for you, using a descriptive title based on the criteria you've set.

The range of dates included in the report—Enter the start and stop dates for transactions you want to include. You can provide whole months, or indicate specific days.

How transactions are subtotaled—Indicate whether they are subtotaled by week, year, class, category, and so forth. Enter a selection or press 1 for Don't subtotal.

The transactions you want included—Indicate either Current, All, or Selected. Current transactions are those only in the currently selected account. All transactions are from accounts. (Note: Many reports are restricted to bank, cash, and credit card accounts.) When using selected accounts, you specify the accounts that contain the transaction you want in your reports, as shown in Figure 10.28. Press the Spacebar to include the account in the report; press it again to exclude it.

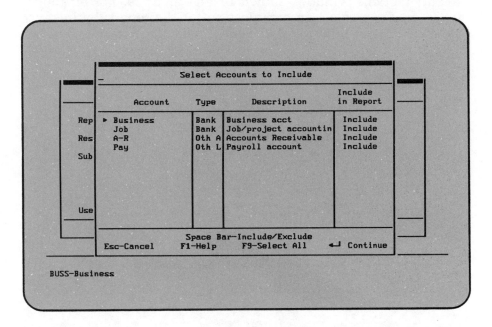

Figure 10.28. Select accounts to include in the report in this window.

In addition, certain Create Report windows expect you to provide other information.

Summary reports allow you to indicate row headings for categories, classes, payees, or accounts. Enter the number of the type of row headings you want.

Summary and budget reports allow you to indicate column headings. Type the number that corresponds to the type or column heading you want.

Account balances reports allow you to specify the intervals at which you want the ending balances to be calculated. The available choices are: one week, two weeks, a half month, a month, a quarter, a half year, or a year.

Setting Report Options

Pressing the F8 key from any Create Report window displays the Report Options window, shown in Figure 10.29. For all report types, you can select an organization for the report (by income/ expense or cash flow basis) and how transfers are to be handled.

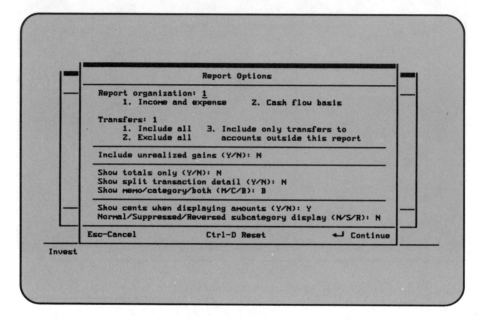

Figure 10.29. The Report Options window.

When the report is organized by income/expense, transactions are grouped by income first, then by expense. When the report is organized by cash flow basis, Quicken groups transactions and transfers by INFLOWS and OUTFLOWS, respectively.

Transaction reports offer five additional selections:

▶ *Show totals only*—Press Y when you want the report to show only the total income and expenses for selected transactions.

▶ *Show split transaction detail*—Press Y to include a rundown of split transactions.

▶ *Show memo/category/both*—Press M or C to include just the memo or category in transaction reports; press B to include them both.

▶ *Shows cents when displaying amounts*—Press Y to show dollars and cents in reports and N to show only dollars.

▶ *Normal/Suppressed/Reversed subcategory display*—Press S to suppress subcategories and subclasses in reports; press R to reverse the order of subcategories (to make it easier to spot budget allocations; for example, change Utility:Phone to Phone:Utility); press N to return the subcategory display to normal.

When you're finished with the Report Options window, press the Enter key to go back to the Create Report window.

Filtering Transactions

241

Pressing the F9 key at any Create Report window displays the Filter Report Transaction window, illustrated in Figure 10.30. Using the options in this window, you can specify the kinds of transactions you want included in the report. Only those transactions that meet *all* of the criteria you have indicated will be processed into the report. You have the following options:

Restrict report to transactions meeting these criteria—Enter a text string for matching with Payee name, memo, category, or class. You can use an exact text match or find text that includes or excludes the text you've indicated. See the section entitled "Transaction Filter Text Matching," below, for more information.

Select categories to include—Press Y if you want to select categories to include in the report. The window in Figure 10.31 appears. Initially, all categories are included; to exclude a category, highlight it with the up and down arrow keys then press the Spacebar.

Select classes to include—Press Y if you want to select classes to include in the report. You include/exclude classes the same as you do categories (see above).

Tax-related categories only—Press Y if you want to include only tax-related categories in the report.

Below/Equal/Above the amount—Press B if you want to include transactions that are below a specified amount or press E or A if you to want to include transactions that are equal to or greater than the specified amount. Indicate the amount, in dollars and cents.

Payments/Deposits/Unprinted checks/All—This option specifies the type of transactions. Press A if you want to include all transactions, press P to include only payments, press D to include only deposits, and press U to include only unprinted checks.

Cleared status is blank—Press Y or N beside both or either of the cleared status symbols to include these transactions in the report. The * clear symbol is for transactions that have been marked clear but haven't been reconciled with the bank statement. The X clear symbol is for transactions that are both marked clear and reconciled.

242

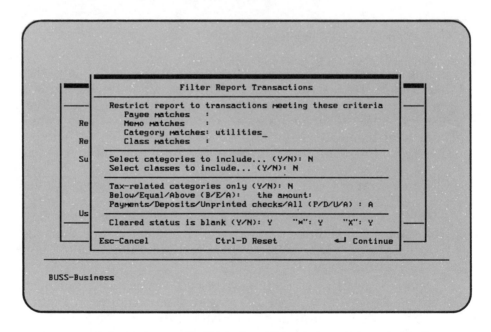

Figure 10.30. Specify the information you want to include in your reports in the Filter Report Transactions window.

When you are finished entering the filter information, press the Enter key to continue. Quicken takes you back to the Create Report window. Alternatively, you can press the F8 key then Ctrl-D to reset all the entries to their default settings. You can now return to the Create Report window or re-enter your custom settings.

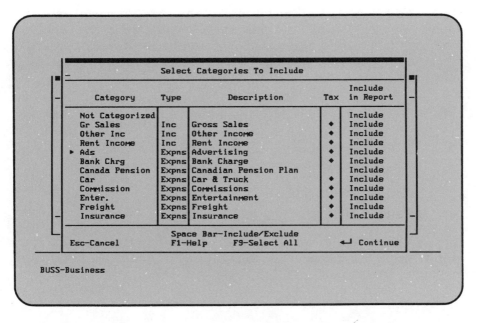

Figure 10.31. The Select Categories to Include window.

Transaction Filter Text Matching

Having Quicken find those transactions that meet certain criteria is the fastest and most accurate way to produce reports. When using the transaction filter options listed above, you can find those transactions that meet only the criteria you specify. That criteria is in the form of a text match. You can locate transactions by payee, memo, category, or class, or a combination of all four.

The most straightforward use of the transaction filter text matching is exact text searches. For example, if you want to include only those transactions that list "Joe's Bar and Grill" as the payee, enter "Joe's Bar and Grill" in the Payee blank within the Filter Report Transactions window. Quicken will search through your accounts and list in its report only the transactions with the text you specify. You can do the same for memos, categories, and classes.

You can also use text matching to find approximate entries. Quicken uses double periods as a "wildcard"; the double periods match up to any text. For example, to find checks written to any of Joe's businesses (Bar and Grill, Bed and Breakfast, and Pool Hall), enter

`Joe's..`

Quicken finds

> Joe's Bar and Grill
> Joe's Bed and Breakfast
> Joe's Pool Hall

An extension of text matches is *excluding* transactions you don't want. Quicken uses the tilde (~) character to mean exclude. The entry

`~Utilities`

will *not* include any transactions with the utilities category. You can combine the double periods and tilde character to build elaborate text-matching schemes. The entry

`~Joe's..`

will *not* include

> Joe's Bar and Grill
> Joe's Bed and Breakfast
> Joe's Pool Hall

244

Examples of Custom Reports

Figures 10.32 through 10.35 illustrate some examples of custom Quicken reports. Because these reports were defined using the customizing options detailed earlier in this chapter, their format and content should only be considered as representative of the types of reports you can produce. You are free to design your own reports any way you desire.

```
                              Sample Custom Transaction
                               1/ 1/90 Through 1/ 9/90
BUSS-All Accounts                                                              Page 1
1/ 9/90


          Date  Acct    Num      Payee      Memo    Category  Clr  Amount
          ----- ------- ------ ------------ ------- --------- - ----------


          1/ 1 Business        Opening Balance        [Business]   X   5,000.00
          1/ 5 Business *****  Pacific Leasing        Rent Paid         -657.00
          1/ 6 Business *****  Bill Computer Sh       Office          -1,498.00
          1/ 6 Business *****  Northern Station       Office             -45.98
          1/ 6 Business *****  Steel Market Ind                         -400.98
          1/ 6 Business *****  Federal Express        Freight           -247.54
          1/ 1 Job             Opening Balance        [Job]        X        0.00
          1/ 2 Job             Parts In               /Prod 100A        -354.98
          1/ 2 Job             Parts In               /Prod 100B        -498.33
          1/ 4 Job             Labor                  /Prod 100A        -100.98
          1/ 4 Job             Labor                  /Prod 100B        -123.09
          1/ 5 Job             Shipping               /Prod 100A         -45.12
          1/ 5 Job             Shipping               /Prod 100B         -10.29
          1/ 6 Job             Misc. Expenses         /Prod 100A        -100.63
          1/ 6 Job             Misc Expenses          /Prod 100B        -187.34
          1/ 1 Pay             Opening Balance        [Pay]                 0.00
          1/ 2 Pay           S Bill Smithers          Payroll:Gross       500.00
                                                      Payroll-FICA        -45.00
                                                      Payroll-Fed        -128.00
                                                      Payroll-Dues        -25.00
                                                      Payroll-Ins          78.76
          1/ 2 Pay           S Arnold Gross           Payroll:Gross       676.90
                                                      Payroll-FICA        -56.98
                                                      Payroll-Fed        -157.00
                                                      Payroll-Dues       -250.00
                                                      Payroll-Ins         -83.00
          1/ 2 Pay           S Tony Abalone           Payroll:Gross       500.00
                                                      Payroll-FICA        -45.00
                                                      Payroll-Fed        -128.00
                                                      Payroll-Dues        -25.00
                                                      Payroll-Ins          78.70
                                                                          100.00
          1/ 2 Pay           S George Stout           Payroll:Gross       750.00
                                                      Payroll-FICA        -75.98
                                                      Payroll-Fed        -166.87
                                                      Payroll-Dues          0.00
                                                      Payroll-Ins         -98.00
                                                                     ----------
                       TOTAL  1/ 1/90 -  1/ 6/90                      2,130.27

          1/ 7 Business        Gorshon Developm                        2,500.00
          1/ 8 Business        Bank charges           Bank Chrg          -34.76
          1/ 7 Job           S Permits                /Prod 100A          45.98
                                                      /Prod 100B         103.00
          1/ 9 A-R             Opening Balance        [A-R]                 0.00
          1/ 9 A-R             Tony's Pizza Sho 10098                    450.00
          1/ 9 A-R             Grimley's Clocks 10099                    200.00
          1/ 9 A-R             Westmore Concret 10100                    689.98
          1/ 9 A-R             Dana's Fried Fis 10101                    200.00
          1/ 9 A-R             Computers R Us                          1,000.00
                                                                     ----------

                              Sample Custom Transaction
                               1/ 1/90 Through 1/ 9/90
BUSS-All Accounts                                                              Page 2
1/ 9/90

          Date  Acct    Num      Payee      Memo    Category  Clr  Amount
          ----- -------- ------ ------------ ------- --------- - ----------

                       TOTAL  1/ 7/90 -  1/ 9/90                      5,154.20


                                                                     ----------
                       OVERALL TOTAL                                  7,284.47
                                                                     ==========


                       TOTAL INFLOWS                                 12,873.32
                       TOTAL OUTFLOWS                                -5,588.85
                                                                     ----------
                       NET TOTAL                                     7,284.47
                                                                     ==========
```

Figure 10.32. A sample custom transaction report.

245

```
                        Sample Summary Report
                        1/ 1/90 Through 1/ 9/90

                                                              OVERALL
          Payee              A-R       Business        Job        Pay      TOTAL
------------------------  ------------  ------------  ------------  ------------  ------------
Arnold Gross                 0.00          0.00          0.00        129.92       129.92
Bank charges                 0.00        -34.76          0.00          0.00       -34.76
Bill Computer Shop           0.00     -1,498.00          0.00          0.00    -1,498.00
Bill Smithers                0.00          0.00          0.00        380.76       380.76
Computers R Us           1,000.00          0.00          0.00          0.00     1,000.00
Dana's Fried Fish Ltd.     200.00          0.00          0.00          0.00       200.00
Federal Express              0.00       -247.54          0.00          0.00      -247.54
George Stout                 0.00          0.00          0.00        409.15       409.15
Gorshon Development          0.00      2,500.00          0.00          0.00     2,500.00
Grimley's Clocks           200.00          0.00          0.00          0.00       200.00
Labor                        0.00          0.00       -224.07          0.00      -224.07
Misc Expenses                0.00          0.00       -187.34          0.00      -187.34
Misc. Expenses               0.00          0.00       -100.63          0.00      -100.63
Northern Stationery          0.00        -45.98          0.00          0.00       -45.98
Opening Balance              0.00      5,000.00          0.00          0.00     5,000.00
Pacific Leasing Co.          0.00       -657.00          0.00          0.00      -657.00
Parts In                     0.00          0.00       -853.31          0.00      -853.31
Permits                      0.00          0.00        148.98          0.00       148.98
Shipping                     0.00          0.00        -55.41          0.00       -55.41
Steel Market Industries      0.00       -400.98          0.00          0.00      -400.98
Tony Abalone                 0.00          0.00          0.00        480.70       480.70
Tony's Pizza Shop          450.00          0.00          0.00          0.00       450.00
Westmore Concrete Co.      689.98          0.00          0.00          0.00       689.98
                        ------------  ------------  ------------  ------------  ------------
OVERALL TOTAL            2,539.98      4,615.74     -1,271.78      1,400.53     7,284.47
                        ============  ============  ============  ============  ============
```

Figure 10.33. A custom summary report.

What You Have Learned

This chapter detailed Quicken's numerous reports and how to make them. Here's what you have learned:

▶ You can view reports on screen or print them out.
▶ Quicken offers five preset personal reports: cash flow, monthly budget, itemized categories, tax summary, and account balances.

```
                              Custom Budget Report
                             1/ 1/90 Through 1/ 9/90

                     1/ 1/90    -     1/ 6/90   1/ 7/90    -     1/ 9/90   1/ 1/90    -     1/ 9/90
   Category Description Actual  Budget  Diff     Actual   Budget   Diff    Actual   Budget   Diff
   ---------------------------- -------------------------- -------------------------- ----------------------------

INCOME/EXPENSE
  EXPENSES
    Automobile Fuel     0.00    8.70   -8.70     0.00     4.35    -4.35    0.00     13.06   -13.06
    Clothing           43.98   19.35   24.63     0.00     9.67    -9.67   43.98     29.03    14.95
    Dining Out         76.98   14.51   62.47     0.00     7.25    -7.25   76.98     21.77    55.21
    Groceries           0.00   67.74  -67.74     0.00    33.87   -33.87    0.00    101.61  -101.61
    Home Repair & Maint. 198.00 19.35  178.65    0.00     9.67    -9.67  198.00     29.03   168.97
    Household Misc. Exp 134.05  14.51  119.54     0.00     7.25    -7.25  134.05     21.77   112.28
    Housing             0.00  241.93 -241.93     0.00   120.96  -120.96    0.00    362.90  -362.90
    Medical & Dental    0.00   14.51  -14.51     0.00     7.25    -7.25    0.00     21.77   -21.77
    Telephone Expense   0.00    9.67   -9.67     0.00     4.83    -4.83    0.00     14.51   -14.51
                       --------- --------- --------- --------- --------- --------- --------- --------- ---------
  TOTAL EXPENSES      453.01  410.27   42.74     0.00   205.10  -205.10  453.01    615.45  -162.44

                       --------- --------- --------- --------- --------- --------- --------- --------- ---------
TOTAL INCOME/EXPENSE -453.01 -410.27  -42.74     0.00  -205.10   205.10 -453.01   -615.45   162.44
                       ========= ========= ========= ========= ========= ========= ========= ========= =========
```

Figure 10.34. A custom budget report.

247

▶ Quicken offers seven preset business reports: P&L statement, cash flow, A/P by vendor, A/R by customer, job/project, payroll, and balance sheet.

▶ You can customize any preset personal or business report.

▶ All reports (including preset personal and business) are based on one of Quicken's main report types: transaction, summary, budget, or account balances.

▶ You can view and print wide reports by changing the number of characters per line from 80 to 132.

▶ Reports saved as a disk file can be opened by word processor and electronic spreadsheet programs.

▶ Filtering allows you to include in your reports only those transactions you specify.

```
                ACCOUNT BALANCES REPORT BY MONTH
                        As of 1/ 9/90
BUSS-All Accounts                                                    Page 1
1/ 9/90
                                        1/ 1/90        1/ 9/90
                    Account             Balance        Balance
------------------------------------- --------------- ---------------
ASSETS
  Cash and Bank Accounts
    Business-Business acct
      Ending Balance                    5,000.00       4,615.74
      plus: Checks Payable                  0.00       2,849.50
                                        ----------    ----------
    Total Business-Business acct        5,000.00       7,465.24
    Job-Job/project accountin               0.00      -1,271.78
                                        ----------    ----------
  Total Cash and Bank Accounts          5,000.00       6,193.46

  Other Assets
    A-R-Accounts Receivable                 0.00       2,539.98
                                        ----------    ----------
  Total Other Assets                        0.00       2,539.98

                                        ----------    ----------
TOTAL ASSETS                            5,000.00       8,733.44

LIABILITIES
  Checks Payable                           0.00       2,849.50

  Other Liabilities
    Pay-Payroll account                     0.00      -1,400.53
                                        ----------    ----------
  Total Other Liabilities                   0.00      -1,400.53

                                        ----------    ----------
TOTAL LIABILITIES                           0.00       1,448.97

                                        ----------    ----------
OVERALL TOTAL                           5,000.00       7,284.47
                                        ==========    ==========
```

Figure 10.35. A custom account balances report.

248

Setting Up a Business Accounting System

In This Chapter

▶ *Concepts of double-entry accounting*
▶ *Cash accounting in Quicken*
▶ *Budgeting payables with cash accounting*
▶ *Accrual accounting in Quicken*
▶ *Receivables and payables accounts*
▶ *Entering transactions*

This chapter gives you the building blocks for creating a complete accounting system in Quicken. You'll learn how to apply Quicken to your business for cash or accrual accounting, and you'll see examples of each type of system. By the end of this chapter, you'll be ready to create important business reports, such as a balance sheet, income statement, and cash analysis statement.

Using Quicken in Business

One of the keys to accurate business accounting is a strict system of codes. Everything gets a number or a code so that entries are consistent. This lets you create reports that group items by the desired code. Quicken's most important code is the category name. Whenever you enter a transaction, you assign it to a category—that's giving it a code, more or less. Later, Quicken can tally all the items that have the same code. This can provide you with totals for expense categories, as well as income categories.

Categories serve another purpose; they allow you to perform double-entry accounting. *Double-entry accounting* is a system of debits and credits that apply to your asset and liability accounts. In a strict accounting sense, each category in the category list is a separate account. And each account is coded—with a number. This is commonly known as your chart of accounts. A business' chart of accounts is, basically, what Quicken calls the *category list*.

Quicken does not need to code its categories because it uses unique name for each one. The name itself is used by Quicken as a code. However, if you're used to coding accounts, you can use numbers instead of names for these categories. You can take them straight off your chart of accounts, which, hopefully, was prepared for you by an accountant.

Using these categories, you can assign debits and credits to each transaction, which keeps your assets and liabilities in balance. That's the purpose of double-entry accounting. *Whenever you credit one category, you must debit another.* (Remember, all accounts are categories as well as those on the category list.) If you make a sale, you usually debit cash and credit inventory.

Now it gets a little confusing because debits are not always increases and credits are not always decreases. The good news is that Quicken takes care of debits and credits for you—as long as you provide the category (code) to which each transaction applies. That's what this chapter is all about. It will show you how to enter transactions for double-entry accounting, using both a cash and an accrual system. Quicken makes it easy.

Cash Accounting with Quicken

A *cash accounting system* deals with transactions that affect your cash balance. You sell a product and receive a check; that's *cash income*. You pay a bill from your checking account; that's a *cash expense*. These types of transactions are simple entries into your various cash account registers or transaction screen (Write Checks screen). As cash comes in, you generate an *income* transaction and as cash goes out, you generate an *expense* transaction.

Income transactions are posted to your check register and are given an income category for tracking purposes, such as Gross Sales or Rent Income. Quicken enters this in the checking register as a deposit. Figure 11.1 shows an example.

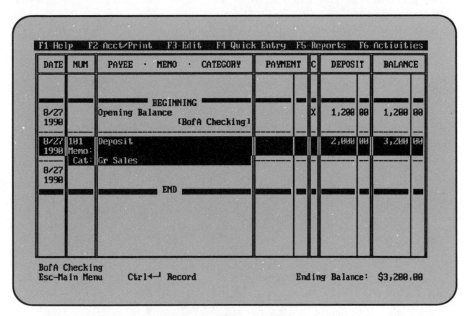

Figure 11.1. Entering a cash deposit as an income transaction with categories.

As mentioned earlier in this chapter, you should take care to always include a category for your transactions—that's what double-entry accounting is all about. It lets you find the balances of various income and expense categories, no matter what types of transactions affect them. The cash entry shown in the figure has just increased the cash balance in the check register and the cash balance in the Gross Sales category (which you will see when you generate a report).

As another example, suppose you write a check to ABC Office Supply and assign it to the Office Expense category. Later, you might use your credit card to purchase office supplies from another company, but you assign the same category (Office Expense) to the credit card transaction, too. Both of these transactions affect the balance of the Office Expense category.

Cash management is handled with checking accounts, credit card accounts, and cash accounts[md]all of these track income and expenses by category. Credit card accounts are a little different from the others because they generate an expense when you make the purchase (use the credit card) and not when you pay the credit card's bill. For example, if you purchase office supplies with your credit card, you may enter a transaction into the credit card journal that looks like the one in Figure 11.2.

252

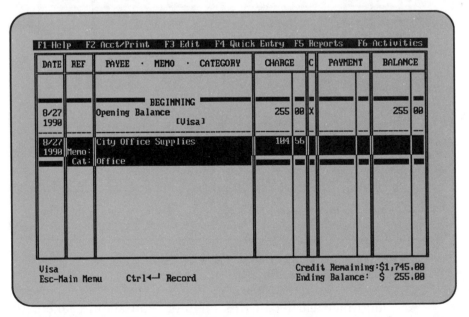

Figure 11.2. Typical credit card transaction.

The Office Expense category has already been affected by this transaction—as has the balance of your credit card account.

When you pay the bill for this, you may use the Write Checks screen for the transaction. This will decrease the balance in the checking account journal, but the category to which it's assigned is the credit card account. Figure 11.3 shows what this check might look like.

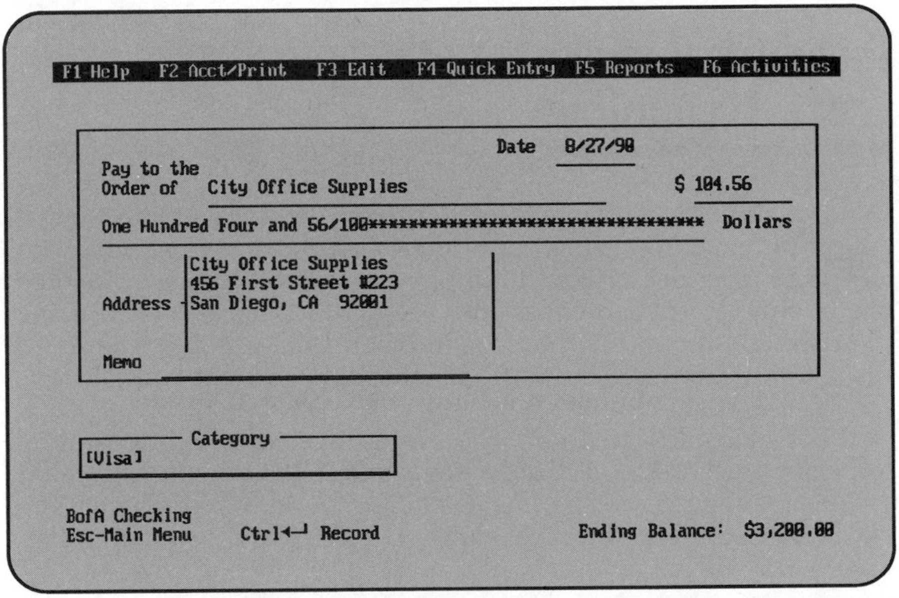

```
 F1 Help   F2 Acct/Print   F3 Edit   F4 Quick Entry  F5 Reports   F6 Activities

                                        Date    8/27/90
      Pay to the
      Order of   City Office Supplies                         $ 104.56

      One Hundred Four and 56/100************************************* Dollars

                  City Office Supplies
                  456 First Street #223
      Address    San Diego, CA  92001

      Memo

      ┌─── Category ───
      [Visa]

   BofA Checking
   Esc-Main Menu      Ctrl↵  Record                Ending Balance:  $3,200.00
```

Figure 11.3. Paying on your credit card account.

Thus, writing a check for the credit card bill decreases the cash balance in the checking account and increases the balance (lowers the balance due) in your credit card account. Paying the credit card bill has no affect on the expense category (Office Expense). It's handled like a transfer between accounts, and transfers do not generate income or expense—they simply change your cash balances.

> ▶ **Tip**: You can choose categories for transactions by pressing Ctrl-C. You can then choose the desired category from the list. Remember that all your accounts are also categories for other accounts.

253

So far so good. When you generate reports from your various registers, you get an accurate picture of your cash position. Likewise, you get balances for all your income and expense categories. This tells you where your money is going and you can compare these balances over several months, if desired.

Payables Budgeting with Cash Accounting

254

Using a simple post-dating technique for checks, you can budget for future expenses using your check register. This provides you with a general idea of your future payables (expenses) and income needs. Simply enter a check into the Write Checks screen, using the date that the bill is due for the date of the check (never enter these transactions directly into the checking account journal).

For example, suppose you have a bill from Quality Printing for some brochures you had printed. This bill is due on November 1, 1991. Although today is September 12, 1991, you enter the check and post-date it for November 1, 1991. This is shown in Figure 11.4.

Notice that the check is written and all categories are filled out, as if you were really paying this bill. The key is that you don't print this check (that is, do not record the transaction). Printing the check adds it to the checking account register—which affects your cash balances. Leaving the check unprinted simply keeps it around in the "checkbook" without ever affecting cash. Use a class entry to store additional information about the payable, such as the invoice number or your P.O. number if you use them. This way, you can generate reports that list payables due by invoice number.

> ▶ **Tip**: If you use the vendor's invoice number as a class, you should also include a unique vendor ID code. This will prevent complications when two vendors have the same invoice numbers. For example, invoice 23308 from Quality Printing might be listed with the class: QP23308.

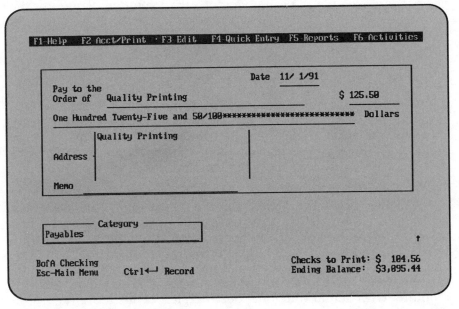

Figure 11.4. Post-dating a check.

Why do this? If you add all the bills that come due for a particular month, Quicken will give you a summary of your total expenses due for that month. In other words, you can create reports based on these post-dated entries. Press the F5 key for Business Reports, A/P by Vendor to generate a total expense report by vendor. This tallies the unprinted checks you've entered and groups them by vendor name (payee). Each month will be broken out into its own column. These will, of course, be accurate only to the extent that you have completely listed the expenses by entering them as post-dated checks. Chapter 12 provides details about creating this report, as well as other business reports.

If you use the post-dated check technique for tracking expenses (payables) or for budgeting, these transactions will not affect the cash reports because they do not affect the journals. In other words, checks are not entered into the check register until you "print" them. Since post-dated checks are not printed, they do not affect the cash reports. When the time comes to actually pay a bill, you can simply print the check that you have post-dated. This creates the expense entry in the check register. If you do not pay the entire amount on the check—or if you use one check to pay several invoices for the same vendor—then remove or modify the post-dated checks and enter a new check for the actual amount you pay.

When you use post-dated checks, Quicken tells you the amount of unprinted checks. This number appears in the Checks to Print summary at the bottom of your screen. The Ending Balance figure now reflects the total balance of funds—after you pay post-dated checks. This will likely be negative if you enter many post-dated checks. The Current Balance amount tells you what the balance is through the current date; this will not include post-dated checks. Again, all these numbers appear at the bottom of the screen.

Besides using the post-dated checks for budgeting, you can use Quicken's budgeting screen for tracking monthly figures. Just select 3 for Reports from the main menu, then press the F7 key twice. This takes you to the Specify Budget Amounts screen. You can break each category into monthly budget amounts. Use this report along with the post-dated checks to compare budget amounts with actual bills due. See Chapter 10 for more details on using the budget report.

256

Accrual Accounting with Quicken

Accrual accounting is a more sophisticated method of tracking income and expense. In addition to tracking cash flows using the cash accounts (checking, cash, and credit card accounts), accrual accounting tracks payables and receivables using the other liability and other asset accounts. Payables is a liability, and receivables is an asset; they both affect your net worth and ability to borrow. They are meant to give you a more accurate picture of your business' disposition, and most financial institutions expect them in a balance sheet report.

However, you should be careful about relying too heavily on payables and receivables data and their related calculations. Small businesses make it or break it based on cash, cash, cash! While a large receivables may help you in obtaining a business loan, you should not forget to generate cash flow reports as well as the balance sheet to get a real-life picture of your cash position.

Payables and receivables are accounts that have their own journals—just like your checking account. But they also become categories for other accounts. When you write a check, you can list Payables as the category. This will allow Quicken to decrease the cash balance in your cash account and increase the payables (reduce the negative amount—resulting in a decrease in the total payables due). This is called *crediting and debiting*. Meanwhile, each entry in your payables register reflects an invoice that you must pay or a payment made on that entry (which has been posted from one of your cash accounts).

How is this different from the post-dated check system? Primarily, the post-dated check technique does not affect the balance sheet. Although you can track payables using post-dated checks, you cannot have the payables figures balance with the other accounts. For example, when you pay a bill, you credit the cash account and debit payables, resulting in a balance of assets and liabilities. In order to add debits and credits to your payables and receivables, you must have payables and receivables accounts. You may want to combine the post-dated check technique with the payables account. More on this later.

A receivables account works in the same way. It maintains its own journal while providing a category for posting from other accounts. The receivables journal can provide aging reports, total receivables reports by customer, invoice number, and date.

When you generate a bill for a customer, you've created a receivable. That amount should be posted to the receivables account and shown as an asset on your balance sheet. This entry should also generate income and expense. This means that, in addition to changing (increasing) the balance of your receivables account, you also must provide a category for the transaction. Providing a category for the transaction lets Quicken post an "offsetting entry" to the category you specify, thus, balancing the accounts. This is commonly known as *debiting and crediting*.

Quicken handles debits and credits differently than a strict bookkeeping system. If you're familiar with bookkeeping principles, you may find Quicken's organization of accounts confusing. For one thing, Quicken's accounts are not really debit and credit accounts. Thus, you might find that debits are not always on the left side of the register. However, Quicken makes things simple for you. It knows how to debit and credit based on your entries. When you post a transaction, it knows to create an equal and opposite entry into the account category you specify. So the important thing is to always include a category for your entry.

257

As an example, suppose your shop sells $1000 worth of merchandise on 30-day terms. You enter this transaction into the receivables journal under the current date. This creates the increase in receivables. The category to which this applies might be Gross Sales. So, you enter Gross Sales as the category for the transaction. You've now balanced the books, and your balance sheet will reflect the receivables as an asset. When the inventory ships, you might create another transaction, which is reflected in your inventory account. (We'll discuss inventory accounts later in this book.) There, you might decrease inventory and list Cost of Goods as the category. The point here is that your cash hasn't changed a bit! When you get paid for the invoice, you generate the cash transaction using the cash journal (i.e., enter a deposit) and list Payables as the category for the cash transaction. This lets Quicken adjust both the cash and the payables balances and balance the accounts.

258

When you list any other asset or other liability account as a category for a cash account, Quicken considers it a transfer. Hence, the transaction does not generate income or expense. In the previous example, the income was generated when you created the invoice in the receivables journal. When the bill is paid, you are simply transferring from receivables to cash and not generating a second income for the same sale. The same is true of the transaction you enter when the inventory is shipped. This type of transfer is known as a *balance sheet transaction* since it affects the balance sheet only. Quicken takes care of the details for you, but it helps to know a little about the theory.

Starting Your Accrual Accounting System

Now that you know some of the theory of accrual accounting, try setting up payables and receivables accounts. If you're starting from scratch (or if you're creating a completely new account group), you should start by selecting Quicken's built-in account categories for business. When you create a new account group, Quicken will offer its standard categories as shown in Figure 11.5. Table 11.1 lists these standard categories.

You can add categories to this list as described in Chapter 6 —just be sure that you properly define them as income or expense categories.

In addition to these categories, all accounts that you create will appear as categories. When you're ready to create accounts, start with all the normal cash accounts as described throughout this book. Include a bank account for each of your business checking or savings accounts. Keep a cash account for cash transactions (even if you don't expect to have many). Chapter 3 provides details about setting up these accounts and creating a new account group.

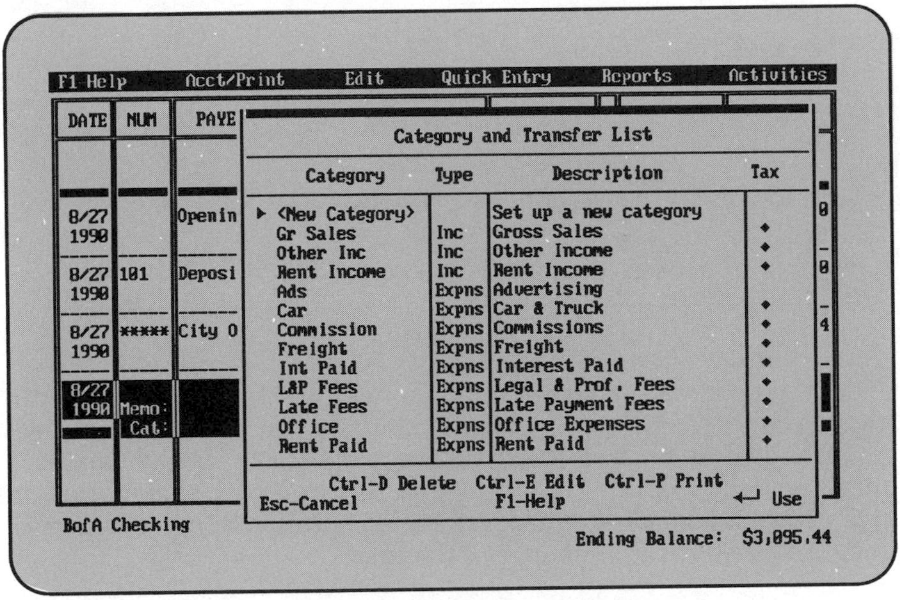

Figure 11.5. Quicken's standard business categories.

Table 11.1. List of Standard Business Categories.

Category	Type	Description	Tax
Gr Sales	Income	Gross sales	X
Other Inc	Income	Other income	X
Rent Income	Income	Rent income	X
Ads	Expense	Advertising	X
Car	Expense	Car/truck	X
Commission	Expense	Commissions	X
Freight	Expense	Freight	X

Continued

Table 11.1   continued

Category	Type	Description	Tax
Int Paid	Expense	Interest paid	X
L&P Fees	Expense	Legal/professional fees	X
Late Fees	Expense	Late payment fees	X
Office	Expense	Office expenses	X
Rent Paid	Expense	Rent paid	X
Repairs	Expense	Repairs	X
Returns	Expense	Returns & allowances	X
Taxes	Expense	Taxes	X
Travel	Expense	Travel expenses	X
Wages	Expense	Wages & job credits	X

260

If you already have your business bank accounts, credit card accounts, and cash accounts started, you can add the payables and receivables to them. Just be sure that you have an adequate category listing—either by entering your own categories or by using Quicken's standard ones. Essentially, these categories reflect your business' chart of accounts.

> ▶ **Note**: Do not add any payables or receivables categories to this list. This includes short-term and long-term notes payable and receivable or any other payables or receivables. These will be handled in their own accounts as described in the rest of this chapter.

Setting Up a Payables Account

At this point you should have your basic cash accounts established. You're ready to add a payables account. You can add this account to your current account group using option 4 for Select Account from the main menu.

Q Creating a Payables Account

1. From the main menu, choose option 4 for Select Account.

   Takes you into the list of existing accounts. Currently, this list should have your cash accounts in it.

2. Select <New Account>.

   Quicken's account types from which you can start a new account appear.

3. Enter 5 to begin another liability account. Press Tab when finished.

4. Enter the name *Payables* for this account and press Tab.

   This name will appear as the account name and as the category name for transfers.

5. Enter zero (0) for the balance, press Tab (change the date if necessary), and then enter the description *Accounts Payable* and press Enter.

   Adds the account to the existing list.

261

Entering Your Current Payables

You started the payables account with a zero balance. Now you must list all payables in the account individually. This requires that you enter each bill you owe into the payables journal. This way, you can produce reports showing open invoices and individual bills by vendor.

You can also tally the amounts you've paid to each vendor. These can be useful reports for business analysis. An opening balance would lump all current payables into one amount and negate the value of the journal. A little extra work here will go a long way.

When you enter a payable into the payables journal, start by changing Quicken's automatic date to the date you received the invoice. This reflects the date that you acknowledge the liability. Once you've entered all existing invoices, you can probably start accepting Quicken's automatic date as the date of receipt.

Next, enter the name of the vendor (supplier) on the top line of the Payee column. Enter the amount of the invoice in the Increase column because you are increasing payables by adding a new debt. Use the Memo line for "off the record" comments or information about the transaction. This can include comments about the service, the name of the employee who generated the expense, or comments on the purpose of the purchase.

Use the Category field to enter the "offsetting entry" for the balance sheet. In other words, this will be the account that you debit to offset the credit that is being applied to payables. If you purchased products for your business, you might use the Inventory category (which you will learn how to create in Chapter 13). If you purchased office equipment, you might apply the debit to Equipment and Machinery, which is a category that does not appear on Quicken's standard list (you can add it). You get the point...you have to apply the debit to some category so you can offset the credit to payables.

262

When you enter a category, Quicken may ask if it should record the transaction. This dialog box is shown in Figure 11.6.

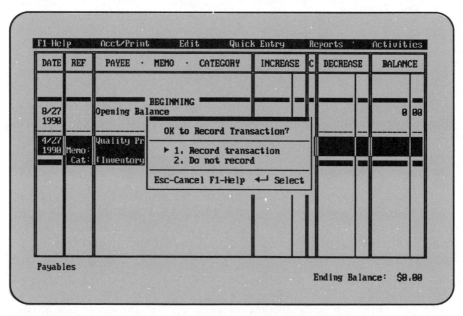

Figure 11.6. Quicken prompts to record a transaction.

Select option 1 to record the transaction; this posts the amount to the proper account (category).

Finally, use a class to enter the invoice number that appears on the vendor's bill. This should include a code for the vendor, plus the invoice number. For example, invoice number 18808 from Quality Printing might be entered as QP18808. All vendor codes should be unique. This will help you distinguish between vendors that have similar invoice numbers, and it will let Quicken produce reports that group these invoice numbers by vendor.

To add a class, leave the cursor in the Category line after you insert the category name. Then, press Ctrl-L and create a new class for the invoice. (Alternatively, you can press the F4 key and choose the Select/Set Up Class option.) This class will now appear in the Class List and can be used for all transactions relating to that invoice. You can also type a slash (\) and then the class entry. Quicken will then offer to add it to the list for you.

If you use a purchase order system for tracking purchases, then enter your company's P.O. number instead of the vendor's ID and invoice number. However, you may still want to enter the vendor ID in front of your P.O. number so you can categorize the invoices by vendor. Figure 11.7 shows a typical invoice entry into the payables journal.

After you've entered all payables, the Ending Balance shown at the bottom of the screen will reflect the total.

Tracking Payables Due

So far, the payables journal has no way of tracking the due date for your bills. You will certainly want to create reports that show when your bills are due—not just how much is due.

For this, you can continue to use the post-dated check technique. When you enter a payable into the payables journal, create a post-dated check for that amount using the Write Checks screen. This will track the due dates for the invoices you owe. But in this case do not enter the category or any category in the Category blank. This will keep Quicken from updating the payables register prematurely. Later, when you actually pay the bill, go back to that check, enter the category, and print the check.

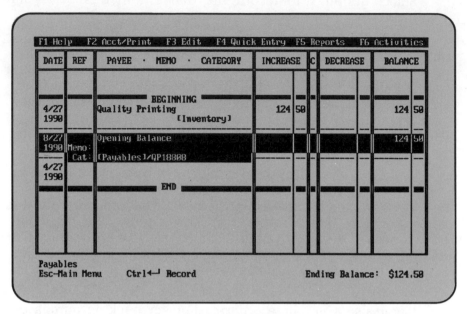

Figure 11.7. Entering a payable with category and class.

Refer to the section "Payables Budgeting with Cash Accounting" earlier in this chapter for additional information on the post-dating technique.

Another way to track due dates is to use a subclass entry to record the date. This will appear on the Category line of the journal along with the category name and the class. Subclasses can be entered in the form:

`Category/Class:Subclass`

Simply type a colon and enter a new class consisting of the due date for the invoice. (If you do not define the subclass first, then Quicken will give you the opportunity to add it to the class list after you enter it on the line.) The due date should be entered in the form:

`YYMMDD`

For example, the date January 21, 1991 should be entered *910121*. This lets you sort the dates chronologically in your reports.

Creating a Receivables Account

Creating a receivables account is just like creating a payables account, except that it must be another asset account. Use the steps listed for creating a payables account, but choose option 4 for Other Asset for the account type (step 3) rather than option 5.

Just as with the payables account, the receivables account should begin with a zero balance, and you should enter all outstanding receivables individually. This lets you track each invoice as well as the total receivables figure.

When you enter a receivable, type the date of the invoice in the Date column. Enter the name of the buyer in the Payee column and the amount of the invoice in the Increase column. Notice that the Increase column is on the right and the Decrease column is on the left. That's because this is an asset account and Quicken places decreases on the left. You might find this a bit unorthodox if you're familiar with traditional accounting systems.

265

Finally, use a class to record your company's invoice number. This will appear alongside the category name for the offsetting entry. Figure 11.8 shows a typical receivables entry.

In this example, the offsetting entry is immediately posted to the Inventory account as a decrease. Figure 11.9 shows this automatic entry.

> ▶ **Note**: Refer to Chapter 13 for details about setting up an inventory account.

> **Caution**: These transaction examples should not be construed as suggesting the proper way to account for your business' assets and liabilities; they are merely examples to show how the system works. Consult your accountant for advise on the proper use of categories.

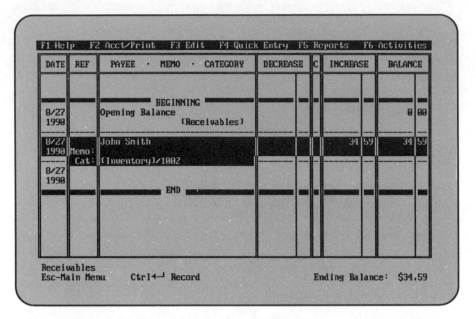

Figure 11.8. Entry showing your company's invoice number.

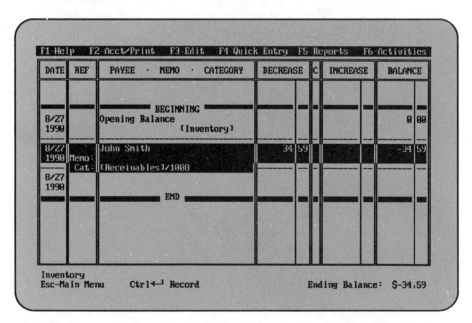

Figure 11.9. Recording an entry in the inventory account.

Other Asset and Liability Accounts

Now that you've used the other asset and other liability accounts, you can continue to add various payables and receivables accounts in the same way. You may need a long-term Notes payable account as well as a short-term notes payable account, for instance. These will all become categories for transactions and will affect your balance sheet.

Transaction Examples

Your system is set. Provided you accurately apply debits and credits to the proper categories, your accounts will provide a wealth of information about your business. Now let's look at some example transactions. This example system includes an inventory account, which is explained in Chapter 13. You may want to turn to that chapter if you plan to include inventory in your system.

267

When income comes in from your sales, you may make daily deposits. If so, just be sure to split the income into it's proper categories when you tally the deposit sheet. A deposit log will help in this. Chances are, most of the income will be attributed to Gross Sales. However, if you have added income categories, you might want to split the deposit further. Suppose today's deposit looks like this:

Gross Sales	$500.00
Other Income	$35.55
Total	$535.55

This is simply a matter of splitting the deposit transaction in your checking account's register. Simply enter the deposit into your checking account and press Ctrl-S to split the categories when you reach the Category line. Figure 11.10 shows the split for the categories.

```
 F1 Help        Acct/Print      Edit       Quick Entry      Reports       Activities
┌─────┬────┬────────────────────────────────┬─────────┬─┬─────────┬─────────┐
│DATE │NUM │ PAYEE  ·  MEMO  ·  CATEGORY     │ PAYMENT │C│ DEPOSIT │ BALANCE │
├─────┼────┼────────────────────────────────┼─────────┼─┼─────────┼─────────┤
│ 8/27│    │Deposit                         │         │ │  535 55 │         │
│ 1990│Memo│                                │         │ │         │         │
│     │Cat │                                │         │ │         │         │
└─────┴────┴────────────────────────────────┴─────────┴─┴─────────┴─────────┘
               Split Transaction

        Category              Description            Amount
   1:Gr Sales                                        500.00
   2:Other Inc                                        35.55
   3:
   4:
   5:
   6:
            Enter categories, descriptions, and amounts
   Esc-Cancel    Ctrl-D Delete    F9-Recalc Transaction Total    Ctrl↵ Done

 BofA Checking

                                        Ending Balance:  $3,095.44
```

Figure 11.10. Splitting a deposit in the check register.

► **Note:** If any of the checks in your deposit apply to outstanding receivables, you should reference Receivables as the category, along with the amount and invoice number. More on this later.

Now let's try receiving a different kind of income: a receivable. Suppose you make a sale for $145.50 on terms. The invoice you give the customer is number 1024.

First, enter the receivables journal for this entry. Then enter the name of the customer in the PAYEE column and invoice amount in the INCREASE column. When you reach the CATEGORY line, press Ctrl-C to view the available categories. Select Inventory (remember, you must create the inventory account before this category appears). Now type a slash (/) and enter your invoice number. Figure 11.11 shows this transaction.

```
 F1 Help   F2 Acct/Print   F3 Edit   F4 Quick Entry  F5 Reports   F6 Activities
┌──────┬─────┬──────────────────────────────┬──────────┬──┬──────────┬──────────┐
│ DATE │ REF │ PAYEE  ·  MEMO  ·  CATEGORY  │ DECREASE │C │ INCREASE │ BALANCE  │
├──────┼─────┼──────────────────────────────┼──────────┼──┼──────────┼──────────┤
│      │     │          BEGINNING           │          │  │          │          │
│ 8/27 │     │Opening Balance               │          │  │          │      0 00│
│ 1990 │     │              [Receivables]   │          │  │          │          │
│ 8/27 │     │John Smith                    │          │  │    34 59 │    34 59 │
│ 1990 │     │            [Inventory]/10·   │          │  │          │          │
│ 8/27 │Memo:│Fry & Jones, Inc.             │          │  │   145 50 │          │
│ 1990 │Cat.:│Inventory/1024                │          │  │          │          │
│      │     │                              │          │  │          │          │
└──────┴─────┴──────────────────────────────┴──────────┴──┴──────────┴──────────┘
 Receivables
 Esc-Main Menu     Ctrl←┘ Record                      Ending Balance:  $34.59
```

Figure 11.11. A receivables transaction.

When you press Enter to complete the transaction, you will be asked if you want to add the invoice number to the Class List. Go ahead and add the number. You will then be asked if you want to record the transaction. Definitely record the transaction.

Now suppose a week has passed and Mr. Jones pays his bill. You deposit his check along with several others. The total deposit is $345.54. Simply enter the deposit into the check register as you did in the earlier example. Split the transaction into its various parts.

In this case the check for $145.50 should be separated into its own category: Receivables/1024. This will cause the transaction to post the amount to the receivables account and reference invoice number 1024 as the class. Later, your "open invoices" report will show this invoice as paid. All amounts posted to receivables should be split in the deposit transaction and shown individually under the Receivables category with the invoice number as the class.

What You Have Learned

This chapter provided details about setting up and using Payables and Receivables accounts in Quicken. The example transactions should give you a practical guide to using these accounts and explain how to handle specific transactions. Here's what you learned:

▶ To use Quicken for double-entry accounting, you must assign a category to each and every transaction you enter.

▶ All cash management is done with your basic cash accounts: Checking, Credit Card, and Cash.

▶ When using a credit card account, enter a category for the expense when you type the transaction. This generates an expense at the time of the purchase—which is the correct method. Later, when you pay the credit card bill, you'll perform a transfer from the checking account to the credit card account.

▶ By entering bills (payables) as post-dated checks, you can use Quicken to track your payables due by date and payee.

▶ The A/P by vendor report shows you which post-dated checks are still open and provides a payables list by vendor name.

▶ Use another asset account to track receivables and an other liability account to track payables. These accounts will also be categories for other accounts.

▶ Payables and receivables should be posted at the time they are generated, even though they have not changed your cash.

▶ Start all payables and receivables accounts with a zero balance—then enter all outstanding payables and receivables as individual transactions. Although this means a little more work, it helps you track payables and receivables by invoice number and name.

▶ When entering payables transactions, use a class entry to store the vendor's invoice number. Add a vendor ID code to their invoice number for best results. You can add a class by typing a slash (\) and then entering the class information.

▶ When entering a receivables transaction, use a class entry to store your company's invoice number.

▶ When customers pay their bills, be sure that each check is entered individually in the deposit transaction. This is done by splitting the transaction. Be sure that each check is entered along with the invoice number being paid. Checks and cash from non-receivables income can be grouped together.

271

272

Chapter 12

Business Reporting with Quicken

In This Chapter

273

- ▶ *Cash flow reports*
- ▶ *Customizing cash flow reports*
- ▶ *The A/P by vendor report*
- ▶ *Creating an open invoices report for payables and receivables*
- ▶ *Account history report*
- ▶ *Trial balances*

This chapter continues with the information presented in Chapter 11. Using the accounts set up in that chapter, you'll learn how to print various business reports, including payables, receivables, and trial balance reports. Many people use custom setups, which are simple variations on built-in reports. By the end of this chapter, you'll be able to customize reports for many business needs.

Cash Flow Reports

Quicken provides a built-in cash flow report that helps you see your overall cash inflows and outflows. This can be useful for keeping your monthly expenses in check—or for seeing trends in income and expenses.

The cash flow report uses your cash journals to produce its summary. This includes your bank accounts, credit card accounts, and cash accounts. The report groups each transaction in your cash journals into income and expense categories, then it provides total income and total expense figures. Just remember that only transactions posted in the registers affect this report; unprinted checks will not be part of this report.

Let's take a look at the example checking account used in Chapter 11. A few transactions, including some unprinted checks listed at the bottom of the screen, are posted in this account. Figure 12.1 shows the transactions in this register.

274

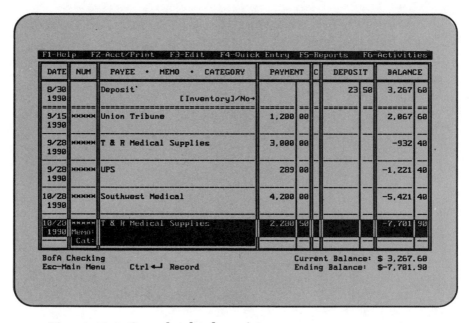

Figure 12.1. Sample check register.

Notice that the current balance and ending balance figures differ. This is due to the unprinted checks listed. Do not use the ending balance when you use the post-dated check system described here.

In addition, the credit card account contains a few transactions that will affect the cash flow report. This includes an opening balance, a purchase, and a payment (see Figure 12.2).

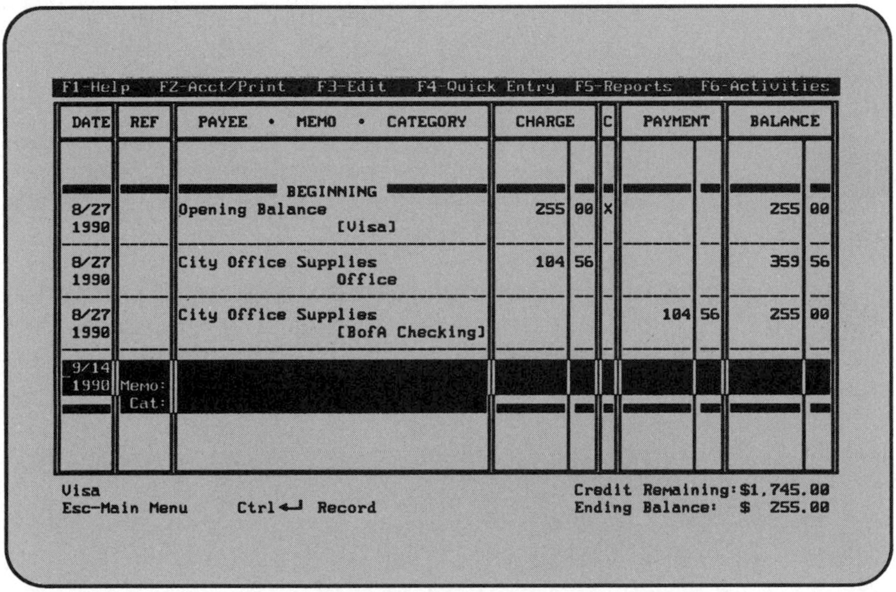

275

```
 F1-Help   F2-Acct/Print   F3-Edit   F4-Quick Entry  F5-Reports   F6-Activities

 DATE  REF   PAYEE • MEMO • CATEGORY    CHARGE   C  PAYMENT   BALANCE


                      ═══ BEGINNING ═══
 8/27       Opening Balance              255 00 X           255 00
 1990                    [Visa]

 8/27       City Office Supplies         104 56            359 56
 1990                    Office

 8/27       City Office Supplies                   104 56  255 00
 1990                    [BofA Checking]

 9/14  Memo:
 1990  Cat:


 Visa                                   Credit Remaining:$1,745.00
 Esc-Main Menu     Ctrl↵  Record        Ending Balance:  $  255.00
```

Figure 12.2. Transaction in a credit card account.

Now let's see what the cash flow report produces. Follow these steps to produce the report.

Q Producing the Cash Flow Report

1. From the main menu,
   select option 3 for Reports.
2. Select option 1 for Personal
   Reports.
3. Select option 1 for Cash
   Flow.

4. Enter a report title if desired. This example uses the title "ABC Cash." Press Enter when you finish with the title. (Note: The report title is optional; you can press Tab or Enter to skip it.)

5. Press Enter twice.

Accepts Quicken's dates. Quicken already knows the date limits for the report—based on the transaction dates in the journals. Usually, you won't need to change these dates, unless you plan to restrict the report to certain dates. □

276

The result of this report is shown in Figure 12.3. Notice that categories are combined from both the checking and credit card journals. Office Expenses, for example, is a total from both journals.

```
                                ABCCASH
                      1/ 1/90 Through 9/30/90
ABC_CORP-Bank,Cash,CC Accounts                                    Page 1
9/14/90
                                          1/ 1/90-
                      Category Description   9/30/90
                      ----------------------  ----------

                      INFLOWS
                        Gross Sales          2,500.00
                        Other Income            35.55
                        FROM Receivables        34.59
                        FROM FEDWITH           120.00
                        FROM FICA              235.50
                        FROM Inventory          23.50
                        FROM STWITH             23.50
                                             ----------
                      TOTAL INFLOWS          2,972.64

                      OUTFLOWS
                        Business FICA          120.55
                        Freight                295.50
                        Gross Payroll        1,459.00
                        Office Expenses        230.54
                        Outflows - Other     4,489.00
                                             ----------
                      TOTAL OUTFLOWS         6,594.59

                                             ----------
                      OVERALL TOTAL         -3,621.95
                                             ==========
```

Figure 12.3. Cash flow report.

Customizing the Cash Flow Report

Now let's look at customizing this report. For one thing, you might want to break out the cash totals into monthly subtotals. You can do this by listing each month across the top of the report as headings for columns. Then, list the categories down the left side with monthly totals in each column.

Ⓠ Customizing the Cash Flow Report

1. From the main menu, select option 3 for Reports.

2. Select option 1 for Personal Reports.

3. Select option 1 for Cash Flow.

    Shows Cash Flow Report screen, where you can enter the report title.

    277

4. Press the F8 key to enter the customization screen.

    The window in Figure 12.4 appears.

5. Press Tab to change the various settings in this screen, as desired.

    This example uses option 5 for Month as the setting for column headings. This will produce monthly subtotals for each category down the left side. This example also restricts transaction dates to match the data in the registers.

6. When finished with the custom settings, press Enter until the report prints.

    ☐

Figure 12.5 shows the final report.

> ▶ **Note:** For more information about printing and customizing reports, see Chapter 10.

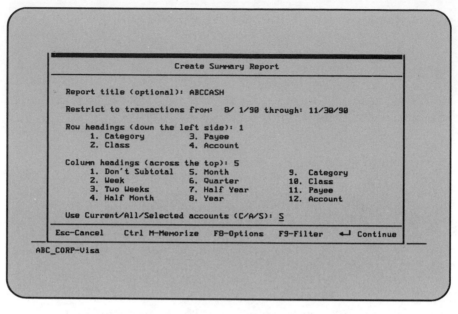

Figure 12.4. Customization options for cash flow report.

278

The A/R and A/P Reports

The accounts payable and accounts receivable reports are summary reports, just like the cash flow report seen earlier in this chapter. A summary report lists items down the left side and subtotals (and totals) across the top. As you saw in the cash flow example, you can use the customization screen to choose the items that are listed down and across the report.

The accounts payable report shows the vendor (or payee) down the left side of the page and months subtotaled across the top. Refer to Figure 12.6 to see the A/P by vendor report, which shows the form specified by the default.

This report is listed in the business reports group and comes from your unprinted checks. The only thing to remember about this report is that you must keep your unprinted checks up to date. Be sure to print checks when you actually pay the bills—or remove them from the register.

```
                              ABCCASH
                    8/ 1/90 Through 11/30/90
ABC_CORP-Selected Accounts                                    Page 1
9/14/90

  Category Description      8/90         9/90        10/90        11/90
-----------------------  ----------  ----------  ----------  ----------
INFLOWS
  Gross Sales             2,500.00        0.00        0.00         0.00
  Other Income               35.55        0.00        0.00         0.00
  FROM Receivables           34.59        0.00        0.00         0.00
  FROM Inventory             23.50        0.00        0.00         0.00
                         ----------  ----------  ----------  ----------
TOTAL INFLOWS             2,593.64        0.00        0.00         0.00

OUTFLOWS
  Freight                   295.50        0.00        0.00         0.00
  Office Expenses           230.54        0.00        0.00         0.00
  Outflows - Other            0.00    4,489.00    6,480.50         0.00
                         ----------  ----------  ----------  ----------
TOTAL OUTFLOWS              526.04    4,489.00    6,480.50         0.00

                         ----------  ----------  ----------  ----------
OVERALL TOTAL             2,067.60   -4,489.00   -6,480.50         0.00
                         ==========  ==========  ==========  ==========
```

279

```
                              ABCCASH
                    8/ 1/90 Through 11/30/90
ABC_CORP-Selected Accounts                                    Page 2
9/14/90
                          OVERALL
  Category Description      TOTAL
-----------------------  ----------
INFLOWS
  Gross Sales             2,500.00
  Other Income               35.55
  FROM Receivables           34.59
  FROM Inventory             23.50
                         ----------
TOTAL INFLOWS             2,593.64

OUTFLOWS
  Freight                   295.50
  Office Expenses           230.54
  Outflows - Other       10,969.50
                         ----------
TOTAL OUTFLOWS           11,495.54

                         ----------
OVERALL TOTAL            -8,901.90
                         ==========
```

Figure 12.5. Final customized report.

Another way to view payables is to customize the job/project report. The job/project report is listed in the business reports group. After you select this report, press the F8 key to customize it. Figure 12.7 shows what the customization screen should look like. When you print the report, Quicken will ask you to select the desired accounts for inclusion. Using the Spacebar, leave all accounts out of the report except payables. That is, select only payables for the report. The result will look something like Figure 12.7.

You can prepare an accounts receivable report by customizing a transaction report. A transaction report does not summarize (or total) categories or classes from various accounts; instead, it lists all transactions that have common categories or classes. Using a transaction report, you can list each invoice in your receivables account and see which have balances due. Here are the steps for creating the receivables report.

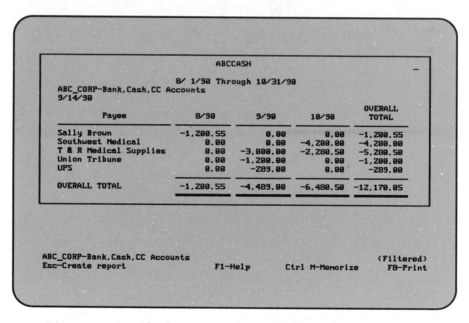

Figure 12.6. Default accounts payable by vendor report.

1. From the main menu, select option 3 for Reports. Then select option 1 for Personal Reports. Finally, select option 3 for Itemized Categories. This gets you to the Itemized Category screen, where you can enter the report title.

2. Press the F8 key to customize the report. The transaction report screen appears; select options for the custom report here.

```
                                    ABCCASH
                         8/ 1/90 Through 11/30/90
ABC_CORP-Payables                                                     Page 1
9/14/90

  Class Description        8/90             9/90            10/90
---------------------  ---------------  ---------------  ---------------
Invoice                    0.00             0.00             0.00
Invoice:
   Inventory Item       -230.00             0.00             0.00
                       -----------      -----------      -----------
Total Invoice          -230.00             0.00             0.00
SM889-334:
   Inventory Item          0.00         -4,200.00            0.00
                       -----------      -----------      -----------
TOTAL SM889-334            0.00         -4,200.00            0.00
TR10012:
   Inventory Item      -5,280.50            0.00             0.00
                       -----------      -----------      -----------
TOTAL TR10012          -5,280.50            0.00             0.00
UPS34-12               -289.00             0.00             0.00
UT2390                -1,200.00            0.00             0.00
                       -----------      -----------      -----------
OVERALL TOTAL         -6,999.50         -4,200.00            0.00
                       ===========      ===========      ===========
```

281

```
                                    ABCCASH
                         8/ 1/90 Through 11/30/90
ABC_CORP-Payables                                                     Page 2
9/14/90
                        OVERALL
  11/90                  TOTAL
---------------  ---------------
    0.00             0.00

    0.00          -230.00
-----------      -----------
    0.00          -230.00

    0.00         -4,200.00
-----------      -----------
    0.00         -4,200.00

    0.00         -5,280.50
-----------      -----------
    0.00         -5,280.50
    0.00          -289.00
    0.00        -1,200.00
-----------      -----------
    0.00        -11,199.50
===========      ===========
```

Figure 12.7. Customized job/project report with invoice numbers.

3. Enter a title and a date range appropriate for the report. Next, choose option 10 for Class for the Subtotal. This will give you a listing of each invoice since invoice numbers are used as the class.

4. Enter an S in the final option to select accounts for the report. Press Enter when finished.

5. Finally, make sure that only the receivables account is included in this report, as shown in Figure 12.8. Quicken will place all other asset accounts into the report. This is not desired. Use the Spacebar to deselect other accounts.

This will display open receivables by invoice number. The final report will look like Figure 12.9. Any item that has a balance due is still open and should be collected.

> ▶ **Tip**: You can use this same report format for an open payables report. Follow the same steps but choose only the payables account for inclusion in the report. You might prefer this report to the A/P by vendor report—although the receivables report has no due dates associated with it. If you use a subclass to hold the due dates (as suggested in the previous chapter), this report will provide all you need.

Another built-in format that you might find useful is the A/R by customer report. This is listed in the business report group, and it organizes the transactions in your other asset accounts by the payee. The payees are listed down the left side of the report, and the months are subtotaled along the top. This provides a history of your receivables, including deposits that are transferred to the receivables account (that is, payments made on the invoices). However, this will not categorize the deposits by invoice number.

Trial Balances

The final report to discuss in this chapter is a simple ending balance printout for each account. You can do this with a transaction report, which is much like the open receivables report created above. In this case, choose option 9 for Category for the Subtotal by option when you get to the customization screen. Select all your accounts for inclusion in the report. This totals all transactions in all accounts by category. This is useful for an ending figure in a trial balance sheet. If you remember not to include the

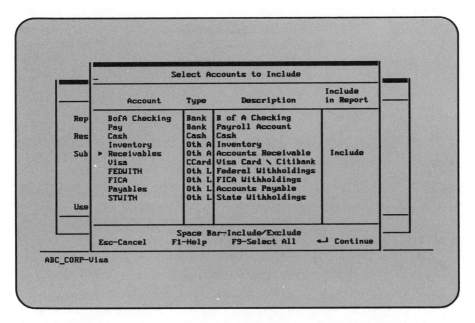

Figure 12.8. The final step in customizing the transaction
report.

```
                                  REPORT
                          8/ 1/90 Through 11/30/90
ABC_CORP-Receivables                                                  Page 1
9/14/90

    Date   Num      Description        Memo        Category     Clr Amount
    -----  ------   ----------------   ----------  -----------  --- --------

           1008
           ----
    8/27            John Smith                     [Inventory]/1008    34.59
    8/29            Deposit                         [BofA Checking]/1  -34.59
                                                                     --------
           TOTAL 1008                                                   0.00

           1024
           ----
    8/27            Fry & Jones, Inc.              [Inventory]/1024   145.50
                                                                     --------
           TOTAL 1024                                                 145.50

           Transactions - Other
           --------------------
    8/27            Opening Balance               [Receivables]        0.00
                                                                     --------
           Total Transactions - Other                                  0.00
                                                                     --------
           OVERALL TOTAL                                              145.50
                                                                     ========
```

Figure 12.9. The final receivables report.

category in post-dated checks, then these checks will appear in this report under "Expenses—Other" and can be ignored. If you include the categories when you create post-dated checks, they will be distributed throughout the report and will throw off the figures. Figure 12.10 shows an example of this report.

What You Have Learned

This chapter discussed business reporting with Quicken. Here's what you learned:

284

▶ The cash flow report summarizes your cash transactions—not including unprinted checks in the check register. This is useful for tracking your cash.

▶ You can customize the cash flow report (and any report) by pressing the F8 key after selecting the report from the list of built-in reports.

▶ There are really only two types of reports in Quicken: summary reports and transaction reports. Most built-in reports are simply variations (customizations) of these two styles.

▶ A customized job/project report can be useful for tracking payables by invoice number.

▶ By customizing the transaction report, you can produce a list of receivables by invoice number or customer.

▶ You can create a report that summarizes the activity in each account. This is often called a trial balance report. Simply customize a transaction report so that it's subtotaled by the category.

```
                              REPORT
                      8/ 1/90 Through 11/30/90
ABC_CORP-Selected Accounts                                    Page 1
9/14/90

  Date   Acct      Num     Description      Memo      Category    Clr  Amount
  -----  --------  ------  ----------------  -----------  ---------------  -  ----------

         INCOME/EXPENSE
           INCOME
             Gross Sales
             -----------
  8/27 BofA Che         Deposit                        Gr Sales         2,000.00
  8/27 BofA Che       S Deposit                        Gr Sales           500.00
                                                                      ----------
             Total Gross Sales                                         2,500.00

             Other Income
             ------------
  8/27 BofA Che       S Deposit                        Other Inc          35.55
                                                                      ----------
             Total Other Income                                           35.55
                                                                      ----------
           TOTAL INCOME                                                2,535.55

           EXPENSES
             Advertising
             -----------
  8/28 Payables            Union Tribune   Three ads   Ads/UT2390      -1,200.00
                                                                      ----------
             Total Advertising                                        -1,200.00

             Business FICA
             -------------
  8/31 Pay        *****S Sally Brown       Company's F  BUSFica          -120.55
                                                                      ----------
             Total Business FICA                                         -120.55

             Freight
             -------
  8/28 BofA Che 103   United Freight S                 Freight          -295.50
  8/28 Payables        UPS                             Freight/UPS34-   -289.00
                                                                      ----------
             Total Freight                                              -584.50

             Gross Payroll
             -------------
  8/31 Pay        *****S Sally Brown       Gross Pay   Payroll        -1,459.00
                                                                      ----------
             Total Gross Payroll                                      -1,459.00

             Office Expenses
```

Figure 12.10. Ending balances for all categories using all accounts.

```
                              REPORT
                     8/ 1/90 Through 11/30/90
ABC_CORP-Selected Accounts                                    Page 2
9/14/90

  Date    Acct    Num    Description     Memo     Category   Clr  Amount
  -----  -------- ------  -------------- -------- ---------- - ----------
                  --------------
  8/28 BofA Che 102      Pac Bell                 Office          -125.98
  8/27 Visa              City Office Supp         Office          -104.56
                                                              ----------
            Total Office Expenses                                -230.54

            Expenses - Other
            ----------------
  9/15 BofA Che *****  Union Tribune                          -1,200.00
  9/28 BofA Che *****  T & R Medical Su                       -3,000.00
  9/28 BofA Che *****  UPS                                      -289.00
 10/28 BofA Che *****  Southwest Medica                       -4,200.00
 10/28 BofA Che *****  T & R Medical Su                       -2,280.50
                                                              ----------
            Total Expenses - Other                           -10,969.50
                                                              ----------
         TOTAL EXPENSES                                       -14,564.09
                                                              ----------

         TOTAL INCOME/EXPENSE                                 ----------
                                                             -12,028.54

         TRANSFERS
            TO Receivables
            ---------------
  8/27 Inventor        John Smith         [Receivables]/        -34.59
  8/27 Inventor        Fry & Jones, Inc   [Receivables]/       -145.50
                                                              ----------
            Total TO Receivables                               -180.09

            TO BofA Checking
            ----------------
  8/30 Inventor        Deposit`           [BofA Checking        -23.50
  8/29 Receivab        Deposit            [BofA Checking        -34.59
                                                              ----------
            Total TO BofA Checking                             -58.09

            TO Inventory
            ------------
  8/28 Payables        T & R Medical Su   [Inventory]/TR     -5,280.50
  8/30 Payables        Billings Medical   [Inventory]/BM       -230.00
  9/12 Payables        Southwest Medica   [Inventory]/SM     -4,200.00
                                                              ----------
            Total TO Inventory                               -9,710.50

            TO Pay
```

Figure 12.10. (continued)

```
                              REPORT
                    8/ 1/90 Through 11/30/90
ABC_CORP-Selected Accounts                              Page 3
9/14/90

  Date   Acct    Num    Description     Memo      Category    Clr  Amount
  -----  ------  -----  -------------   --------  ----------  ---  --------
         ------
  8/31 FEDWITH          Sally Brown               [Pay]            -120.00
  8/31 FICA             Sally Brown               [Pay]            -235.50
  8/31 STWITH           Sally Brown               [Pay]             -23.50
                                                                  ---------
            Total TO Pay                                          -379.00

            TO Visa
            -------
  8/27 BofA Che 101     City Office Supp          [Visa]           -104.56
                                                                  ---------
            Total TO Visa                                         -104.56

            FROM Payables
            -------------
  8/28 Inventor         T & R Medical Su          [Payables]/TR1  5,280.50
  8/30 Inventor         Billings Medical          [Payables]/BMS    230.00
  9/12 Inventor         Southwest Medica          [Payables]/SM8  4,200.00
                                                                  ---------
            Total FROM Payables                                  9,710.50

            FROM Receivables
            ----------------
  8/29 BofA Che         Deposit                   [Receivables]/     34.59
                                                                  ---------
            Total FROM Receivables                                  34.59

            FROM BofA Checking
            ------------------
  8/27 Visa             City Office Supp          [BofA Checking    104.56
                                                                  ---------
            Total FROM BofA Checking                               104.56

            FROM FEDWITH
            ------------
  8/31 Pay       *****S Sally Brown  Federal Wit  [FEDWITH]         120.00
                                                                  ---------
            TOTAL FROM FEDWITH                                      120.00

            FROM FICA
            ---------
  8/31 Pay       *****S Sally Brown  Fica With    [FICA]            235.50
                                                                  ---------
            TOTAL FROM FICA                                         235.50

            FROM Inventory
```

Figure 12.10. (continued)

```
                                    REPORT
                           8/ 1/90 Through 11/30/90
     ABC_CORP-Selected Accounts                                      Page 4
     9/14/90

     Date    Acct     Num    Description      Memo      Category  Clr  Amount
     -----  --------  ------ --------------- ----------- --------------- - ----------
            --------------
     8/30 BofA Che          Deposit'                    [Inventory]/No      23.50
     8/27 Receivab          John Smith                  [Inventory]/10      34.59
     8/27 Receivab          Fry & Jones, Inc            [Inventory]/10     145.50
                                                                        ----------
            Total FROM Inventory                                           203.59

            FROM STWITH
            -----------
     8/31 Pay       *****S Sally Brown     State With   [STWITH]            23.50
                                                                        ----------
            TOTAL FROM STWITH                                               23.50
                                                                        ----------
            TOTAL TRANSFERS                                                  0.00

            BALANCE FORWARD
              Payables
              --------
     8/27 Payables          Opening Balance             [Payables]/QP1       0.00
                                                                        ----------
            Total Payables                                                   0.00

            Receivables
            -----------
     8/27 Receivab          Opening Balance             [Receivables]        0.00
                                                                        ----------
            Total Receivables                                                0.00

            BofA Checking
            -------------
     8/27 BofA Che          Opening Balance             [BofA Checking X 1,200.00
                                                                        ----------
            Total BofA Checking                                          1,200.00

            Cash
            ----
     8/27 Cash              Opening Balance             [Cash]             100.00
                                                                        ----------
            Total Cash                                                     100.00

            FEDWITH
            -------
     8/31 FEDWITH           Opening Balance             [FEDWITH]            0.00
                                                                        ----------
            TOTAL FEDWITH                                                    0.00
```

288

Figure 12.10. (continued)

```
                              REPORT
                    8/ 1/90 Through 11/30/90
ABC_CORP-Selected Accounts                              Page 5
9/14/90
   Date   Acct    Num    Description    Memo    Category   Clr  Amount
   -----  ------- ------  --------------  ---------- --------------- -  ----------

          FICA
          ----
   8/31 FICA              Opening Balance         [FICA]             0.00
                                                                ----------
          TOTAL FICA                                                0.00

          Inventory
          ---------
   8/27 Inventor         Opening Balance         [Inventory]        0.00
   8/30 Inventor         Southwest Medica        [Inventory]/No   124.50
   8/30 Inventor         Medical Supplier        [Inventory]/No   450.00
   8/30 Inventor         Medical Supplier        [Inventory]/No   200.00
                                                                ----------
          Total Inventory                                        774.50

          Pay
          ---
   8/31 Pay              Opening Balance         [Pay]       X 10,000.00
                                                                ----------
          Total Pay                                          10,000.00

          STWITH
          ------
   8/31 STWITH           Opening Balance         [STWITH]           0.00
                                                                ----------
          TOTAL STWITH                                             0.00

          Visa
          ----
   8/27 Visa             Opening Balance         [Visa]      X  -255.00
                                                                ----------
          Total Visa                                          -255.00
                                                                ----------
          TOTAL BALANCE FORWARD                             11,819.50

                                                                ----------
          OVERALL TOTAL                                       -209.04
                                                                ==========
```

289

Figure 12.10. (continued)

290

Quicken Applications

In This Chapter

▶ Home/personal inventory
▶ Business inventory
▶ Tracking home repairs and improvements
▶ Budgeting expenses
▶ Managing rental properties
▶ Managing payroll
▶ Non-account applications of Quicken

There's practically no limit to the ways you can use Quicken. Although Quicken is primarily a check register program for the home and small business, its versatility lets you use it to track all kinds of financial records. Business examples include handling payroll, tracking inventory, and managing rental properties.

In this chapter, you'll discover some additional business uses for Quicken, as well as some interesting personal uses. You'll learn how to use Quicken to track your business inventory (primarily for balance sheet preparation), to budget expenses, and to maintain payroll records.

Home/Personal Inventory

Take a mental journey through your home and catalog your personal belongings. Even if you spend hours on this exercise, you would probably miss thousands of dollars in personal property—a camera that's stuffed away in a closet somewhere, a large record collection that you simply take for granted, summer and fall clothes stashed away in a cedar closet.

In the event of a fire, flood, burglary, or other catastrophe, would you remember about all your belongings and recall their worth? More importantly, would your insurance company reimburse you for personal belongings you say you had, but have no record of?

292

You can use Quicken to maintain an inventory of everything you own. You can catalog all of your personal belongings in one account or create several accounts—one for furniture, one for jewelry, one for clothes, and so forth. Figure 13.1 shows an example of a Quicken Other Asset register used to record entries of a video movie collection.

The register lets you record many details about your personal belongings. As shown in the example, you can use the date column to indicate the date of acquisition. If you don't care about when you bought an item—or can't remember—use the current date. The reference column can be used to code items. If you're creating one large register, for example, you can use the REF column to indicate the type of item being cataloged —JEWEL for jewelry, CLOTH for clothes, COIN for coins in a coin collection, and ELEC for electronic items like keyboards, TVs, radios, and stereos.

The PAYEE/MEMO/CATEGORY column is used to describe the item. Enter a description, such as "Microwave Oven" or "Fur coat," in the top line of the PAYEE/MEMO/CATEGORY column. You can enter an additional description in the second (memo) line.

The use of categories is up to you. You probably don't need to use categories if you're separating your belongings into individual accounts. If you're compiling one large account that lists all your personal property, you may wish to identify them by using categories and subcategories.

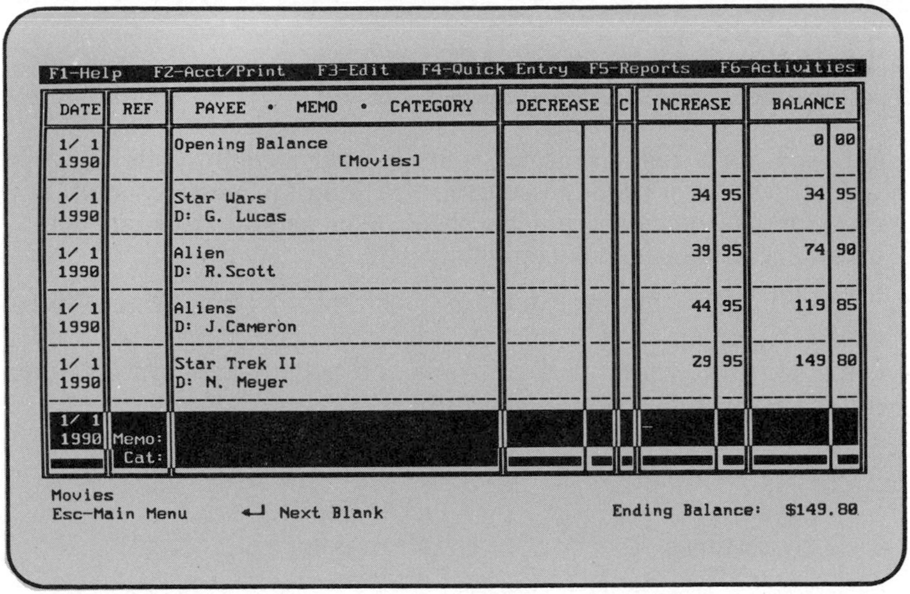

Figure 13.1. Video movie collection example.

Your personal belongings add to your worth, so enter a value (if appropriate) into the INCREASE column of the register. Use the most accurate value you can—whenever possible, avoid estimating the value of your property. With each major purpose, record the item in the register and enter the price you paid. You should probably keep the receipt, especially if the item is covered by a warranty. If you're cataloging jewelry or collectibles, you may need to consult an appraiser or obtain current market values from collector's price books. These price books are available at most book stores, antique shops, and public libraries.

If you don't care about the value of the item, but rather just want to catalog it, leave the INCREASE column blank. Quicken will allow you to record a transaction with the INCREASE and DECREASE columns blank. Alternatively, you may wish to enter a "0.00" in the INCREASE column to indicate that you specifically entered the item without a value.

When you sell or give away a piece of personal property, you should not delete the entry in the register. If you posted a value for the item, replace it with "0.00" so that it won't show up in the Ending Balance for the inventory.

For reference, you can print the register or produce reports, as desired.

Tracking Business Inventory

Quicken does not account for individual inventory items very well. Instead, Quicken is useful for tracking inventory account figures for use on your balance sheet. You should track an actual inventory of hard goods separately.

Quicken uses an inventory account to track transactions made involving your goods. As an account, it can be used as a category from your other journals. To set up this system, you must have the following accounts:

Account Name	Account Type
Payables	Other liability
Receivables	Other asset
Inventory	Other asset

In addition, you should create a COG (Cost of Goods) category as an expense category. You may want to use subcategories to break cost of goods into its various parts, such as shipping, goods, and warehouse expenses:

COG:Shipping
COG:Goods
COG:Other

This creates the appropriate account for categorizing inventory reductions. When it comes to tracking business inventory, there are a few special considerations. For one thing, your inventory journal is being used as an account (or category) for posting transactions from other journals. When you purchase inventory, for example, you write a check for the purchase. This means that you enter the transaction into your checking account journal. The category you specify for the transaction is Inventory. Quicken will decrease the balance in your checking account and increase the amount of inventory you have by the same amount. If you used credit to purchase the items, then you would enter the transaction into the payables journal as a liability. Quicken will increase the liability (payables balance) and increase the inventory amount.

The next transaction occurs when you make a sale. Often, inventory is not shipped at the time of a sale; but even if it ships the same day, your transaction will record the sale to the customer in the form of a receivable or a cash deposit. This transaction will list Gross Sales as the category. When the inventory is shipped, you would create a transaction in the inventory journal that would reduce inventory and list Cost of Goods as the category.

> Ⓝ **Caution**: Remember to check with your accountant for the appropriate use of these accounts in your business. Additional accounts or transactions may be required in this scenario, such as a liability account for unfulfilled sales or an account for returns and allowances that will reduce your gross sales figure. Your accountant will be able to show you the best setup for your business.

295

Suppose a customer purchases an item from inventory for $100. Now that same item was purchased for only $40 and the inventory account shows an increase of $40 back when the item was purchased. Following is the flow of transactions that you would take:

1. If you paid cash for the inventory, enter the transaction in the checking account journal (or appropriate cash journal) and list Inventory as the category. If you have shipping or stocking fees included in the purchase, then split the transaction: List the item's cost as Inventory and the shipping cost as COG:Shipping.

   If you purchased the inventory on credit, enter the transaction in the payables journal and list Inventory as the category with the invoice number as the subcategory. If you have shipping or stocking fees included in the purchase, then split the transaction: List the item's cost as Inventory and the shipping cost as COG:Shipping.

2. When you make a cash sale, list the transaction in the checking account as a deposit and use Gross Sales as the category. This should reflect the total amount of the sale.

   If you make a sale as a receivable, then enter the transaction into the receivables journal and list Gross Sales as the category with your invoice number as the subcategory.

3. When the inventory ships, enter the transaction into the inventory journal for the amount of the inventory (that is, the amount that you paid for the inventory) and list COG:Goods as the category.

> ▶ **Note**: You will have a difference in the ending cost of goods figure and the gross sales figure. This is because you sell items for more than you paid for them. The difference is your gross profit! This will be visible on your balance sheet. At the end of the accounting period, you can transfer gross profit into an asset account, such as equity. Do this by making an adjusting entry in the equity account —another asset account.

296

That's great for balancing the books, but it doesn't track inventory. Somewhere, you'll need a listing of inventory items that can be updated when you purchase new items or sell out of inventory. For example, when you increase the inventory account because of a purchase recorded in the checking account, you should also be able to track specific inventory items. You can do this in Quicken only if you don't use classes to hold invoice numbers (as suggested in this book). This frees the class to be used for listing the inventory items. In this case, when you list Inventory as a category, you can always include a class:

Inventory/Gloves
Inventory/Hats

This technique lets you produce reports that list each inventory item and its balance in the inventory account. This will show you how many of these items are remaining in inventory. However, this is not recommended because it does not let you track payables and receivables by invoice number—because these invoice numbers are listed as the class:

Inventory/SWM1002
Inventory/QP18808

Tracking Home Repairs and Improvements

For most of us, our home is our single most important investment. When you bought your house, you knew it would most likely appreciate in value. Depending on where you live and when you bought your property, your house may earn back enough money that your monthly payments are reimbursed. The net result: you live in your house rent free.

But appreciation doesn't always come swiftly or surely. And taxes often take a big chunk out of any capital gains you may realize on the sale of your home.

One of the best ways to increase the value of your home, while decreasing your taxes when you sell it, is to keep faithful records of your home improvements. Let's say you installed ceiling fans in all three bedrooms, skylights in the living room and entry hall, and new carpeting throughout the house. These items increase the value of your home (beyond the immediate living comfort you enjoy).

297

By recording them—and keeping receipts as backups—you can deduct their cost from the tax basis when the house is sold. If your profit on the house is $10,000, for example, and these improvements cost $3,500, then you're taxed on only $6,500.

Maintaining accurate records of home improvements also helps in increasing the appraised value of your home. An independent appraiser may tack on just $1,500 for the spa you added, even though it's a deluxe $6,000 model with a $2,000 redwood gazebo. Certain types of home improvements may be tax deductible or offer tax rebates. This includes city or state rebates for solar energy panels, water savers, and so forth. Be sure to catalog these as well.

To track home improvements, create an other assets account and enter each improvement as a separate transaction (see Figure 13.2). Enter the date of the improvement (such as the date of completion or purchase date), a description, and the actual cost. If you're adding a substantial upgrade to your house—putting in a family room, for example—use the split transaction feature to catalog the individual costs of the addition. For instance, if the total cost of the addition was $10,000, you might enter $8,700 for labor and materials, $350 for permits, $500 for plumbing hookup, and $450 for paint and materials you bought to finish the inside.

Repairs you make to your home don't affect its tax basis when you sell it, but major repairs should be recorded. This helps when selling your home and also provides you with an accurate accounting of the cost of maintaining your home. You may find, for example, that the fixer-upper you thought you could affordably turn into a cozy cottage is costing you thousands of dollars more each year to repair and maintain. That information could help you decide if you want to keep the house or look for another that doesn't need so much attention.

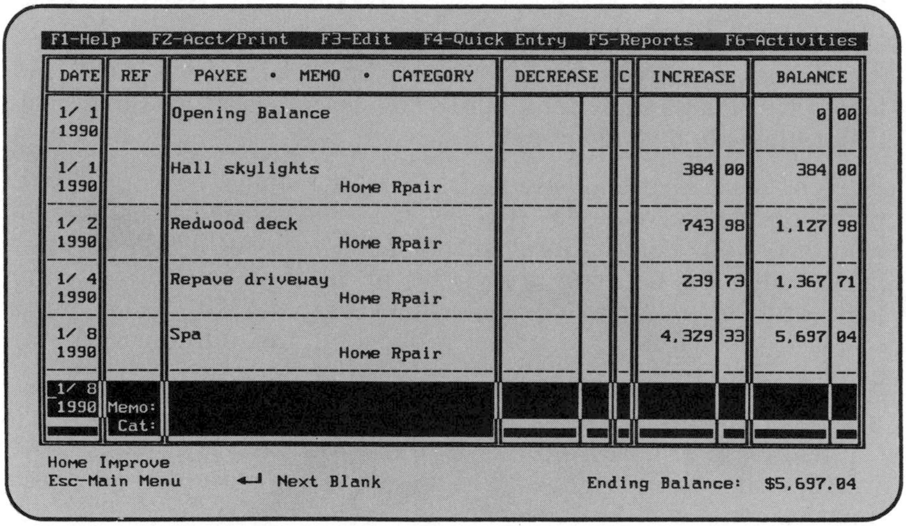

298

DATE	REF	PAYEE • MEMO • CATEGORY	DECREASE	C	INCREASE	BALANCE
1/ 1 1990		Opening Balance				0 00
1/ 1 1990		Hall skylights Home Rpair			384 00	384 00
1/ 2 1990		Redwood deck Home Rpair			743 98	1,127 98
1/ 4 1990		Repave driveway Home Rpair			239 73	1,367 71
1/ 8 1990		Spa Home Rpair			4,329 33	5,697 04
1/ 8 1990		Memo: Cat:				

F1-Help   F2-Acct/Print   F3-Edit   F4-Quick Entry   F5-Reports   F6-Activities

Home Improve
Esc-Main Menu   ↵ Next Blank   Ending Balance: $5,697.04

Figure 13.2. Home Improvements register.

Budgeting Expenses

One of the most useful applications of Quicken is using the program as a "watchdog." If you're on a budget (and who isn't?), you can budget your spending and use Quicken's registers and reports to spot over- and under-spending.

The key to budgeting your expenses is to make sure your transactions are categorized (at least the transactions you want budgeted, like food, clothing, and entertainment). Without the categories, Quicken has no way of knowing how you're spending your money.

The monthly budget report, one of the five preset personal report types Quicken offers, lets you assign budget amounts to the categories you are using. Before printing the report, indicate a monthly budget for those categories (expenses) you want to track. If needed, you can assign a different budgeted amount for each month of the year, as explained in more detail in Chapter 10.

Only those categories that you budgeted will appear in the report. You can have as many or as few budgeted expense categories as you wish. Typical budgeted categories include auto fuel, utilities, dining out, groceries, and home repair and maintenance. Unless you need to keep tabs on them, there's little need to budget for those expenses that are are the same every month. This includes rent, mortgage payment, and car payment.

Quicken's budget reports also include income. This is helpful if you don't get a regular paycheck or supplement your income from other sources. In a given month (or other period of time) you can view your total income and note significant peaks and dips.

299

If you desire, you can create custom monthly budgets. To create a custom budget report, choose Budget at the Report menu and fill in the Create Budget Report window, as shown in Figure 13.3. Indicate the report title and date range for transactions. Also, indicate how you want the columns organized—by week, two weeks, month, year, or none. You can print a report on just the currently selected account, on all accounts, or just on accounts that you identify.

Managing Rental Properties

If you own real estate that you rent to others, you can use Quicken to keep track of your income and expenses. You should maintain each property you own in a separate other assets account. If you own an apartment building, one account can track all the units. You'll need to develop a system whereby you can identify each of the apartments, for rental and expense purposes.

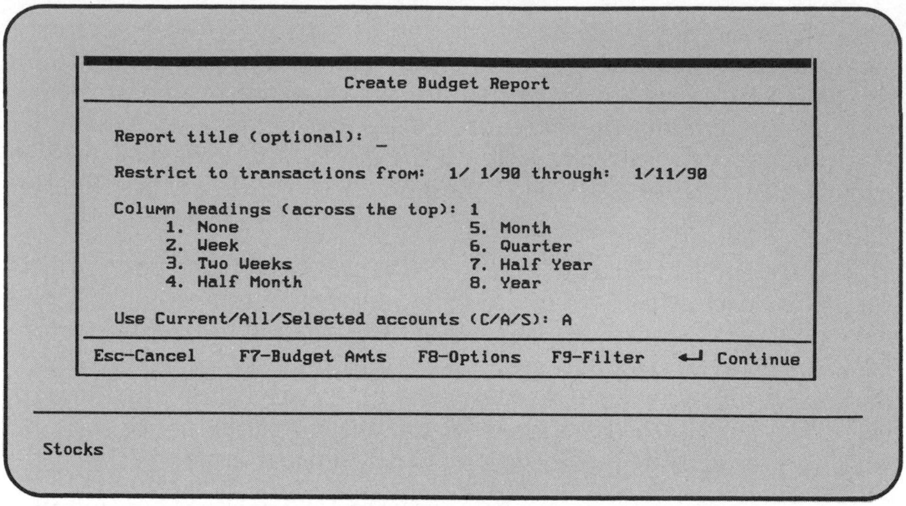

```
                          Create Budget Report

        Report title (optional):  _

        Restrict to transactions from:  1/ 1/90 through:  1/11/90

        Column headings (across the top): 1
             1. None                  5. Month
             2. Week                  6. Quarter
             3. Two Weeks             7. Half Year
             4. Half Month            8. Year

        Use Current/All/Selected accounts (C/A/S): A

        Esc-Cancel    F7-Budget Amts    F8-Options    F9-Filter    ↵ Continue


  Stocks
```

Figure 13.3. Create Budget Report window.

300

You can use a single other assets account to manage all your rental property, but you should use classes to readily identify the income or expense of a specific property. For example, suppose you own two office spaces, one on Hyde Street and the other on Jekyll Ave. When entering income and expense transactions, you can refer to these properties as classes:

Rent payment/Jekyll Ave.	Rental income, Jekyll Ave.
Repairs/Hyde St.	Repairs expenses, Hyde St.
Utilities/Jekyll Ave.	Utilities expenses, Jekyll Ave.

As always, you must create classes before assigning them to transactions. You can create classes directly in the Class List window or when recording the transaction. When recording the transaction, Quicken will note that the class name you've provided doesn't exist; you can add the class to the list or select another from from the list.

When you receive a rent check, enter the transaction and provide the amount in the INCREASE column. You should enter expenses in the DECREASE column.

Quicken's summary report helps you identify properties that are making or losing money for you. As shown in Figure 13.4, each property is listed in its own column, with income and expense items separated. If a property is consistently costing

more money than it's bringing in, you can decide if it's worth
keeping.

```
                              Income & Expense
                           1/ 1/90 Through 1/11/90
Rental                                                          Page 1
1/11/90

                                                              OVERALL
   Category Description      Hyde St    Jekyll Ave    Other      TOTAL
   --------------------     ---------   ----------   -------   --------

INCOME/EXPENSE
   INCOME
      Painting                 0.00       245.80       0.00     245.80
      Repairs                 98.73       233.93       0.00     332.66
                           ---------   ----------   -------   --------

   TOTAL INCOME               98.73       479.73       0.00     578.46


   EXPENSES
      Rent Income           -900.00      -750.00       0.00  -1,650.00
      Water, Gas, Electric   -10.98        -9.33       0.00     -20.31
                           ---------   ----------   -------   --------

   TOTAL EXPENSES           -910.98      -759.33       0.00  -1,670.31


                           ---------   ----------   -------   --------
TOTAL INCOME/EXPENSE       1,009.71     1,239.06       0.00   2,248.77


BALANCE FORWARD
   Rental                     0.00         0.00        0.00       0.00
                           ---------   ----------   -------   --------
TOTAL BALANCE FORWARD         0.00         0.00        0.00       0.00


                           ---------   ----------   -------   --------
OVERALL TOTAL              1,009.71     1,239.06       0.00   2,248.77
                           =========   ==========   =======   ========
```

Figure 13.4. Rental property summary report.

Managing Payroll

Payroll is a difficult task for most companies. The task of maintaining accurate payroll records can become so difficult that many

301

firms have outside accounting companies track payroll records; some even prepare the paychecks, using a cash fund established by the employer.

Quicken paves the way to simplifying the payroll task. It does not actually calculate the payroll amounts for you; rather, it tracks payroll expenses and withholdings for reporting and tax purposes. You can use the pop-up calculator or a spreadsheet to calculate the tax withholdings.

The journey starts with the creation of several other liability accounts, created just for the purposes of containing payroll information. Each transaction is a separate paycheck. Deductions, including federal withholding tax, state tax, social security, union dues, and so forth, are handled as transfers to the other liability accounts. In addition to these accounts, which will contain amounts withheld from paychecks, you'll need at least two expense categories: one to track gross pay and another to track the company's portion of the FICA withholding (since both the company and the employee pay this amount). So, your accounts and new categories will include the following:

Categories	Accounts
FICA	Other liability
FEDWITH	Other liability
STWITH	Other liability
Payroll	Expense
BUSFica	Expense

Other accounts and categories might be required, depending on your payroll needs. Some companies offer withholdings for insurance, savings plans, and a host of other sponsored activities. Each withholding should get a new other liability account.

Finally, it's recommended that you use a separate checking account for payroll. This will require a new checking account in Quicken. Keeping payroll separate from your regular company account is a good way of keeping track of payroll expense. Balancing the payroll account is as easy as balancing a checkbook.

When you enter a paycheck into the Write Checks screen, split the transaction using Ctrl-S. Enter the itemizations into the Split Transaction screen as follows:

1. Enter the gross payroll amount for the employee and assign it to the category Payroll.

302

2. Enter the company's portion of the FICA amount paid on this check. This will be a percentage of the total FICA due since the employee and company share this payment. Assign this to the category BUSFica.

3. Enter the total FICA payment (the sum of the company's portion and the employee's portion) as a negative amount. Assign this to the FICA other liability account.

4. Enter the state withholding, federal withholding, and any other withholding amounts as individual entries assigned to the appropriate other activities accounts. Each should have its own account. Be sure to enter these amounts as negative numbers.

If you sum the split entries for the check, you should end up with the appropriate net pay, which is the amount that goes onto the check itself. Figure 13.5 shows an example of a payroll entry.

303

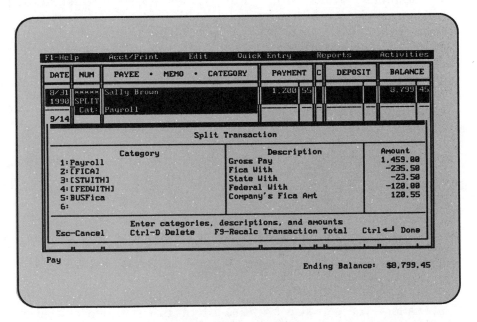

Figure 13.5. A split payroll transaction.

▶ **Tip:** Since all paychecks will use the same split transaction, try using a memorized transaction to create paychecks. This can save much time and help you avoid errors.

The built-in payroll report is useful for tracking gross pay by employee. This report is located in the business reports group and totals all Payroll category transactions in all your accounts. You might also want to see a listing of each payroll category. For this, you should customize the payroll report by removing the filtering that is automatically applied. This is done with the F9 key after you press the F8 key to customize the report. Experiment for best results.

Finally, note that with payroll you must make adjusting entries to the accounts when you pay the withholdings to the government. When you write a check for FICA, for example, be sure to list FICA as the category for the check (not BUSFica). This creates the appropriate balance sheet transaction and reduces your FICA account to zero. Similarly, you should list FEDWITH and STWITH as categories for checks written on these withholding amounts. The BUSFica remains as a business expense category for tax matters.

304

The summary, transaction, and payroll reports furnished by Quicken can be an aid in completing W-2 forms at the start of the next calendar year. Quicken will not print the required information in the W-2 forms; you must do that manually or enter the data Quicken provides into a tax preparation program. Many such programs accept imported data either in the Lotus 1-2-3 PRN or DOS ASCII formats. If the tax preparation program accepts imported data, save your payroll reports as a disk file. If you have only a few W-2 forms to complete, the conversion from Quicken to the tax program probably won't be worth the effort. But the more employees you have, the more time and energy you will save.

Non-Account Applications of Quicken

While Quicken is expressly designed to be used to manage financial matters, you can also use it as a form of simplified computer database. You are limited to entering data in the column and row format Quicken imposes on financial transactions, but for many applications, this restriction is of no consequence. Armed with the program's text search features, you can locate specific data records, or groups of data records, in a flash, and even list them in custom reports.

Maintaining inventories (where no value is assigned to the items) is a popular use of Quicken as a database. You can use either an other asset or other liability account; it doesn't matter which if you won't be using the account to tally monetary worth. Use the Payee and Memo blanks to describe the item. You can use categories, when desired, to classify the item. An example of a Quicken register as database is shown in Figure 13.6.

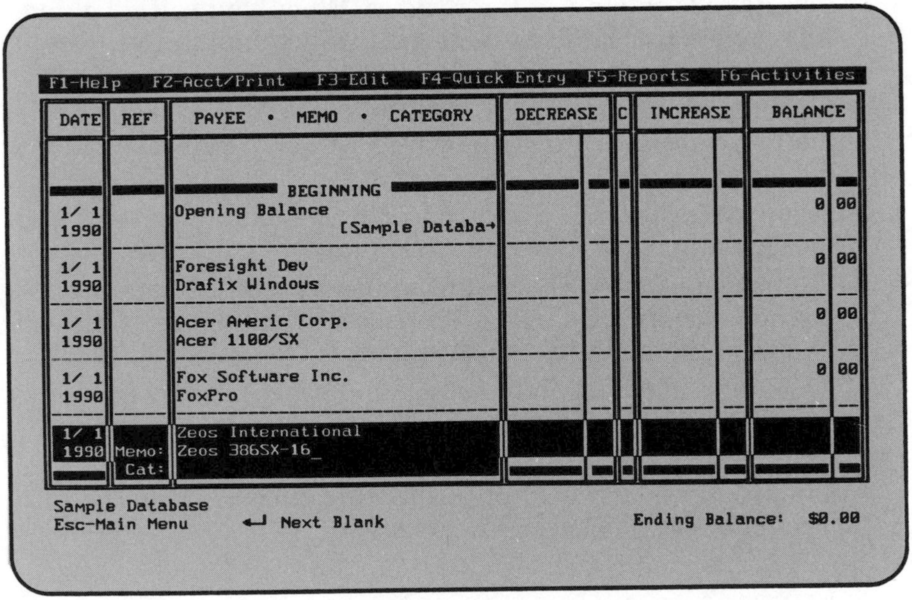

Figure 13.6. An example of using Quicken as a database.

At any time, you can print the database (choose the Print Register command from the Acct/Print menu) or prepare one of the many reports Quicken offers. If you've assigned each transaction to a particular category, you can use the itemized category report to obtain a birds-eye view of the database.

What You Have Learned

This chapter discussed numerous home and business applications for Quicken. Here's what you have learned:

► You can use Quicken to monitor the inventory in your home, including clothes, jewelry, and electronic items.

► Personal property should be recorded in an other asset account.

► Enter the value of your personal belongings in the INCREASE column of the register. When you sell a belonging, delete the value in the INCREASE column or replace it with a "0.00."

► Recording improvements you make to your own home helps decrease its tax basis, which can help you save money when you sell it.

► Maintaining accurate records of home improvements also helps to increase the appraised value of your home.

► To use Quicken for budgeting expenses, record transactions using categories and identify those categories as budgeted items in the monthly budget report.

► Quicken's checking, other asset, and other liability accounts can be used to maintain accounts receivable and accounts payable registers for business.

► Quicken uses a system of post-dating checks to track future accounts payable cash flow needs.

Standard Quicken Account Categories

This appendix lists the standard categories provided by Quicken. Home and business categories are separated. You can use these categories as is or create your own to fit your needs. You can also edit the standard categories—change the category name, type, description, or tax-time notation.

Standard Home Categories

Category	Type	Description	Tax
Bonus	Income	Bonus income	X
Canada Pen	Income	Canadian pension	X
Div Income	Income	Dividend income	X
Family Allow	Income	Family allowance	X
Gift Received	Income	Gift received	X
Int Inc	Income	Interest income	X
Investment Inc	Income	Investment income	X
Oldage pen	Income	Old age pension	X

Continued

Category	Type	Description	Tax
Other Inc	Income	Other Income	X
Salary	Income	Salary	X
Auto Fuel	Expense	Automobile fuel	
Auto Other	Expense	Automobile expense	
Auto Serv	Expense	Automobile servicing	
Auto Loan	Expense	Automobile bank loan	
Bank Chrg	Expense	Bank charge	
Charity	Expense	Charitable donations	X
Childcare	Expense	Childcare expense	
Christmas	Expense	Christmas expenses	
Clothing	Expense	Clothing	
Dining	Expense	Dining out	
Dues	Expense	Dues	
Education	Expense	Education	
Entertain	Expense	Entertainment	
Gifts	Expense	Gift expenses	
Groceries	Expense	Groceries	
Home Repair	Expense	Home repair/ maintenance	
Household	Expense	Household miscellaneous expense	
Housing	Expense	Housing	
Insurance	Expense	Insurance	
Int Exp	Expense	Interest expense	X
Invest Exp	Expense	Investment expense	X
Medical	Expense	Medical/dental	X
Misc	Expense	Miscellaneous expense	
Mort Int	Expense	Mortgage interest	X
Mort Prin	Expense	Mortgage principal	

Continued

308

Category	Type	Description	Tax
Other Exp	Expense	Other expenses	
Recreation	Expense	Recreation	
RRSP	Expense	Regular retirement savings	
Subscriptions	Expense	Subscriptions	
Supplies	Expense	Supplies	X
Tax Fed	Expense	Federal tax withholding	X
Tax FICA	Expense	Social Security tax	X
Tax Other	Expense	Miscellaneous taxes	X
Tax Prop	Expense	Property tax	X
Tax State	Expense	State withholding tax	X
Telephone	Expense	Telephone expense	
UIC	Expense	Unemployment insurance	X
Utilities	Expense	Water, gas, electric	

309

Standard Business Categories

Category	Type	Description	Tax
Gr Sales	Income	Gross sales	X
Other Inc	Income	Other income	X
Rent Income	Income	Rent income	X
Ads	Expense	Advertising	X
Car	Expense	Car/truck	X
Commission	Expense	Commissions	X
Freight	Expense	Freight	X
Int Paid	Expense	Interest paid	X

Continued

Category	Type	Description	Tax
L&P Fees	Expense	Legal/professional fees	X
Late Fees	Expense	Late payment fees	X
Office	Expense	Office expenses	X
Rent Paid	Expense	Rent paid	X
Repairs	Expense	Repairs	X
Returns	Expense	Returns and allowances	X
Taxes	Expense	Taxes	X
Travel	Expense	Travel expenses	X
Wages	Expense	Wages and job credits	X

310

Special Categories for Investment Accounts

Note: These categories appear only when you have created an investment account.

Category	Type	Description	Tax
_DivInc	Income	Dividend income	X
_IntInc	Income	Interest income	X
_LT CapGnDst	Income	Long-term capital gains distribution	X
_RlzdGain	Income	Realized gain/loss	X
_ST CapGnDst	Income	Short-term capital gains distribution	X
_UnrlzdGain	Income	Unrealized gain/loss	X
_IntExp	Expense	Investment interest expense	X

Suggested Additional Home Categories (as needed)

Category	Type	Description	Tax
Alimony Inc	Income	Alimony income	X
Alimony Exp	Expense	Alimony expense	X
Cas&Theft	Expense	Casualty and theft	X
Emp Bus	Expense	Employee business expenses	X
Legal	Expense	Legal/professional fees	X
Moving	Expense	Moving expenses	X
Penalty	Expense	Penalty/early withdrawal	X
Tax Prep	Expense	Professional tax preparation	X
Union	Expense	Union/professional dues	X

311

Suggested Additional Business Categories (as needed)

Category	Type	Description	Tax
Bad Debt	Expense	Bad debt (write-off)	X
Bank Chrg	Expense	Bank charges	X
Benefit	Expense	Employee benefit	X
Copy	Expense	Copy/repro expenses	X
Dep	Expense	Depreciable expense	X
Dep Exp	Expense	Depreciation expense	X

Continued

Category	Type	Description	Tax
Entertain	Expense	Entertainment	X
Insurance	Expense	Insurance	X
Postage	Expense	Postage	X
Supplies	Expense	Supplies	X

312

Appendix B
On-Line Help Topics

The following is a quick reference of the topics covered by Quicken's on-line help feature.

Account Group Activities
Account group, selecting one to use
Account group, setting up new one
Account types
Account, setting up new one
Acct/Print Menu
Activities Menu
Balance Sheet, business report
Beginning to use Quicken, part 1
Beginning to use Quicken, part 2
Business Reports Menu
Calculator, using
Change Settings menu
CheckFree electronic payment service
CheckFree, importing data from
Classes
Copy single account

314

Transfers
Transfers in reports
Writing checks
Year-end procedures

315

316

Appendix C

Starting Quicken with Command-Line Options

Ordinarily, you start Quicken simply by typing

Q

at the DOS prompt and then pressing Enter. You can also start Quicken using one of several command-line options. You type these options at the DOS prompt to invoke special features when you run Quicken. These command-line switches allow you to:

▶ Automatically open an account, account group, or main menu item when you start Quicken.

▶ Use large accounts or request large reports.

▶ Specify preference between two keystroke styles.

The command-line options for Quicken are:

At the DOS Prompt	What It Does
Q Check	Starts Quicken and loads the account named Check. If the account name includes a space character, place it in quotes, as in Q "Check Acct."

At the DOS Prompt	What It Does
Q Check QDATA	Starts Quicken and loads the account named Check, which resides in the QDATA account group.
Q 5	Starts Quicken and automatically selects the 5 main menu option (Options Settings). Quicken opens the account last used.
Q Check 5	Starts Quicken, loads the Check account, and selects the 5 main menu option (Options Settings).

Note that you can include all three types of command line switches at once. For consistency, enter the account name first, followed by the account group, and finally the main menu number.

Two additional command-line options allow you to set aside extra memory for data, and to specify the action of the Home and End keys.

318

Option	Effect
Q /N	Sets aside extra RAM for data.
Q /A	Use Quicken version 3.0 key definitions for Home and End keys.
Q /S	Use Quicken version 4.0 key definitions for Home and End keys

The following is a summary of the action of the Home and End keys in Quicken versions 3.0 and 4.0:

Key	Quicken 4.0	Quicken 3.0
Home	Start of current blank	Top of register
End	End of current blank	End of register
Ctrl-Home	Top of register	Top of register
Ctrl-End	Bottom of register	Bottom of register*
Home Home	Go to first blank	None
End End	Go to last blank	None
Ctrl-F10	End reconcile	None

Note:
* When reconciling an account in version 3.0, pressing Ctrl-End ends the reconciliation process.

Index

319

320

321

323

325

Reader Feedback Card

Thank you for purchasing this book from Howard W. Sams & Company's FIRST BOOK series. Our intent with this series is to bring you timely, authoritative information that you can reference quickly and easily. You can help us by taking a minute to complete and return this card. We appreciate your comments and will use the information to better serve your needs.

1. Where did you purchase this book?

☐ Chain bookstore (Walden, B. Dalton) ☐ Direct mail
☐ Independent bookstore ☐ Book club
☐ Computer/Software store ☐ School bookstore
☐ Other _____

2. Why did you choose this book? (Check as many as apply.)

☐ Price ☐ Appearance of book
☐ Author's reputation ☐ Howard W. Sam's reputation
☐ Quick and easy treatment of subject ☐ Only book available on subject

3. How do you use this book? (Check as many as apply.)

☐ As a supplement to the product manual ☐ As a reference
☐ In place of the product manual ☐ At home
☐ For self-instruction ☐ At work

4. Please rate this book in the categories below. G = Good; N = Needs improvement; U = Category is unimportant.

☐ Price ☐ Appearance
☐ Amount of information ☐ Accuracy
☐ Examples ☐ Quick Steps
☐ Inside cover reference ☐ Second color
☐ Table of contents ☐ Index
☐ Tips and cautions ☐ Illustrations
☐ Length of book
☐ How can we improve this book? _____

5. How many computer books do you normally buy in a year?

☐ 1—5　　　☐ 5—10　　　☐ More than 10
☐ I rarely purchase more than one book on a subject.
☐ I may purchase a beginning and an advanced book on the same subject.
☐ I may purchase several books on particular subjects.
(such as _____)

6. Have you purchased other Howard W. Sams or Hayden books in the past year? _____
If yes, how many? _____

7. Would you purchase another book in the FIRST BOOK series? _____

8. What are your primary areas of interest in business software?
   - [ ] Word processing (particularly _____)
   - [ ] Spreadsheet (particularly _____)
   - [ ] Database (particularly _____)
   - [ ] Graphics (particularly _____)
   - [ ] Personal finance/accounting (particularly _____)
   - [ ] Other (please specify _____)

Other comments on this book or the Howard W. Sams book line: _____
_____

Name _____
Company _____
Address _____
City _____ State _____ Zip _____
Daytime telephone number _____
Title of this book _____

Fold here

- -